International Banking and Financial Centers

International Banking and Financial Centers

edited by

Yoon S. Park
School of Government and Business Administration
George Washington University

Musa Essayyad
School of Business
University of Alaska, Anchorage

Kluwer Academic Publishers
Boston/Dordrecht/London

Distributors for North America:
Kluwer Academic Publishers
101 Philip Drive
Assinippi Park
Norwell, Massachusetts 02061 USA

Distributors for all other countries:
Kluwer Academic Publishers Group
Distribution Centre
Post Office Box 322
3300 AH Dordrecht, THE NETHERLANDS

Library of Congress Cataloging-in-Publication Data

International banking and financial centers / [edited by] Yoon S. Park, Musa Essayyad.
p. cm.
Based on papers presented at a conference held in Anchorage, July 1987.
Includes index.
ISBN 0-7923-9016-4
1. Banks and banking. International. 2. International finance.
I. Park, Yoon S., 1935- . II. Essayyad, Musa.
HG3881.I575125 1989
332.1'5—dc20 89-8096
CIP

Second Printing 1990

Printed in the United States of America.

TABLE OF CONTENTS

PREFACE

The development of international financial centers (IFCs) has paralleled the rapid expansion of international banking and Eurocurrency activities. During the past decade and a half, the international banking and financial markets have experienced phenomenal growth along with the parallel expansion of IFCs. The size of the Eurocurrency market grew from $110 billion in 1970 to over $4,000 billion by 1987, while the total international assets of all banking institutions rose from $130 billion to $4,800 billion during the same period. Some of the preeminent IFCs are playing a major role in the international financial markets, as demonstrated by the size of their international assets: Bahamas ($144 billion), Cayman Islands ($174 billion), Singapore ($150 billion), Hong Kong ($130 billion), Bahrain ($46 billion), and Panama ($32 billion). The patterns of Euroborrowing and Eurolending activities in these IFCs have been undergoing major changes. These changes came about as a result of the introduction of the floating exchange rate system in 1973, recent financial deregulation, internationalization of the financial markets, securitization of financial assets and liabilities, and global financial innovations.

Since the pioneering work of Kindleberger in 1974 on the formation of financial centers, there has not been a comprehensive study to reflect the recent developments, trends and the mystique that have surrounded the IFCs' functions and operations in the international money and capital markets. The purpose of this book is, therefore, to bridge this literature gap by providing scholars, financial executives, bankers, and graduate and senior students of international finance and banking a comprehensive in-depth look into the various aspects of IFC fabric: definition; organization; competition; innovations, and evaluation of their contributions to international financing and investment and to the economies of host countries.

This book, which consists of sixteen articles, provides specific answers to the following questions:

* What are the economic, financial, legal and managerial requirements of establishing a successful international financial center in certain countries?

* What are the benefits of setting up an IFC to the host country?

* What are the cost elements of hosting an IFC?

* What are the current comparative advantages of IFC in the Pacific Rim nations such as Hong Kong and Singapore vis-a-vis other IFCs in Panama, Bahrain and Bahamas?

* What is the economic impact of recent developments in some IFCs, such as Hong Kong's future relationship with China, political turmoil in Panama, and the effect of the Persian Gulf war on Bahrain?

* What are the new developments concerning International Banking Facilities (IBFs)?

* What are the benefits and costs of setting up an IBF department at a U.S. bank?

To answer these and other questions, the book is divided into four parts. Part I discusses the recent developments that characterized the functions of IFCs. Part II analyzes the costs and benefits of IFCs. Part III takes a fresh look into the performance of International Banking Facilities. Part IV provides a global perspective on the IFCs.

This book is designed to be a reference book for bankers, financial executives, public finance officers, economists at international financial organizations, and other scholars in this field. In addition, it can also be used as a supplement to a textbook on international finance at the advanced undergraduate and graduate levels.

This volume has evolved from the papers presented in July 1987 by distinguished experts at an international banking and finance conference on IFCs, organized in Anchorage by the Alaska Center for International Business and co-sponsored by other public and private organizations. We would especially like to express our gratitude to the Honorable Steve Cowper, the Governor of the State of Alaska, Mr. Tony Knowles, the former Mayor of Anchorage, Dr. Ron Lehr, Executive Director of Alaska Housing Finance Corporation, Mr. Bert Wagnon, Executive Director of Alaska Development and Export Authority, and Mr. Ronald Bosi, President and CEO of Rainier Bank Alaska, for their organizations' generous moral and financial support in organizing the conference.

Finally, our special thanks go to Mr. Zachary Rolnik, editor at Kluwer Academic Publisher for his advice and counsel in editing this volume and to Ms. Mary J. Barry for her hard work and patience in transforming the manuscripts into readable products with her word processing skill.

John Choon Kim, Executive Director
ACIB (Project Sponsor)

Editors:
Musa Essayyad, University of Alaska Anchorage
Yoon S. Park, The George Washington University

NOTES ON CONTRIBUTORS

Bhattacharya, Anindya K. Dr. Bhattacharya is an economist at the U.S. General Accounting Office. He did his graduate work in international relations at the London School of Economics, John Hopkins University, and Columbia University. He earned his undergraduate degree at Cambridge University in England. Dr. Bhattacharya has taught at SUNY, Pace University, and Adelphi University. He has served as a consultant for numerous institutions including many United Nations agencies, Chase Manhattan Bank, and Central Bank of Barbados. He is a prolific writer and has published seven books and numerous articles about international finance and banking. Of particular importance to our book is Dr. Bhattacharya's excellent published work and experience in cost/benefit analysis of offshore banking centers including Bombay and Singapore.

Chang, Soon Young. Dr. Chang is an assistant professor of international business at Han Yang University in Seoul, Korea. He received his M.B.A. and Ph.D. degrees from The George Washington University. Professor Chang has published a book entitled *New Financial Instruments in International Capital Markets* (in Korean). He has also written widely in the field of international finance in Korea.

Essayyad, Musa. Dr. Essayyad is the William H. Seward Professor of International Finance at the University of Alaska Anchorage. Prior to teaching business finance, investment, and international finance at UAA, he worked as the economic advisor to Qatar's Permanent Mission to the United Nations in Geneva, and at the First National Bank of Chicago in London. During his assignment in Geneva he participated and chaired numerous international meetings dealing with international monetary and financial issues, commodities agreements, and shipping financing. He was the alternate governor of Qatar for the World Bank (1976 IMF-IBRD Joint meetings); member of OPEC Economic Commission (1976); member of the Governing Council of International Fund for Agricultural Development, Rome (1978); and member of the Board of Trustees of Arab Planning Institute, Kuwait (1976). Dr. Essayyad earned his M.A. and Ph.D. in finance at the University of Alabama and did his undergraduate work in accounting at Beirut Arab University. His research interests are international portfolio diversification, foreign exchange forecasting, and development of offshore banking centers. He has published many articles on international finance, banking, and economics.

Goldberg, Michael A. Dr. Goldberg is currently the Herbert B. Fullerton Chair Professor of Urbank Land Policy at the University of British Columbia. He obtained his M.A. and Ph.D. in economics from the University of California, Berkeley. He lectured at 28 universities in Canada, United States, Singapore, Australia, China, and Germany. He served as economic and finance consultant to numerous corporations and government organizations. He published nine books, more than 60 journal articles, and more than 20 book articles.

Helsley, Robert W. Dr. Helsley is an assistant professor of economics at the University of British Columbia. He earned his M.A. and Ph.D. at Princeton University. He worked as economic consultant to ECO Northwest Ltd. in Oregon and has published in the area of international financial center development.

Key, Sydney J. Dr. Key is an economist in the Federal Reserve Board's Division of International Finance, where she specializes in current issues in international banking. She is also responsible for monitoring and analyzing developments in the European Community as it moves toward the goal of completing the internal market by 1992. Dr. Key worked on the Board's regulations providing for the establishment of International Banking Facilities in the United States and has published a number of articles on this subject. She has also written articles and chapters on foreign banking in the United States, the most recent of which was co-authored with Gary M. Welsh and published in the 1988 edition of *The Bankers' Handbook*. Dr. Key has also published articles on employee group pension plans and the federal tax treatment of married two-earner couples; she served as a member of the President's Interdepartmental Task Force on Women in 1979-80. Dr. Key received both her A.B. and Ph.D. degrees in economics from Harvard University.

Khoury, Sarkis J. Dr. Khoury is a professor of finance at the University of California, Riverside. He received his MBA in finance and economics at Boston University and his Ph.D. in international finance at the Wharton School. Prior to his current position, he taught international finance and speculative markets at the University of Notre Dame, Bucknell University, and Drexel University. His professional business experience includes investment broker at Paine, Webber, Jackson & Curtis; cashier at the Central Bank of Lebanon; and consultant for many corporations on mergers and acquisitions, portfolio strategy, and international debt restructuring. He has published nine books and monographs and numerous articles about international banking and finance.

Levi, Maurice D. Dr. Levi is the Bank of Montreal Professor of International Finance at the University of British Columbia in Canada. He was born in London and earned his B.A. in economics at the University of Manchester and M.A. and Ph.D. in economics at the University of Chicago. He has taught at the London Business School, M.I.T., Hebrew University of Jerusalem, University of California, Berkeley, Roosevelt University, Indiana University, and University of Chicago. He worked for First National City Bank and Shell Oil Company. He has published nine books, including an excellent textbook on international finance and numerous articles in leading economics and finance journals.

Li, David K.P. The Honorable David K.P. Li is Director and the Chief Executive Officer of the Bank of East Asia, Limited. Mr. Li is a Member of both the Legislative Council of Hong Kong, and the Exchange Fund Advisory Committee, and Vice-Chairman of the basic Law Drafting Committee, the body responsible for drafting the future laws of Hong Kong to be adopted after territorial sovereignty reverts to China in 1997. Mr. Li is also a member of the Investment Committee of The Hong Kong Special Administrative Region Government Land Fund trust, which was established to determine investment policies for public funds in Hong Kong after 1997. He is a graduate of the University of Cambridge in Economics and Law and a Fellow of the Institute of Chartered Accountants in England and Wales. Mr. Li is the Chairman of the Chinese Banks' Association in Hong Kong, a member of the Economic Review Committee and the Banking Advisory Committee of the Hong Kong Government, and a member of the Executive Committee of the Hong Kong Association of Banks.

Moffett, Michael H. Professor Moffett is currently teaching international economics and monetary theory at Oregon State University. His graduate work in international economics was done at the University of Colorado and his undergraduate work was completed at the University of Texas, Austin. He has worked as staff economist at Tekenkron Research Inc., Berkeley, California, and was a research fellow at the Brookings Institution, Washington, D.C. He has presented many papers at different national and international business conventions. His research interests are cost/benefit analysis of International Banking Facilities, and assessment of the risk of Asian Pacific borrowers.

Nashashibi, Hikmat S. Mr. Nashashibi is the Chairman of Moseley Capital Markets Limited, London; Vice-Chairman of Moseley Holding Corporation, New York. He is also Chairman of the Arab Bankers Association, London, and Executive Director of Arab Financial Services Company, Bahrain. Prior to these positions, Mr. Nashashibi was the General Manager of Kuwait International Investment Company, Kuwait, and Investment Manager of the Arab Fund for Economic and Social Development. After graduating from the American University of Beirut in 1966, he was appointed head of the Foreign Trade of Kuwait Chamber of Commerce and Industry. He then worked for an American brokerage firm as a stockbroker on Wall Street. Mr. Nashashibi has published extensive works in English and Arabic on the subject of OPEC investments, including three Arabic books on developing Arab capital markets and investing Arab financial surpluses. He has been commissioned to undertake a number of studies on Arab Financial Markets to organizations such as United Nations Conference on Trade and Development (UNCTAD), Board of Governors of Arab Central Banks, United Nations Industrial Development Organization (UNIDO), and the League of Arab States.

Park, Yoon S. Dr. Park is a professor of business administration at The George Washington University, Washington, D.C. He earned his M.B.A. in finance from Fairleigh Dickinson University; D.B.A. in international finance from Harvard Business School; and M.A. and Ph.D. in economics from The George Washington University. Dr. Park has served as professorial lecturer in international finance at The George Washington University and Georgetown University (1975-77), a senior economist at the World Bank (1970-77), and advisor to The Samsung Group, Seoul, Korea (1978-79). He has also served as a consultant to many organizations including the Institute of Banking and Finance (Mexico), Central Bank for Cooperatives, Royal Bank of Canada, American Express International Banking Co., The World Bank, Korea Institute for International Economics. Dr. Park's publications include seven books, numerous articles, papers, and reports on international banking and finance. Dr. Park has been selected as one of the ten distinguished international finance experts by the outgoing Chairman of the NYSE.

Reed, Howard Curtis. Dr. Reed is the Managing Director and Chief Executive Officer of Curt Reed and Co., an international cash management concern. He is also the chairman of ISSARK, Inc.'s board. His banking experience includes positions with Irving Trust Company and Morgan Guaranty Trust Company in New York. He obtained his Ph.D. in international business and Japanese Area Studies at the University of Washington, and M.A. in economics at the City University of New York. Dr. Reed earned his B.A. in mathematics from the University of Arkansas, where he is currently a member of its Board of Trustees. Dr. Reed has published numerous articles and a book on international financial centers.

Sing, Francis P. Dr. Sing is the President of FPS International, Inc., a worldwide business consulting company, that is specialized in the promotion of joint ventures and licensing agreement projects in Asia. In 1985 and again in 1986, Dr. Sing was invited by the United Nations to lecture in China. Prior to his current position, Dr. Sing was a professor of economics and finance for over twenty-three years at many universities including Georgetown and John Hopkins. He obtained his Ph.D. in financial economics at New York University. Before that he had been a security analyst with the Manufacturers Hanover Trust Company of New York City. He has also served as an editorial consultant to McGraw-Hill Book Company, The Reston Publishing Company, Richard D. Irwin, Inc., and the Ronald Press Company.

Stonehill, Arthur I. Dr. Stonehill is Professor of International Business at Oregon State University. He did his graduate work in international business, finance, and economics at Harvard University, University of Oslo (Norway), and University of California, Berkeley. His undergraduate education in history and French was completed at Yale. He has taught at many U.S. and European universities. In addition to being founder and director of several computer and land development concerns, he has served as consultant to many corporations in the U.S., Denmark, United Kingdom, the Netherlands, Hong Kong, China, Italy, and Norway. He has published seven books, five monographs, and numerous articles and cases about international finance and business.

Terrell, Henry S. Dr. Terrell is a Senior Economist in the Division of International Finance at the Federal Reserve Board. He has a B.A. from Williams College (1964) and a Ph.D. from Stanford University (1969) and joined the staff of the Federal Reserve Board in 1969 as an Economist in the Division of Research and Statistics. From 1974 to 1985 he served as

Chief of the International Banking Section in the Division of International Finance. Dr. Terrell has held visiting positions at the Federal Reserve Bank of San Francisco and at the Fletcher School of Law and Diplomacy at Tufts University, and has served as a consultant to an AID mission to study Egyptian private sector finance. Dr. Terrell has published numerous articles on international banking and financial topics, the most recent of which is "The Determinants of the Growth of Multinational Banks: 1972-1986," co-authored with Professor Robert S. Dohner of the Fletcher School.

Tschoegl, Adrian Edward. Dr. Tschoegl is currently an executive at SBCI Securities (Asia) in Tokyo. He earned his doctorate in international business at M.I.T., and his M.P.A. and B.A. at U.C.L.A. Prior to his present job he taught at the University of Michigan for many years. He was a visiting scholar at the Institute of Monetary and Economics Studies of the Bank of Japan, and worked at the Security Pacific National Bank at Los Angeles and T.S. Kollerich & Cie. in England, Switzerland and United Arab Emirates. Dr. Tschoegl is an authority on the cost/benefit analysis of IFCs. He has published extensively in leading journals in this field.

Wu, Hsiu-Kwant. Dr. Wu is the Lee Bidgood Professor of Finance and Economics at the University of Alabama. Dr. Wu did his graduate work in economics at the Wharton School and his undergraduate work in international affairs at Princeton. Dr. Wu taught at universities of Boston, Harvard, M.I.T., Chicago, and Peking. He served as economic advisor to the Office of the Comptroller of the Currency (1975-1980), consultant to many institutions including SEC and NYSE; was a member of the U.S. delegation to the U.N. Conference on Investment in Fisheries in Rome; and was a member of the Alabama Trade Mission to Japan/U.S. Southeastern Association meeting in Japan. Dr. Wu was appointed, along with Henry Kissinger and David Rockefeller, as a member of the U.S./China Task Force on Bilateral Relations. He has published a book, monographs, and articles in leading finance and investment journals.

PART I

RECENT DEVELOPMENTS IN INTERNATIONAL FINANCIAL CENTERS

1. INTRODUCTION TO INTERNATIONAL FINANCIAL CENTERS: THEIR ORIGIN AND RECENT DEVELOPMENTS

Yoon S. Park
The George Washington University

INTRODUCTION

In recent years the volume of cross-border international financial flows has risen sharply, dwarfing that of international trade. While the total world trade volume has reached the $4 trillion mark a year, the total cross-border international financial flows are about fifty times as much, estimated at $200 trillion per year. Thus, unlike in earlier decades the engine of growth in international financial flows is no longer the world trading activities but the accelerating momentum of international financial market activities. The huge volume of cross-border financial flows is directly related to the enormous size of the international financial market system. As of the end of 1987 the gross size of the Eurocurrency market was $4.4 trillion, while the total amount of funds raised on international financial markets reached $384 billion in 1987.[1]

Concomitant with the expansion of international financial markets, the international banking system has experienced a robust growth during the past two decades. The total cross-border banking assets had risen from $2.7 trillion in 1982 to $4.7 trillion by the end of 1987.[2] Expansion of international banking and finance in recent decades was accompanied by the emergence of a number of important international financial centers around the globe. These financial centers have served as the focus of banking and financial activities on an international scale. They have attracted a large number of financial institutions from around the world, which engage in deposit collection, funding and inter-bank trading, foreign exchange operations, currency and interest rate swaps, financial futures trading, and other financial activities on a worldwide scale. Thus, these financial centers have played a central role in the evolution and expansion of international financial markets.

DEFINITION

The importance of international financial centers has been widely recognized for the last decade and a half, and scholastic interest has been generally active, as witnessed by the number of studies in this field. Consequently, a significant body of literature on the topic has emerged. In addition, the popular business press and journals report frequently on financial centers. The topic has also been the subject of interest to regulators and law makers, who are concerned with the potential financial and regulatory impact of such centers. For example, various committees of U.S. Congress have looked into the potential abuses of offshore financial centers by U.S. residents in violation of U.S. tax and other laws.[3]

There have been various attempts to define international financial centers since the early 1970s, as their role in international financial markets has risen remarkably. There have been different uses of the term "international financial center", such as world financial center (WFC), regional financial center (RFC), international financial center (IFC), offshore financial center (OFC), international banking center (IBC), offshore banking center (OBC), etc. Johnson (1976) uses the term "regional financial centers" as the host centers in which are concentrated financial activities -banking, insurance, and ancillary types of financial business enterprises - that cater to clients in outside regions.[4] Dufey and Giddy (1978) define "offshore centers" as international financial centers that host financial intermediation activities primarily for non-resident borrowers and depositors.[5]

McCarthy (1979, p. 49) defines offshore banking centers as:

> cities, areas, or countries which have made a conscious effort to attract offshore banking business, i.e. nonresident foreign currency-denominated business, by allowing relatively free entry and by adopting a flexible attitude where taxes, levies, and regulations are concerned.

Favorable treatment in the regulations is viewed as one of the most important contributing factors in the growth of international financial centers. Many countries actively provide a favorable regulatory environment for foreign financial institutions with the objective to develop one of its cities as a financial center. Dufey (1983) called some of them "aggressive" centers (e.g. Singapore), distinguished from "reluctant" centers (e.g. Tokyo) which arise more naturally, or even against the wishes of the government authorities there.[6] In this sense, McCarthy's definition of offshore banking centers is equivalent to Dufey's aggressive centers.

Almost all authors, particularly Kindleberger and Reed, seem to think that financial markets are organized in a hierarchical form, and an international financial center indicates the apex of the hierarchy.[7] Some authors view an international financial center as identical to, or interchangeable with, an offshore financial center. For example, Park (1982) observes that:

> since all international financial centers deal in external or 'offshore' currencies as compared to the domestic or 'onshore' currency of a national financial center, I will call them offshore financial centers.

Park classifies four different types of these financial centers: primary centers such as London and New York that serve worldwide clients and each possess predominant sources and uses of funds within its market area; booking centers that act as the location for shell branches to book both outside sources and uses of funds, such as Nassau and the Cayman Islands; funding centers that channel offshore funds collected from outside their market regions into their own market areas through inward intermediation, such as Singapore and Panama; and collection centers such as Bahrain that intermediate the channeling of surplus funds collected inside their regions to outside users.

The significance of the presence of foreign financial sector in the host country determines classification of a financial center as either national or international. Thus, such financial centers as Los Angeles and San Francisco may be classified as national centers, while others such as Bahrain and Panama may be considered international. Development of financial centers can be either demand-driven as a natural accompaniment to the economic and trading growth in the center region, or supply-driven with conscious policy initiatives by the government authorities to promote the emergence of a financial center within its borders. In general, both primary and funding centers belong to the former category, while booking and collection centers belong to the latter.

ECONOMIC EFFECTS

There have been various studies on the impact of financial centers on the local economy: Johnson (1976) on Panama, Cheng (1976) on the U.S. West Coast, particularly Los Angeles and San Francisco; Hodjera (1978) on Singapore; Jao (1979) on Hong Kong; Grubel (1980) on Nairobi; Choi (1984) and Chang (1985) on several important financial centers both in the United States and abroad. In this book, a couple of new studies are included with the purpose of developing both the theoretical as well as practical framework to evaluate the benefits and costs of hosting international financial centers.

The findings of these and other studies generally seem to agree that international financial centers have several distinct benefits, some substantial in relative terms and some not, which can be summarized in the following ways:

(1) Optimization of allocational efficiency - Hosting of an international financial center is likely to remove local and sectoral monopoly and monopsony and promotes the formation of savings and their international pooling by the integration of the local capital markets with the more efficient regional or global markets. An optimization of financial resource allocation is achieved on a regional or even global basis.

(2) Increase in local employment - International financial centers give an impetus to the development of financial and related industries such as legal, accounting, printing and the air and surface transportation sectors. This development in turn expands job opportunities for local as well as expatriate personnel in these industries. In addition, the increased economic activities of these industries affect other

sectors, thus resulting in a spill-over effect on the total economy.

(3) Provision of additional tax revenues - International financial centers generate additional tax revenues for host governments. These tax revenues include personal income tax on local and expatriate employees, registration fees on foreign financial institutions, and stamp duties and transfer taxes on securities being traded. Estate taxes and capital gains taxes can also increase as a center attracts the pool of investment capital to be managed by the financial institutions located there.

(4) Promotion of internationalization of the local economy - Location of international financial centers encourages foreign investment in the local economy either in the form of joint ventures or other direct investments. They also accelerate the flow of valuable information on finance, commerce, and industry from overseas. Foreign investment and the flow of international business information promote the internationalization of the local economy.

(5) Increase in the financial activities of MNCs - International financial centers are also used as location for holding companies as well as the financial subsidiaries of multinational companies which take full advantage of the favorable fiscal and regulatory climate of the offshore centers. It is well known that many captive insurance companies are located in offshore financial centers by large foreign corporations in order to increase their financial flexibility.

However, there can be some potential costs for host countries associated with these financial centers. Implementation of domestic monetary policies may become more difficult due to internalization of offshore funds and the resulting excess money supply growth. Thus, monetary policy may be countermanded through some leakage in the domestic banking system in the presence of offshore funds. The potential also exists for capital outflows from the domestic market since there are generally no taxes levied on deposits in the offshore center.

PROSPECTS

Both financial flows and financial activities are extremely sensitive to external forces, especially political and social instability. History has shown us that financial centers come and go, as their regional economies as well as political fortunes shift over the years. It is instructive to reflect on the fact that both Tangier in North Africa and Havana in the Caribbean once served as international financial centers before the onset of the World War. Recently, we have witnessed the decline of Beirut and the subsequent emergence of Bahrain as the Middle East financial center due to the ongoing civil war in Lebanon. The current political conflicts between U.S. and Panamanian governments have significantly dampened the prospect of Panama as an international financial center.

Establishment of International Banking Facilities (IBFs) in the United States since early 1980s has had some adverse impact on the growth of financial centers in the Caribbean, though the exact magnitude of the financial flows from the Caribbean centers to U.S. IBFs cannot be estimated accurately. It is interesting to note that some observers such as Morgan Guaranty Trust Company of New York include U.S. IBF assets as part of the Eurocurrency market, since the dollar-denominated deposits at IBFs are treated exactly as Eurodollar deposits by U.S. authorities even though they are located inside the United States.[8] Furthermore, the interest rates for IBF-related operations are more closely linked to the Eurocurrency market than to the domestic U.S. CD market.

As international financial markets are integrated into one global market with 24-hour trading operations, the importance of international financial centers is likely to persist and even strengthen further. Key cities with convenient time zone linkages with the major financial centers of the world can enhance their prospect to develop into the financial centers on their own. Unless the cities themselves already enjoy significant trade and investment activities, the development of a viable international financial center requires a conscious effort and coordinated planning on the part of the host cities and countries in the realm of taxes, regulations and other infrastructure necessary to an international financial center.

Since the benefit-cost equation appears favorable for hosting international financial centers, it is possible, indeed probable, to expect continuation of efforts by various countries and cities to develop international financial centers in their own regions. The supply of new centers, however, may ultimately depend upon the demand for new financial centers. On the one hand, the development of improved telecommunications may render it easier than before to operate global financial operations with a fewer number of financial centers. On the other hand, the recent move by the Group of Ten and the European Common Market to strengthen their banking regulations by introducing risk-based capital ratios may enhance the attractiveness of new offshore financial centers which are willing to waive such regulations.[9] No matter how the result may be decided on the total number of international financial centers, however, the prospect of continuing expansion in cross-border financial activities in the coming years indicates that the role of international financial centers will continue to grow in the foreseeable future.

NOTES

1. See *World financial markets*. 1988. Morgan Guaranty Trust Company. Issue 3, July, and *Financial market trends*. 1988. OECD, May:5.

2. IMF. 1988. *International financial statistics*. July:51.

3. U.S. Congress. 1985. *Crime and secrecy: The use of offshore banks and companies*. Report by the Permanent Subcommittee on Investigations of the Committee on Governmental Affairs, United States Senate. Washington.

4. Harry G. Johnson. 1976. Panama as a regional financial center. *Economic Development and Cultural Change*. January:262.

5. Gunter Dufey and Ian Giddy. 1978. *The international money market*. Englewood Cliffs, New Jersey: Prentice Hall:24.

6. Gunter Dufey. 1983. Banking in the Asian Pacific area. In R. Moxon, J. F. Truitt and T. Roehl (eds.), *Asia Pacific dynamics*, Greenwich, CT: JAI Press.

7. See Charles P. Kindleberger. 1974. *The formation of financial center: A study in comparative economic history*, Princeton, NJ: Princeton University Press. See also Howard Curtis Reed. 1981. *The preeminence of international financial centers*. New York: Praeger Publishers.

8. *World Financial Markets*, 1988. Morgan Guaranty Trust Company, March 18:26.

9. Basle committee proposes standards for bank capital levels and measurement. *IMF Survey*, January 25, 1988, and Banks' new minimum capital rules add to international bankers' worries. *The Wall Street Journal*, July 12, 1988.

REFERENCES

Chang, Soon Young. 1985. *The economic impact of offshore banking centers on the host countries*. DBA dissertation, The George Washington University.

Choi, Sang-Rim. 1984. *Economic rationale and consequences of international banking and financial centers*. PhD dissertation, The University of Michigan.

Dufey, Gunter, and Ian Giddy. 1978. *The international money market*. Englewood Cliffs, NJ: Prentice Hall.

Dufey, Gunter. 1983. Banking in the Asian Pacific area, in R. Moxon, J.F. Truitt and T. Roehl (eds.), *Asia Pacific dynamics*. Greenwich, CT: JAI Press.

Financial market trends, OECD. May 1988.

Grubel, Herbert G. 1980. A proposal to establish an Afro-currency market in Nairobi. In John S. Chipman and Charles P. Kindleberger (eds.), *Flexible exchange rates and the balance of payments: Essays in memory of Egon Sohmen*, Studies in International Economics, vol. 7, Amsterdam: North-Holland Publishing Co.

Hodjera, Zoran. 1978. The Asian currency market: Singapore as a regional financial center. *IMF Staff Papers*, vol. 25.

International financial statistics. 1988. IMF, July.

Jao, Y. C. 1979. The rise of Hong Kong as a financial center. *Asian Survey*. July.

Johnson, Harry G. 1976. Panama as a regional financial center. *Economic Development and Cultural Change*, January.

Kindleberger, Charles P. 1974. *The formation of financial centers: A study in comparative economic history*, Princeton, N.J.: Princeton University Press.

McCarthy, Ian. 1983. Offshore in the Asian Pacific area in R. Moxon, J. F. Truitt and T. Roehl (eds.), *Asia Pacific dynamics*, Greenwich, CT: Jai Press.

Park, Yoon S. 1982. The economics of offshore financial center. *Columbia Journal of World Business*, Winter:31.

U.S. Congress. 1985. *Crime and secrecy: The use of offshore banks and companies*, Report by the Permanent Subcommittee on Investigations of the Committee on Governmental Affairs, United States Senate, Washington.

World Financial Markets. 1988. Morgan Guaranty Trust Company, March 18:26.

World Financial Markets. 1988. Morgan Guaranty Trust Company, Issue 3, July.

2. THE FEASIBILITY OF ESTABLISHING AN INTERNATIONAL FINANCIAL CENTER: THE CASE OF ANCHORAGE

Musa Essayyad
University of Alaska Anchorage

INTRODUCTION

In his first state-of-the-state address of January 1986, Governor of Alaska, Steve Cowper, outlined an economic plan to alleviate a state economy plagued by the persistent fluctuation and uncertainties that have lately engulfed world oil prices. According to the Governor's plan, the State of Alaska should take positive steps to diversify its energy-based economy and to rid itself of the dangers of relying on oil as the premiere source of state income. Governor Cowper envisioned, among other things, the need for promotion of international trade in Alaska's natural resources and other products through export credit guarantee facilities that may be offered by the Alaska Industrial Development and Export Authority (AIDEA); establishment of a statewide international trade center that would conduct in-depth marketing studies; establishment of a foreign trade zone in Anchorage; and promotion of the highly promising tourism sector. The institutionalized umbrella under which these promotional needs would be addressed is called "Trade Alaska." The working blueprint for this promotional and educational organization entails developing a strategy to meet the goal of diversification.

Another idea also suggested by the Governor was to set up an international financial center in Anchorage. The proposed center would function as an interbank market, comprised of foreign and local financial institutions, in which short-term, medium-term and long-term international lending and borrowing, denominated in Eurocurrencies--for purposes of investment, financing, hedging, and speculation--are consummated. Lenders and borrowers would include multinational corporations, banks, and governments.

The center has three objectives: first, to help interbank participants to spread risk through loan syndication and generate profits that may be derived from spreads, margins, service charges, commissions, capital gains, dividends and interest income; second, to finance Alaska's international trade; and third, to offer Alaskan entrepreneurs access to foreign capital to finance Alaskan projects at reasonably low cost. Although short-term benefits might be meager, the realization of profits through the international financial center is a long-term objective. Once operational, the center is expected to have a positive economic spill-over effect on local employment and business activities in travel, hotels, restaurants, utilities, real estate, and other sectors.

The profits generated by the center participants would be augmented by cost savings derived, first, from the wholesale nature of the Euromarket, which leads to smaller spread and economies of scale, and, second, from the absence of stringent restrictions in terms of taxes, reserve requirements on deposits, interest rate ceilings, deposit insurance premiums, transfers of funds, and government intervention in the credit market.

The purpose of this paper is to consider the economic feasibility of such an international financial center in Anchorage. The remaining part of the paper is divided into two major sections. The first section discusses the categorization of international financial centers in the developed and developing countries; and the second section examines the different comparative advantages with which Anchorage is endowed and why the city may or may not be competitive as an international financial center. The paper concludes with a summary and general evaluation of the feasibility.

CATEGORIZATION OF INTERNATIONAL FINANCIAL CENTERS

The above prelude on the definition, functions, and objectives of an international financial center (IFC) is formulated in terms of its relationship to Anchorage and reflects our aspirations as Alaskans to diversify the state's energy-based economy. The exact nature of IFCs is still debatable and needs further research. Financial economists have introduced many academic definitions that may be regarded as complementary. Kindleberger's (1974) pioneering work on IFCs defines the concept by pointing out that IFCs perform a medium of exchange, while they also have an interspacial store-of-value function. He argues that the specialized function of international payments and foreign lending or borrowing is best performed at one central place that is also the specialized center for domestic inter-regional payments.

Different authors suggest different classifications for IFCs. Despite heterogeneity of those classifications, the functional services and general requirements for establishing IFCs are relatively similar. McCarthy (1979) classifies IFCs as either "functional" or "paper." While the former refers to a full-fledged IFC that facilitates the channelling of surplus Eurocurrencies from primary world centers to final borrowers, a "paper" center is a location of record. McCarthy points out that both offshore types have common characteristics: they require low capital, low license fees, ease of entry, and low taxes and levies on offshore business.

Although Cheng (1976) uses the terms, "regional," "international," and "regional international," interchangeably and without serious distinction, Johnson (1976) rightly distinguishes between "regional" and "international" centers by arguing that a center is "regional" if it derives its role from its geographic proximity to its customers, and from the safety and ease of operation of the foreign banks' branches. The "international" center, on the other hand, serves as a magnet for financial powers whose financial, banking, and insurance activities serve the whole world or a major part of it. In another categorization, Park (1982) classifies IFCs into four types:

primary offshore centers that provide worldwide Eurocredits, such as London and New York; booking centers for shell branches of multinational banks such as the Bahamas and Cayman Islands; funding centers that perform the functions of inward financial intermediation, such as Panama and Singapore; and collection centers that carry out the functions of outward financial intermediation, as in Bahrain. In his research on the role of IFCs in developing countries, Gorostiaga (1984) distinguishes between the "traditional" and the "new" IFCs. Traditional IFCs have gained preeminence because of their capacity for generating capital based on domestic savings and international trade, such as London, New York, Frankfurt, Zurich, etc. The "new" IFCs, on the other hand, lack financial autonomy and are typically intermediate regional centers; they are regarded as a geographical extension of the "traditional" centers operating in different time zones.

Reed (1981) has identified hierarchical relationships among different IFCs. His taxonomy is based on five levels, namely host IFC (e.g., Alexandria, Geneva, Shanghai, Seattle); IFC (e.g., Bahrain, Los Angeles, Moscow); supranational financial center of the second order (e.g., Amsterdam, Chicago, San Francisco); supranational financial center of the first order (e.g., New York and London); and supranational financial center (e.g., London). Dufey and Giddy (1978) argue differently by pointing out that IFCs develop as extensions of domestic centers. Due to their efficiency, which is based on economies of scale, international communications, geographic locations, and financial services, domestic centers develop rapidly and become recognized as international financial centers. The development and efficiency of local banks, according to Dufey and Giddy, is conducive to a successful IFC in any center, including Anchorage, provided that local banks have wholeheartedly supported it. Furthermore, Wasserman (1963) suggests a distinction between "world" and "international" financial centers. "World" centers offer more extensive services than those provided by "international." (For an excellent review, see Howard Curtis Reed, 1980).

WHAT MAKES ANCHORAGE AN INTERNATIONAL FINANCIAL CENTER

Researchers suggest an endless number of variables that may contribute to the emergence of a successful IFC. Fortunately, in-depth studies on IFCs have mushroomed during the 1970s, setting the stage for a clearer explanation of this phenomenon. Generally, the common factor determining this financial phenomenon is explained by Robert Aliber's (1976) rationalization based primarily on either of the two theories: the industrial organization theory or the classical pure theory of international trade. According to the former, an IFC may survive market competition and develop thereafter if its borrowing-lending spread is reasonably narrow, thus implying that the IfC is more efficient than other competitors. Relative efficiency may be related to the concentration ratio of banks operating at a particular IFC. The higher the concentration ratio, the more competitive and profitable the IFC, and vice versa.

Nadler (1955) highlighted the following factors deemed prerequisite for a successful IFC: a stable convertible currency; stable and sustained demand and supply of this currency; a well-adjusted balance of payments that reflects the stability of the currency; the availability of local financial institutions with expertise in handling international banking and finance transactions; the presence of branches of multinational banks that function without government restrictions; and the existence of a central bank or office of a central bank at the IFC. Conninx (1987), executive director of DIBC (UK), a London-based international and banking consulting firm, and an author of books on foreign exchange, points out that bankers as well as corporate and private investors are usually drawn to places which are politically stable, have excellent communications, have a supply of qualified human resources (unless it is a postbox), fall within a time zone permitting at least minimal daytime contact, and have something special to offer, like low or no taxes (e.g., the Bahamas, Channel Islands), a banking secrecy law (e.g., Switzerland and Panama), or an activity in which they have a very strong, almost monopolistic position (e.g., financial futures in Chicago, currency options in Philadelphia, etc.).

While Kindleberger (1974) attaches great importance to the number, size, and international sophistication of local banks in building up a reputation for the IFC, Haegele (1975) places more emphasis on the historical role of the IFC, i.e., the IFC must have a recognized historical involvement in international trade in order to establish its international reputation, and this reputation can be bolstered if the IFC has historically been a restriction-free market. Citing New York port as a case in point, Vernon (1960) emphasizes the importance of successful international trade involvement as a prerequisite for a viable IFC. In an article on industrial organization of banking, Giddy (1983) pointed out that to have a well-developed IFC, there is a need for a free transferability of funds, free movement of some banks, and availability of regulatory-burden differences. In his study on the preeminence of IFCs, Reed (1980) discusses forty-one factors that are identified in the literature which are deemed important in considering the definition, eminence, and formulation of IFCs. His study is unique because he was the first researcher to utilize multivariate discriminant analyses in his research. Prior work was mainly descriptive in nature.

In summary, there are many factors that jointly play a decisive role in developing a competitive and surviving IFC. Despite the multitude of factors suggested by various scholars, these factors are complementary. The relative weight of each variable vis-a-vis others, nevertheless, is still debatable. The less controversial factors regarded by scholars and practitioners as prerequisites for a successful IFC are discussed here in terms of their relationships to Anchorage.

Availability of Developed Financial Infrastructure

Scholars and practitioners alike agree on the need for a sophisticated telecommunication network linking the IFC with other worldwide IFCs, active international air transportation with frequent scheduled flights to and from the other IFCs, and seasoned local financial expertise in international banking, finance, accounting, and business law.

Telecommunications. There is no doubt that Anchorage is equipped with a sophisticated telecommunication system operated by local companies. In addition to handling different types of international calls, local companies can also handle the increased demand for overseas data transmission. Currently, there are several options in Anchorage. Western Union offers an "Easy Link" facility, which is an electronic mailbox (the user accesses it through computer and modem) and Telex can send messages immediately or can be programmed to send them later. The latter is important for international transactions where time differences are extremely important. Moreover, there is a "Facsimile" facility which is popular in Japan and other Pacific Rim countries. "Dial Network" is a system in which the dial tone carries both voice and data transmissions to the recipient. And "Dedicated 24-Hour Circuit" resembles the "Dial Network" but differs in that the user purchases a "private line."

Air Transportation. For Anchorage to be a viable IFC, it must have an active international airport that bustles with many air carriers serving frequently scheduled flights to other financial centers. Currently, the international terminal of Anchorage Airport serves the following weekly number of scheduled flights: to Brussels, 2; Copenhagen, 3; Frankfurt, 5; London, 4; Paris, 3; Taipei, 3: and Tokyo, 19. There are many unscheduled overseas flights, also. In addition to international flights, the number of scheduled flights to the financial centers in the lower 48--i.e., Los Angeles, San Francisco, Seattle, Chicago, Miami, and New York--are adequate.

Anchorage International Airport is considered a medium-sized air-traffic hub. In 1983, it was the second largest of all 36 medium-sized airports in the United States in terms of passenger enplanements, and it was the largest in terms of foreign enplanements. In 1984, total passenger traffic had risen to 4 million passengers, in comparison to 10.5 million passengers at Seattle-Tacoma International Airport. According to the Alaska Department of Transportation, the number of foreign passengers enplaning at Anchorage is projected to grow at an annual rate of 6% through 1996. Planners at the airport foresee no critical problems for the next ten years in staying ahead of airport traffic. However, international growth may be hampered by looming uncertainties. One of the present problems is that fare discounting on the routes through Anchorage has been discontinued by the carriers. Another problem is that, in 1989, advanced space technology will economically justify the introduction of longer-range jets which will be able to skip Anchorage as a convenient refueling stop. Moreover, the Soviet Union has announced it will allow carriers to utilize Soviet airspace on non-stop flights between Tokyo and Europe. Following this course, carriers will be able to save three hours in flight time. British Airways and Air France have decided already to utilize the new route and Japan Air Lines has announced that it will be using this route more frequently in the future. Other sources of uncertainty that may affect the future growth of traffic at Anchorage International Airport are the increased competition from other airports and routes and the unpredictable future of U.S. military involvement in the Pacific region.

Anchorage Expertise in International Banking, Finance, Accounting, and Law. Rainier Bank Alaska, National Bank of Alaska, Alaska Housing Finance Corporation, Alaska Industrial Development and Export Authority, Alaska Power Authority, SOHIO, and other exporting and importing local businesses and agencies have all developed some expertise in international finance. Their involvement has either been through export-import financing, floating a very few Eurobonds in international capital markets, or financing local projects or mortgages. Although major U.S. brokerage houses in Anchorage are capable of handling trading futures contracts and stock options, they generally lack international expertise. The affiliation of local brokerage houses and some local banks with large and sound financial institutions in the lower 48 can help tremendously in the training and retraining of personnel in international banking and finance. Furthermore, despite some resource constraints, the University of Alaska Anchorage can be used as the nucleus for a more comprehensive international finance and banking training program aimed at meeting the needs of the proposed IFC. With a joint effort by the local financial community and the University, this program can eliminate many constraints. This will contribute to a long-term sustained human capital formation in the field of international banking and finance in Alaska. This approach is far superior to letting individual financial institutions train their personnel on a short-term *ad hoc* basis.

Structure of Anchorage's Banking Market

One of the major requirements of a developed, successful international financial center is the existence of efficient financial institutions that are genuinely desirous of making up an interbank money market conducive to risk-spreading. Therefore, this section of the study will survey Anchorage banks in terms of their types, their international banking delivery systems and services, their concentration, and the historical evaluation of their performances.

As of January 1, 1987, there were seventeen banks in Alaska -- ten state commercial banks, one state mutual savings bank, five national commercial banks, and one national savings bank. Assets and liabilities of banks have grown with the state economy, but remain a small fraction of the state gross domestic product (GDP). Table 1 shows that, despite the economic boom that came about with the dramatic increase of oil prices during the late seventies and early eighties and the Alaskan Oil Pipeline rush, the total-assets-to-GDP ratio grew from 13 percent in 1980 to only 18 percent in 1984 (data on state GDP for the period 1985-1986 is not available). In the period 1980-1984, bank assets have risen at a

TABLE 1
Alaska Banks Assets/GDP Ratios
(in U.S. $ million)

Year	Total Assets	GDP	Assets/GDP
1980	2539.85	20061.30	.13
1981	2782.38	25643.00	.11
1982	3484.64	25687.10	.14
1983	4323.33	25582.90	.17
1984	4853.33	26432.20	.18
1985	5341.65	NA*	-
1986	5439.08	NA*	-

Sources: Division of Banking, Securities, and Corporations, Department of Commerce and Economic Development, and Institute for Social and Economic Research, University of Alaska Anchorage.

*NA denotes not available data.

compounded annual growth rate of 13 percent compared to 6 percent in the state GDP. The growth rate of bank assets for the period 1980-1986, however, was as low as 11 percent. Although these assets grew during the collapse of oil prices in 1985 and 1986, the growth rate was not pronounced, since it was increasing at a decreasing rate.

Types and Classes of Anchorage Banks. Focusing on the types and classes of commercial banks in Anchorage, Table 2 indicates that after the merger of Security National Bank with Rainier Bank Alaska that followed the former's bankruptcy in 1986, only ten banks remain to make up the banking market in this city. Despite the international banking potential and the availability of a State Banking Statute that provides for and entices the establishment of foreign banks, there are no foreign banks in Anchorage. Of the ten domestic banks in the city, four are nationally chartered, two are state charters, and four are state-insured, non-member banks. Regarding the structure of Anchorage banks, there are one unit bank, three branch banks, and seven holding-company banks. United Bank Alaska is both a branch and a holding-company bank. Anchorage banks, with the exception of Alaska National Bank of the North, which is retail-oriented, are both wholesale- and retail-oriented. Ownership of all banks, with the exception of Alaska State Bank, is public held. Furthermore, all banks but one are incorporated in Alaska: National Bank of Alaska is incorporated in Delaware.

International Banking Delivery Systems and Services. Table 3 indicates that five banks in Anchorage render international banking services via money-center correspondent banks; three house small international departments having, on an average, three employees. Notwithstanding the small size of those departments, Rainier Bank Alaska, and, to a lesser extent, Alaska Pacific Bank and First Interstate Bank of Alaska are better equipped to handle international banking services. Rainier's comparative

TABLE 2
Classification of Banks in Anchorage

	Alaska Pacific Bank	Rainier Bank Alaska	National Bank of Alaska	United Bank Alaska	Ak. Natl Bank of the North	Alaska Mutual Bank	1st Interstate Bk of Ak	Alaska Statebank	Alaska Conti-nental Bk	1st Ntl Bk of Anchorage
Charter Type										
Nationally Char-tered (OCC)		X	X		X					X
State Chartered (FRS)	X						X			
State Insured				X		X		X	X	
Non-member Bank (FDIC)										
State Non-insured Bank										
Banks or BHC, 500 or More Shareholders (SEC)			X	X		X				
Bank Structure										
Unit Bank								X		
Branch Bank				X	X					X
Holding Company Bank	X	X	X	X		X	X		X	
Type of Business										
Wholesale Bank										
Retail Bank					X					
Wholesale/Retail Bank	X	X	X	X		X	X	X	X	X

(Continued)

TABLE 2 (Continued)
Classification of Banks in Anchorage

	Alaska Pacific Bank	Rainier Bank Alaska	National Bank of Alaska	United Bank Alaska	Ak. Natl Bank of the North	Alaska Mutual Bank	1st Interstate Bk of Ak	Alaska Statebank	Alaska Conti-nental Bk	1st Ntl Bk of Anchorage
Ownership										
Alaskan owned									X	
Alaskan owned but affiliated with other lower 48 banks										
Closely held								X		
Publicly held	X		X	X	X	X	X		X	X
Other		X								
Incorporation										
Alaska	X	X		X	X	X	X	X	X	X
Delaware			X							
Other States										
Foreign Country										
Number of Employees	150	100	700	245	204	280	218	150	47	671

TABLE 3
International Banking Delivery System
In Anchorage

Availability of International Banking Delivery Systems	Alaska Pacific Bank	Rainier Bank Alaska	National Bank of Alaska	Ak. Natl Bank of the North	Alaska Mutual Bank	1st Interstate Bk of Ak	Alaska Statebank
Correspondent - Bank Relationship		X	X	X		X	X
International Department	X	X	X				
Participation		X	X				
Representative Office		X					
Overseas Branch		X					
Edge Act Incorporation		X	X				
Agreement Corporation							
Foreign Affiliate							
International Banking Facility (IBF)		*1					

*1 Note - Rainier Bank Alaska parent corporation has several International Banking Facilities along the west coast.

TABLE 4
International Banking Delivery Services
in Anchorage

	Alaska Pacific Bank	Rainier Bank Alaska	National Bank of Alaska	Ak. Natl Bank of the North	Alaska Mutual Bank	1st Interstate Bk of Ak	Alaska Statebank
Export/Import Services and Financing							
Reimbursement letters of credit		X	X			X	
Export/import letters of credit	X	X	X			X	
Standby letters of credit	X	X	X			X	
Other - Trade Financing		X					
Other - Documentary Collections			X				
Money Transfer Services							
Foreign remittance	Drafts	X	X			X	X
International money orders		X	X	X			
Foreign currency bought/sold		X	X	X			
Other - Foreign Collections	X	X	X				
Other - Wire Transfers		X		X	X		

(Continued)

TABLE 4 (Continued)
International Banking Delivery Services
in Anchorage

Other International Services	Alaska Pacific Bank	Rainier Bank Alaska	National Bank of Alaska	Ak. Natl Bank of the North	Alaska Mutual Bank	1st Interstate Bk of Ak	Alaska Statebank
Eurodollar/Eurocurrency transactions		X					
International bank statement spreads		X					
Foreign credit information		X					
Foreign exchange trading		X					
Foreign exchange advisory service		X					
Other - Lock Box, Netting, & Other		X					
Other - Collection			X				

*1 Note - Alaska Continental Bank, First National Bank of Anchorage and United Bank Alaska do not offer any international banking services

TABLE 5
Five Year Summary of Performance of Alaskan Banks

Percentile Ranking (PCT)
within Reset Size Group *86
within State *85
*84

99% - Highest Percentile *83
0% - Lowest Percentile *82

Bank City	Assets $(000)	Asset Size Group	PROFITABILITY: Return on Average Assets (R.O.R./PCT	PROFITABILITY: Return on Average Equity (R.O.E.)/PCT	CAPITAL: Primary Capital --------- Assets/PCT	INTEREST SPREADS: Net Interest Spread (Tax Adj.)/PCT	NONINTEREST INCOME AND EXPENSE: Non-Interest Income -------- Average Assets /PCT	NONINTEREST INCOME AND EXPENSE: Over-head ------- Average Assets/PCT
1 ALASKA CONTINENTAL BK		5	-2.86/32	-37.25/32	7.85/65	4.76/65	2.91/99	6.87/65
ANCHORAGE	52105	5	0.27/99	2.84/99	9.99/99	5.78/65	3.46/99	7.63/32
		5	0.50/99	4.77/65	9.64/65	6.68/65	2.22/65	6.91/65
		6	1.67/99	7.72/99	13.56/99	12.75/99	0.27/99	8.75/99
		8	-1.70/99	-1.86/99	83.25/99	1.51/99	0.00/99	3.11/99
2 ALASKA MUTUAL BK		3	-5.08/49	xxxx/49	4.13/49	2.85/49	0.63/49	2.75/99
ANCHORAGE	619335	3	1.19/49	19.41/99	7.18/49	4.83/49	1.22/49	2.64/99
		3	1.19/49	18.08/99	6.71/49	5.08/49	0.56/49	2.82/99
		3	1.12/32	16.66/65	7.48/32	4.94/32	0.40/32	2.75/99
		4	1.27/56	13.79/27	6.58/27	2.88/13	0.65/27	3.32/99
3 ALASKA PACIFIC BK		4	1.32/74	20.34/99	7.57/49	6.04/61	1.05/49	3.85/86
ANCHORAGE	354586	4	1.17/74	18.28/74	7.35/24	6.17/49	1.04/49	3.88/86
		4	1.65/84	24.94/84	7.43/27	7.06/41	1.38/84	4.13/70
		4	1.29/27	19.18/41	7.55/56	7.61/84	1.23/56	4.75/70
		4	1.03/27	15.00/41	7.47/41	8.27/70	1.07/41	5.39/56
4 ALASKA STATEBANK		4	0.52/61	4.72/61	11.00/99	7.93/99	0.86/36	6.86/24
ANCHORAGE	156694	4	1.09/61	10.73/49	11.96/86	8.52/99	0.98/36	6.16/36
		4	1.22/27	15.29/27	9.04/99	7.55/84	0.87/13	5.39/27
		4	1.56/41	20.85/56	7.65/70	6.15/13	3.04/99	6.31/27
		4	1.21/41	15.11/56	8.48/84	9.80/84	1.11/56	6.95/13
5 FIRST INTERSTATE BK AK		4	-3.65/24	-46.27/36	7.37/26	5.46/36	1.30/86	6.63/36
ANCHORAGE	376054	4	1.08/49	13.07/61	9.50/74	7.10/74	1.46/61	5.00/49
		4	1.46/70	20.48/70	8.04/70	7.24/70	1.33/70	4.84/41
		4	1.58/56	21.89/70	7.27/27	7.49/70	1.27/70	4.75/56
		4	1.41/70	18.32/70	8.42/70	7.54/41	1.16/70	5.22/70
6 FIRST NB OF ANCHORAGE		3	1.83/99	10.16/99	18.00/99	8.47/99	1.69/99	4.72/49
ANCHORAGE	765116	3	2.36/99	13.58/49	18.03/99	9.27/99	1.81/99	5.01/49
		3	2.71/99	17.23/49	17.55/99	9.51/99	1.71/99	4.82/49
		3	2.67/99	19.87/99	14.72/99	9.60/99	1.51/65	4.57/65
		3	2.35/99	19.20/99	12.85/99	8.83/99	1.29/49	4.33/99

TABLE 5, continued
Five Year Summary of Performance of Alaskan Banks

Percentile Ranking (PCT)
within Reset Size Group
within State

*86
*85
*84
*83
*82

99% - Highest Percentile
0% - Lowest Percentile

Bank City	Assets $(000)	Asset Size Group	PROFITABILITY: Return on Average Assets (R.O.R.)/PCT	PROFITABILITY: Return on Average Equity (R.O.E.)/PCT	CAPITAL: Primary Capital ------- Assets/PCT	INTEREST SPREADS: Net Interest Spread (Tax Adj.)/PCT	NONINTEREST INCOME AND EXPENSE: Non-Interest Income -------- Average Assets/PCT	NONINTEREST INCOME AND EXPENSE: Over-head ------- Average Assets/PCT
7 NATIONAL BK OF ALASKA		2	1.60/99	12.54/99	13.74/99	6.90/99	1.71/99	4.59/99
ANCHORAGE	1160573	2	1.79/99	15.09/99	12.78/99	7.36/99	1.70/99	4.55/99
		2	1.81/99	15.95/99	12.27/99	7.45/99	1.73/99	4.62/99
		3	1.71/65	15.66/32	11.61/65	7.34/65	1.79/99	4.85/32
		3	1.74/49	16.10/49	11.39/49	8.49/49	1.58/99	5.24/49
8 RAINIER BK ALASKA		4	0.32/49	3.43/49	8.34/61	6.26/74	1.22/74	5.32/49
ANCHORAGE		4	0.42/24	3.55/24	12.62/99	5.84/36	3.14/99	6.99/24
		5	0.09/32	0.65/32	14.46/99	6.93/99	3.88/99	9.22/32
		5	0.05/49	0.38/49	15.57/99	9.75/99	2.53/99	9.52/49
		5	1.29/65	15.43/65	9.20/99	13.07.99	2.45/99	10.01/32
9 UNITED BK ALASKA		4	-5.20/11	xxxx/11	3.71/11	2.06/11	0.66/11	4.62/74
ANCHORAGE	429385	4	0.44/36	6.13/36	7.48/49	5.38/11	0.72/11	4.12/74
		4	1.45/56	18.22/56	8.11/84	6.92/27	1.11/56	4.08/84
		4	1.65/84	19.15/27	9.06/99	7.34/56	0.55/13	4.13/99
		4	1.59/84	18.97/84	9.10/99	7.57/56	0.51/13	4.20/84
10 ALASKA NB OF THE NORTH		4	-3.52/36	-62.43/24	6.14/24	5.38/24	2.60/99	8.95/11
FAIRBANKS	234441	4	0.11/11	1.67/11	6.84/11	6.73/61	2.59/86	7.31/11
		4	0.77/13	13.44/13	7.41/13	7.18/56	2.76/99	7.28/13
		4	0.57/13	12.91/13	5.51/13	6.80/27	2.56/84	6.64/13
		4	0.40/13	9.73/13	4.85/13	6.93/27	1.68/99	6.49/41
11 DENALI ST BK		7	-2.78/99	-7.94/99	24.18/99	5.91/99	0.42/99	8.78/99
FAIRBANKS	20422							
12 FIRST NB OF FAIRBANKS		4	1.37/86	20.16/86	8.35/74	7.37/85	1.19/61	4.78/61
FAIRBANKS	225305	4	1.79/99	26.38/99	7.41/36	8.03/86	0.95/24	4.48/61
		4	2.14/99	29.81/99	7.89/56	8.65/99	1.09/41	4.56/56
		4	1.88/99	25.37/99	8.12/84	9.54/99	1.01/41	5.26/41
		4	2.26/99	29.42/99	8.21/56	11.49/99	1.52/84	6.78/27

TABLE 5, continued
Five Year Summary of Performance of Alaskan Banks

Percentile Ranking (PCT)
within Reset Size Group
within State

99% - Highest Percentile
0% - Lowest Percentile

Bank City	Assets $(000)	Year	Asset Size Group	PROFITABILITY: Return on Average Assets (R.O.R.)/PCT	PROFITABILITY: Return on Average Equity (R.O.E.)/PCT	CAPITAL: Primary Capital ------- Assets/PCT	INTEREST SPREADS: Net Interest Spread (Tax Adj.)/PCT	NONINTEREST INCOME AND EXPENSE: Non-Interest Income -------- Average Assets/PCT	NONINTEREST INCOME AND EXPENSE: Over-head ------- Average Assets/PCT
13 B M BEHRENDS BK		*86	5	-1.97/99	-26.79/99	6.73/32	5.59/99	1.34/65	7.54/32
JUNEAU	62075	*85	5	0.19/65	2.46/65	8.72/32	6.49/99	1.21/65	6.10/65
		*84	5	0.40/65	5.30/99	8.15/32	6.51/32	1.21/32	5.96/99
		*83	5	0.24/99	3.31/99	7.67/49	7.13/49	0.59/49	5.24/99
		*82	5	1.16/32	15.14/32	8.01/65	7.66/65	0.57/32	4.67/65
14 UNITED BK ALASKA S EASTE		*86	5	-2.80/65	-30.80/65	8.14/99	3.30/32	0.53/32	5.37/99
JUNEAU	51815	*85	5	-0.70/32	-8.69/32	9.71/65	4.84/32	0.19/32	4.99/99
		*84	6	-2.01/99	-10.64/99	11.77/99	2.08/99	0.07/99	6.47/99
15 FIRST BK		*86	4	1.40/99	18.20/74	8.40.86	6.03/49	0.71/24	3.53/99
KETCHIKAN	156326	*85	4	1.62/86	22.07/86	8.14/61	5.84/24	1.51/74	3.77/99
		*84	4	1.29/41	18.20/41	7.78/41	5.74/13	0.99/27	3.71/99
		*83	4	1.60/70	23.80/84	7.48/41	7.31/41	0.73/27	4.23/84
		*82	5	1.96/99	32.86/99	6.92/32	6.20/32	2.12/32	3.99/99

Source: Sheshunoff & Co., **The Banks of the Pacific Northwest**, Austin, Texas. Reprinted by permission.

TABLE 6
Five Year Summary of Performance of Alaskan Banks

Percentile Ranking (PCT)
within Reset Size Group
within State

99% - Highest Percentile
0% - Lowest Percentile

*86
*85
*84
*83
*82

Bank City	Assets $(000)	Asset Size Group	LOANS: Domestic Loans to Deposits -Public Funds/PCT	Domestic Loan Growth /PCT	Net Charge-Offs ------- Average Loans /PCT	NONPERFORMING: Nonperforming Loans ------ Gross Loans /PCT
1 ALASKA CONTINENTAL BK		5	83.4/67	3.2/99	2.36/65	12.3/34
ANCHORAGE	52105	5	98.1/67	6.5/65	0.50/32	6.0/ 0
		5	88.2/34	33.9/99	0.79/32	8.4/ 0
		6	106.1/ 0	xxxx/xx	0.00/99	0.2/ 0
		8	186.8/ 0	xxxx/xx	0.00/99	
2 ALASKA MUTUAL BK		3	93.3/50	-0.5/49	3.94/49	17.9/ 0
ANCHORAGE	819335	3	152.3/50	29.1/99	0.19/99	3.9/50
		3	168.6/50	25.5/99	0.08/49	2.7/50
		3	171.0/67	49.3/99	0.08/99	2.2/ 0
		4	185.2/86	xxxx/xx	0.00/99	
3 ALASKA PACIFIC BK		4	116.9/88	20.4/99	0.41/86	3.4/75
ANCHORAGE	354586	4	110.8/25	21.5/86	0.52/49	1.5/88
		4	111.2/72	32.8/70	0.25/41	0.8/86
		4	93.3/58	29.3/41	0.47/41	2.0/58
		4	87.3/43	35.3/49	0.92/13	
4 ALASKA STATEBANK		4	81.4/13	-9.6/36	0.53/74	12.1/38
ANCHORAGE	156694	4	86.9/13	5.4/24	0.25/86	5.4/25
		4	86.2/15	0.6/27	0.10/99	7.4/ 0
		4	85.8/29	44.6/70	0.47/27	2.8/29
		4	70.2/ 0	13.7/15	0.45/70	
5 FIRST INTERSTATE BK AK		4	110.5/50	1.7/61	2.29/11	14.9/25
ANCHORAGE	378054	4	125.2/63	4.9/11	1.58/11	4.4/38
		4	105.0/43	22.2/56	0.15/84	6.0/15
		4	98.1/72	40.2/56	0.13/70	6.0/15
		4	102.9/58	49.2/65	0.45/56	
6 FIRST NB OF ANCHORAGE		3	73.6/ 0	4.9/99	1.75/99	2.5/50
ANCHORAGE	765116	3	71.8/ 0	-0.5/49	0.78/49	5.3/ 0
		3	73.1/ 0	11.1/49	0.05/99	3.3/ 0
		3	66.8/ 0	28.0/65	0.34/32	0.8/67
		3	54.7/ 0	17.2/99	0.30/49	

TABLE 6 Cont'd

Five Year Summary of Performance of Alaskan Banks

Percentile Ranking (PCT) within Reset Size Group within State

99% - Highest Percentile
0% - Lowest Percentile

*86 *85 *84 *83 *82

Bank / City	Assets $(000)	Asset Size Group	LOANS: Domestic Loans to Deposits -Public Funds/PCT	LOANS: Domestic Loan Growth /PCT	LOANS: Net Charge-Offs ------- Average Loans /PCT	NONPERFORMING: Nonperforming Loans ------ Gross Loans /PCT
7 NATIONAL BK OF ALASKA		2	94.6/ 0	-7.0/99	0.27/99	3.3/ 0
ANCHORAGE	1160573	2	96.2/ 0	15.7/99	0.09/99	1.2/ 0
		2	87.9/ 0	36.5/99	0.02/99	3.1/ 0
		3	68.1/34	17.7/32	0.10/65	1.3/34
		3	66.4/50	14.7/49	0.15/99	
8 RAINIER BK ALASKA NA		4	112.3/75	15.3/86	0.32/99	8.2/50
ANCHORAGE	167036	4	163.7/88	50.5/99	0.07/99	1.7/75
		5	127.4/67	21.4/65	-0.04/99	1.6/67
		5	87.0/50	44.7/99	0.16/99	1.9/50
		5	81.4/34	34.8/99	0.38/65	
9 UNITED BK ALASKA		4	84.4/25	-12.5/24	2.14/24	28.9/ 0
ANCHORAGE	429385	4	133.9/75	10.6/49	0.31/74	13.1/ 0
		4	149.7/86	35.0/84	0.20/56	3.6/29
		4	125.0/86	58.3/99	0.18/56	2.0/86
		4	156.2/72	54.6/82	0.60/41	
10 ALASKA NB OF THE NORTH		4	103.8/38	-28.5/11	1.75/36	16.5/13
FAIRBANKS	234441	4	116.8/50	5.8/36	0.80/36	10.1/13
		4	104.5/29	53.9/99	0.52/27	3.5/43
		4	66.3/15	-1.9/13	0.73/13	6.2/ 0
		4	76.8/15	16.7/32	0.69/27	
11 DENALI ST BK		7	56.8/ 0	xxxx/xx	0.03/99	0.0/ 0
FAIRBANKS	20422					
12 FIRST NB OF FAIRBANKS		4	111.0/63	0.6/49	0.90/61	5.3/63
FAIRBANKS	225305	4	113.8/38	20.8/74	0.42/61	3.0/63
		4	110.6/58	19.9/41	0.16/70	1.7/72
		4	91.9/43	55.0/84	0.06/84	2.0/72
		4	79.9/29	54.9/99	0.03/84	

TABLE 6 Cont'd
Five Year Summary of Performance of Alaskan Banks

Percentile Ranking (PCT) within Reset Size Group within State

99% - Highest Percentile
0% - Lowest Percentile

*86 *85 *84 *83 *82

Bank City	Assets $(000)	Asset Size Group	LOANS: Domestic Loans to Deposits -Public Funds/PCT	Domestic Loan Growth /PCT	Net Charge-Offs ------- Average Loans /PCT	NONPER-FORMING: Nonperforming Loans ------ Gross Loans /PCT
13 B M BEHRENDS BK		5	80.6/34	-5.7/65	1.40/99	7.9/67
JUNEAU	62075	5	92.0/34	1.9/32	0.28/65	3.5/67
		5	84.3/ 0	-0.1/32	0.51/65	5.6/34
		5	81.7/ 0	-9.2/49	1.41/49	6.0/ 0
		5	113.1/67	29.6/65	0.22/99	
14 UNITED BK ALASKA S EASTE		5	64.7/ 0	-17.1/32	2.62/32	14.0/ 0
JUNEAU	51815	5	79.5/ 0	50.0/99	0.10/99	5.3/34
		6	95.8/ 0	xxxx/xx	0.00/99	0.0/ 0
15 FIRST BK		4	63.3/ 0	5.1/74	1.13/49	2.5/88
KETCHIKAN	156326	4	65.4/ 0	18.4/61	1.30/24	3.1/50
		4	55.3/ 0	-3.0/13	0.59/13	3.0/58
		4	57.4/ 0	24.1/27	-0.19/99	2.1/43
		5	51.7/ 0	7.2/32	1.13/32	

Source: Sheshunoff & Co., **The Banks of the Pacific Northwest**, Austin, Texas. Reprinted by permission.

TABLE 7

Deposits, Loans and Profits of Alaskan Banks

			Domestic Deposits		Domestic Loans		Income Before		Loan Quality		Capital Adequacy	
Bank	City	Total Assets $(000)	Dec. 1986 $(000)	% Change Dec. '85 to Dec. '86	Dec. 1986 $(000)	% Change Dec. '85 to Dec. '86	Dec. 1986 $(000)	% Change Dec. '85 to Dec. '86	Nonperforming Loans ----- Gross Loans	Charge-Offs ------- Average Loans	Primary Capital ------ Assets	Nonperforming Loans ------- Primary Capital
1 NATIONAL BK OF ALASKA	ANCHORAGE	1160573	884525	-0.7	704115	-7.0	18076	-7.4	3.30	0.27	13.74	14.7
2 ALASKA MUTUAL BK	ANCHORAGE	819335	692427	8.6	593620	-0.5	-42017	xxxx	17.90	3.94	4.13	285.0
3 FIRST NB OF ANCHORAGE	ANCHORAGE	765116	527849	11.3	330042	4.9	12902	-17.6	2.48	1.75	18.00	6.1
4 UNITED BK ALASKA	ANCHORAGE	429385	392975	-2.0	276666	-12.5	-23664	xxxx	28.87	2.14	3.71	484.8
5 FIRST INTERSTATE BK AK	ANCHORAGE	378054	329504	4.7	246888	1.7	-14268	xxxx	14.91	2.29	7.37	121.2
6 ALASKA PACIFIC BK	ANCHORAGE	354586	310812	20.4	256845	20.4	4414	31.3	3.38	0.41	7.57	31.8
7 ALASKA NB OF THE NORTH	FAIRBANKS	234441	187440	-26.4	138700	-28.5	-10049	xxxx	16.54	1.75	6.14	150.2
8 FIRST NB OF FAIRBANKS	FAIRBANKS	225305	191725	14.8	145472	0.6	3025	-17.1	5.29	0.90	8.35	41.4
9 RAINIER BK ALASKA NA	ANCHORAGE	167036	110743	68.5	116675	15.3	418	2.0	8.23	0.32	8.34	72.6
10 ALASKA STATEBANK	ANCHORAGE	156694	128799	3.6	89682	-9.6	818	-53.7	12.08	0.53	11.00	61.1
11 FIRST BK	KETCHIKAN	156326	139126	16.2	56656	5.1	2051	-1.3	2.51	1.13	8.40	11.1
12 B M BEHRENDS BK	JUNEAU	62075	57899	4.4	40266	-5.7	-1226	xxxx	7.90	1.40	6.73	74.4
13 ALASKA CONTINENTAL BK	ANCHORAGE	52105	47276	18.8	39381	3.2	-1534	xxxx	12.30	2.36	7.85	114.4
14 UNITED BK ALASKA S EAST'N	JUNEAU	51815	47006	-13.1	27523	-17.1	-1664	xxxx	13.98	2.62	8.14	83.4
15 DENALI ST BK	FAIRBANKS	20422	15749	xxxx	8926	xxxx	-380	xxxx	0.00	0.03	24.18	0.0

Source: Sheshunoff & Co., **The Banks of the Pacific Northwest**, Austin, Texas.
Reprinted by permission.

advantage vis-a-vis others in handling international services emanates from its affiliation with Rainier Bancorporation, a Seattle-based bank holding company. Rainier Bancorporation has merged recently with Security Pacific.

Moreover, Table 4 shows that banks in Anchorage generate their international business primarily from export-import financing and, to a lesser extent, from money transfer services that do not require an advanced level of international banking sophistication. The emphasis on export-import financing in those banks is attributable to the increased role of international trade in Alaska's economy. The largest trading partners of Alaska are Japan, Canada, and Korea.

Performance Evaluation. Prior to the November 1985 collapse in world oil prices, most of the banks' performance measures have shown that Alaska banks were reaping the benefits of high and stable oil prices, the increased disposable personal income of Alaskans that accompanied the $8-billion Alaska Oil Pipeline project, and the resulting explosive growth of demand on real estate assets. Table 5 shows that prior to 1986 all ten banks reported ratios of positive return on assets and return on equity--the measures of bank profitability--that in many cases exceeded national averages. The primary capital-to-assets ratio, the measure of bank capital adequacy, indicates that prior to 1986 all local banks were appropriately capitalized, safe and secure. A bank is required to maintain a primary capital level of at least 5.5% to 6%, depending on the types of stock and debt it has issued. All banks except Alaska National Bank of the North in Fairbanks have reported higher primary capital levels, which were favorable to the financial results of the banks. Other important measures are ratios of nonperforming loans to assets and nonperforming loans to gross loans. Table 6 shows that both ratios are low, indicating low rates of loan delinquency.

This rosy picture of Alaskan banks--and of the banks of other oil states--has changed with the recession that followed the collapse of world oil prices in November 1985. As a result, some financial institutions were forced to incur losses, seek mergers, or resort to Chapter 11 bankruptcy. The reasons are:

(1) The dramatic decline in world oil prices from a high of $30 per barrel in November 1985 to a low of $10 per barrel in April 1986, which has left the whole state in a severe recession.

(2) Deep involvement of banks and savings and loan associations in real estate loans that were not able to weather the shock of the decline in oil prices. Table 7 shows that the 1986 construction and land development loans as a percentage of domestic loans were extremely high for Alaska Mutual Bank (47.8%), United Bank Alaska (47.4%), United Bank of Alaska Southeastern in Juneau (39.6%); and First Interstate Bank of Alaska (24.5%). The first three banks were involved in an FDIC-arranged merger that would provide for the infusion of $295 million in aid by the FDIC. With

additional help from the Hallwood group, the three banks merged in 1987 into a new entity called Alliance Bank. In 1987, Bank of the North and First Interstate merged with the National Bank of Alaska. On July 17, 1988, the state of Alaska, on the advise of the FDIC took over the management of Alaska Continental Bank. If family residential housing loans and nonfarm and nonresidential loans are taken into account, 1986 real estate loans as a percentage of domestic loans would be substantially higher. Table 7 indicates that the percentage of nonperforming loans, where interest is past due 90 days or isn't being paid on schedule, is generally higher than the national average of 1.94%. Nonperforming loan levels range from an average 0.48% of total loans in North Carolina to 6.51% in Alaska.

(3) Dwindling primary capital levels. Apart from Alaska Mutual Bank, United Bank Alaska, and Bank of the North, it seems that the 1986 primary capital-to-assets ratios of Alaskan banks were higher than the nationally required level of at least 5.5% to 6% (depending on the types of stock and debt the bank has issued).

In assessing the future direction of Alaskan banks, it is imperative to throw light on some of the pertinent economic and financial elements that would influence the state of their survival, competition, and general performance. First, oil prices. World oil prices have risen during the first half of 1987 to the $18 per barrel level, and have stabilized. Given this recent price trend, supply and demand conditions, and the inherent interest of industrial countries in maintaining stability of world oil prices despite the unabated Iraqi-Irani war, it can be safely predicted that oil prices will be stable at the $15-$18 range. In the long run, however, oil prices are governed by a more complex array of political, economic and expectational forces. The unpredictability of politics in the Middle East, whether in the Israeli-Arab front or the Iraqi-Irani front, may lessen substantially the accuracy of a long-term prediction of oil prices. Second, there is the controversy surrounding the Arctic National Wildlife Refuge (ANWR). A fierce debate exists between the environmentalists and pro development camp on the possibility of tapping ANWR's oil riches. Based on the realities of Alaska's economic problems, many observers believe that this debate will be settled, sooner or later, in favor of the pro development camp. If materialized, the pro development plan would be translated into a greater oil production capacity, putting Alaska at the top of the list of U.S. oil-producing states. Third, there is the possibility of the $8-11 billion Trans-Alaska Gas System. The objective of the proposed project is to give the Yukon Pacific Corporation the right to transport North Slope natural gas through the pipeline to Valdez, where it would be liquified and then moved by ships to Japan, South Korea, and Taiwan. Economically, these countries, particularly Japan, are not yet convinced of the viability. and the Corporation has a great deal of political lobbying to do to convince these countries to buy the liquified gas. If the plan succeeds, there will be tremendous business opportunities that are reminiscent of those provided by the Trans-Alaska Oil Pipeline. Fourth, there are the intact assets of the

Permanent Fund. Political tampering with the fate of the Permanent Fund by trying to slice its earnings to finance current government projects is a malignant action and would jeopardize the benefits for future generations. The more the Fund's earning and assets are kept intact, the greater the future benefits that would be accrued to local financial institutions. Fifth, there is the issue of long-term versus short-term planning. Future performance of banks will rely heavily on whether bank management is oriented toward short-term or long-term profits and growth. The former is myopic and self destructive. Long-term planning is a prerequisite for economic survival and growth. Domestic and probably international portfolio diversification should be addressed in any long-term planning if local banks wish to weather any more shocks associated with loans concentrated in one sector, such as real estate.

Concentration Measures of Anchorage Banks in 1986. In the beginning of this paper, reference was made to Aliber's (1976) explanation of international banking phenomena. He rationalizes that the success of international banking is based on the banks' relative efficiency, as measured by the concentration ratios of these banks. In fact, this theory is not confined in its application to international banking. Efficiency of domestic banking can also be measured by concentration measures. Table 8 shows that, while CR4, CR8, and CRE measures are high and, therefore, support the hypothesis that Anchorage banks are highly *locally* concentrated, *locally* competitive, and thus *locally* efficient, the H^2 measure provides weaker evidence for this premise. Since there is no competition from foreign or lower 48 banks, caution should be used, however, in interpreting the results.

Political Stability

Political stability is one of the most important factors determining the feasibility of setting up and developing a successful international financial center. Assessing political or sovereign risk is a cumbersome task. In fact, this is the very reason for the present immense problems of U.S. and other multinational banks in accumulating nonperforming loans in the developing countries. Those loans represent the bulk of the $62 billion in Third World debt. Measuring sovereign risk is far from accurate. A recognition of the importance of coexisting with this dilemma is evident in the initiative taken by Citicorp when it daringly pioneered the move to set aside an initial $3 billion in additional reserves to cover losses on its Third World loans. Many major banks have followed suit.

Anchorage is far more politically stable than those IFCs situated in developing countries, such as the Bahamas, Bahrain, Hong Kong, Manila, Panama, and Singapore. Consider the case of the *Bahamas*, whose 1984 Royal Commission of Inquiry probe found drug corruption to be widespread in the government of Prime Minister Lynden Pindling. The recent resounding election victory of Pindling was attributed by Bahamian officials to grass-roots resentment against America's interference. Pindling's party is accusing American right-wingers and some members of Congress of trying

TABLE 8

Concentration Measures of Anchorage Banks in 1986

Bank	Loans (in U.S. $ thousand)	Deposits
Continental	38,181	47,276
Alaska State	88,767	128,799
Alaska Pacific	252,717	310,812
First Interstate	234,653	329,504
United	266,666	392,975
Mutual	562,900	692,427
Rainier	115,162	110,743
Bank of the North	133,701	187,440
First N.B. of Anchorage	327,601	527,849
National Bank of Alaska	699,837	885,992
CR4	0.68	0.69
CR8	0.95	0.96
H^2	0.15	0.15
CRE	0.80	0.80

Source: Division of Banking, Securities, and Corporations, Department of Commerce and Economic Development

Notes: All the measures described below can take on values that range between zero and one. The higher the value, the greater the degree of concentration.

CR4 is the proportion of the relevant total amount accounted for by the four banks with the largest individual amounts.

CR8 is constructed in the same manner as CR4, but reflects the proportion held by the top eight banks.

H^2 is the Hirschman-Herfindahl index.

CRE is a modification of Thiel's entropy measure.

to replace Pindling with the opposition leader, who pledged to clean up government corruption.

Furthermore, consider the case of *Bahrain*. Its past preeminence as an IFC is linked to some factors. First, there is the fact of the abundance of surplus funds in the neighboring oil countries of Saudi Arabia, Kuwait, Qatar, the United Arab Emirates, and the Sultanate of Oman. The quadruple hike of oil prices in the late seventies and early eighties that led to the accumulation of huge petrodollar surpluses in these neighboring countries, coupled with the weak absorptive capacity of their markets, had encouraged them to channel their surplus funds through the Bahrain offshore banking center. Second, the breakout of the Lebanese civil war that led to the unfortunate setback in Beirut's position as an IFC had contributed indirectly to the emergence of Bahrain as the new Middle Eastern IFC.

Yet, we sense the perils of political instability in Bahrain. The Iran-Iraq war of attrition, which broke out in 1979, does not seem to be abating. The war has magnified the uncertainty element in the already unpredictable region. The recent development of an increased U.S. military presence in the area, through the reflagging of Kuwaiti oil tankers; the threat of Iranian reprisal; and the danger of more Soviet involvement--all have contributed to the escalation of risk. Such a volatile atmosphere is not conducive to continued flourishing of international financial activities. Although political risk in Bahrain seems high, it is not the only factor that may lead to the weakened position of the country as an IFC. The slump in oil markets and the resulting shrinkage of oil countries' surpluses which represent the "bread and butter" of Bahrain's IFC is an additional factor that may lead to its retreat as one of the forerunners in the IFC race. Cognizant of the ramifications of these developments, the Government of Bahrain has recently commissioned the United Nations Conference on Trade and Development (UNCTAD) to undertake a study aimed at recommending ways and means to foster other service industries in Bahrain.

The situation in *Hong Kong* is also lacking in stability. Political risk in this country may emanate from the unpredictable ramifications of the recent conclusion of the British-Hong Kong Treaty that would revert Hong Kong's territorial sovereignty to China in 1997. Some observers find it discouraging to link the future of Hong Kong to that of the communist People's Republic of China, whose recent political upheavals and harsh government crackdowns on pro-Western elements may distort the image of Hong Kong as a sound IFC, and may deter multinational financial institutions from heavily transacting business there. Others optimistically argue that the new treaty will improve the image of China more than it will hurt the image of Hong Kong. Through Hong Kong, China will have a great opportunity to gain access to the colony's capital markets in order to finance, at reasonable low cost, its industrial, agricultural and service projects.

Political unrest in *Manila* is also a cause for alarm. The overthrow of the Marcos regime has proved that the dictator's rule was not the only problem facing the Philippines. The unfortunate sporadic fighting, kidnapping, and continuous retaliation between the military and the insurgents in the south are still part of the Philippines' daily life. The resulting political instability engulfing this nation is not conducive in any way to the financial stability necessary to maintain a viable IFC in the capital city of Manila.

The picture of *Panama's* political risk is no different. The U.S. administration has been accusing Panama's military leader, Gen. Manuel Antonio Noriega, of murder, drug activities, electoral fraud, and intelligence dealings with Cuban authorities that are inimical to U.S. security interests. Recently, riots and violent protests erupted against the military leadership, resulting in death and injury to hundreds.

Although *Singapore* is relatively stable, its political and economic fabrics may not make it as stable as Anchorage. Recently, the government of Prime Minister Lee Kuan Yew detained without trial 16 people charged with communist connections in Sri Lanka, the Philippines, and Europe. Opposition groups do not believe there is an internal communist threat in Singapore, because the standard of living is very high. This incident has shocked Singaporeans and provoked international protests. The European Parliament, members of the U.S. Congress, and several human-rights organizations have called for the detainees' release or trial. The crash of the Singapore Stock Exchange that took place two years ago is another manifestation of the country's fragile economy and political structures.

In capsule, we have shown that Alaska is more politically stable than the IFCs in the developing countries of the Bahamas, Bahrain, Manila, Hong Kong, Panama and Singapore. However, political stability is not confined to Alaska. It is also alive and strong in western U.S. and Canadian financial centers, particularly those in Seattle, San Francisco, Los Angeles and Vancouver, whose high degree of sophistication and competitiveness in international banking are too colossal to ignore.

Anchorage Time Zone Advantage

For an IFC to be successful, it should fall within a time zone permitting, at least, minimal daytime contact to consummate financial transactions with other existing financial centers. This requirement is essential. Table 9 shows a ten-hour time difference between Anchorage and most financial centers in Europe. Therefore, with no overlap of daytime contact, there can be no possible trading between Anchorage and those centers (assuming Anchorage's working hours to be from 9:00 a.m. to 5:00 p.m. local time). Despite the one-day lag (costing one working day a week), the time difference between Anchorage and the Asian Pacific financial centers, however, is favorable. An Anchorage IFC, if established, can transact business for two hours with Hong Kong, Manila, Peking, and Singapore; three hours with Osaka, Yokohama, and Tokyo; and four hours with Melbourne and Sydney, Australia. During those hours, Chicago, New York, and Miami will be closed. The Anchorage time zone advantage can be nullified, however, by competition from the western financial centers in San Francisco, Los Angeles, Seattle and Vancouver. Moreover, Anchorage's comparative advantage in this regard may not be that pronounced, since the Chicago Board of Trade recently extended its trading hours from 7 to 10 p.m. EDT Monday through Thursday. While the volume of trading has not been huge, compared to daytime trading, it still represents a source of competition as far as the time difference is concerned. Some skeptics fear that evening trading at the Chicago Board of Trade will be a money loser for the exchange and smaller firms alike. The CBOT extension of evening hours was intended to meet the Japanese demand for trading of U.S. Treasury bonds and notes futures.

The prospects of Anchorage as an IFC are strongly linked to the future emergence of international financial markets that would develop into one global marketplace with a 24-hour trading. Fortunately, this possibility is not remote. With the increased integration of international capital markets as a result of the advanced computer and communication technologies, Anchorage might, in the long run, benefit from those future developments. Another possible approach that can be adopted by Anchorage's future Eurocurrency dealers to circumvent some of the limitation of time zone differences with major financial centers is to extend their working hours beyond 5 p.m. or to start their working day in the afternoon. The latter approach is not outlandish to the Alaskan way of life: currently, stock brokers at local brokerage houses start their trading at 5 a.m.

Tax Considerations

Taxes in Some International Financial Centers. Zero or low income tax rates are among the most important factors that have allowed countries like Bahrain, Bahamas, Hong Kong, Cayman Islands, Singapore and Panama to flourish and prosper as IFCs. In general, multinational banks and corporations are attracted to those nations because of the tax deferral provisions of the corporate income tax codes of their parent countries. The corporate and individual tax rates for Bahrain, Hong Kong, British Columbia, Canada, Panama, Alaska, and the United States

TABLE 9
Time Difference Between Anchorage and Some Selected International and Regional Financial Centers

Anchorage @ 09:00 a.m.

Amsterdam	19:00
Antwerp	19:00
Bahrain	21.00
Bangkok	01:00*
Barcelona	19:00
Basel	19:00
Brussels	19:00
Buenos Aires	15:00
Cape Town	20:00
Chicago	12:00
Copenhagen	19:00
Frankfurt	19:00
Geneva	19:00
Hong Kong	01:00 *
Jakarta	01:00 *
Johannesburg	20:00
Kobe	03:00 *
Kuala Lumpar	03:00 *
London	18:00
Los Angeles	10:00
Luxembourg	19:00
Madrid	20:00
Manila	02:00 *
Melbourne	04:00 *
Montreal	13:00
Moscow	21:00
New York	13:00
Osaka	03:00 *
Paris	19:00
Peking	02:00 *
Rio de Janeiro	15:00
Rome	19:00
San Francisco	10:00
Seattle	10:00
Seoul	03:00 *
Shanghai	02:00 *
Singapore	02:00 *
Stockholm	19:00
Sydney	04:00 *
Tokyo	03:00 *
Venice	19:00
Vienna	19:00
Yokohama	03:00 *
Zurich	19:00

Asterisk (*) indicates morning of the following day

are compared in the next section. The comparison is applicable only to foreign banks operating at IFCs.

Bahrain does not have any corporate income tax on financial institutions registered at its offshore banking center. It does charge, however, a significant annual registration fee that varies with the type of services and nationality of the bank's ownership. Also, Bahrain does not have any personal income tax on residents and nonresidents.

Income for financial institutions arising from syndicated offshore activities in *Singapore* may be tax-exempt. Interest on deposits with an approved bank, paid to a company not carrying on business or having a permanent establishment in Singapore, is also exempt from income tax. All individuals are taxed on incomegenerated in Singapore. Individuals normally are taxed at 40%, with some provisions for reduced rates depending on the workers' situations.

Hong Kong has a corporate rate of 18.5% on all profits arising from or derived from business activities in Hong Kong. Individuals are taxed on Hong Kong-based income with tax rates varying from 5% to 25%

Panama has variable tax rates for corporations ranging from 20% to 50% on all income earned within the country. The interest earned on Panamanian government securities or on savings and time deposits with banks established in Panama is not taxable. Nonresidents are taxed only on income from Panamanian sources, with rates varying from 22% to 56%.

The *Canadian* national basic rate is 46%, with a 10% provincial abatement for a net federal rate of 36%. British Columbia, among the Canadian provinces closest to Alaska, has a rate of 16% for a total effective rate on corporations of 52%. Corporations in Canada are subject to tax on their worldwide income and tax credits are available for payment of foreign taxes. The highest combined federal and provincial tax rate in British Columbia is 55%. There are also a surtax and a local tax.

The traditional tax haven has been *Switzerland.* Multinational corporations and banks are attracted by the low Swiss income tax rate of about 10%.

Taxes in the U.S. and Alaska. The highest federal corporate tax in the United States is now 34%. If net income is above $100,000, then a 5% surcharge is added, yielding an effective rate of 39%. Corporations are taxed on their worldwide income. The personal income tax rate ranges from 11% to 38.5% while the tax on income of foreign corporations is assessed at 30% unless tax treaties specify a lower tax rate.

The corporate tax rate in Alaska ranges from 1% to 9.4%, with the maximum rate applied to profits above $90,000. Currently, there is no personal income tax in Alaska. The recent deterioration of oil prices and its adverse impact on the local economy has pushed some politicians to ask for reinstatement of the individual income tax. To attract foreign multinational corporations to Alaska, Governor Cowper has called for repeal of the unitary tax that is payable by those corporations based in Alaska on their profits earned worldwide.

Furthermore, foreign banks which do not maintain a place of business in Alaska for the receipt of deposits and which do not engage in any banking business are exempt from laws and taxation in Alaska. This means that multinational banks can open shell branches in Alaska (Alaska Statute, Sec. 06.10.010, of Chapter 10 on Model Foreign Bank Loan Act).

Alaska versus Delaware. More than half of the Fortune 500 companies and more than 40% of New York Stock Exchange companies are incorporated in Delaware. Of particular interest to Alaskans is the fact that the National Bank of Alaska is also incorporated in Delaware. This section explores the reasons, including the issue of taxes, that Delaware can attract those corporations, and the ways Alaska can emulate and compete with Delaware in attracting companies to be incorporated in Alaska.

Incorporation in Delaware is attractive partly because of low state and local taxes, but mostly because of its laws and regulations. Delaware has a history of low stable tax policies, while many other states' taxes are higher and their policies frequently change. Delaware's tax rate is regressive. A firm pays 8.7% on a net income of $30 million or less, and only 2.7% on a net income above $30 million. In Alaska, a firm pays 9.4% on income that is greater than $90,000.

To incorporate a bank in Alaska, a minimum of a $250,000 is required as paid-in capital. While other states may have different minimum requirements, Delaware has none. Another incentive for incorporation in Delaware is that it has the only separate business court system with a long record of pro-management decisions. Observers argue that the outcome of litigation in Delaware is more predictable than in the legal systems of other states, and, because of the business court specialty, litigation is not time-consuming. Furthermore, transactions related to a bank's own stock are less regulated than in Alaska, as each transaction must be approved by the Alaska Department of Commerce and Economic Development. In Delaware, new corporations can be set up within a week at a cost of $200.00. Incorporating in Alaska, on the other hand, can be a time-consuming and expensive process. The Department of Commerce and Economic Development decides, among other things, whether the new bank will serve the needs of the public. The population density and economic characteristics of the area to be served is examined, along with the character and fitness of the applicant. Clearing those steps can take up to a year and would is quite costly.

The objective in presenting the above comparison is to illustrate what kind of regulation we in Alaska should consider relaxing in order to be more competitive. The governor's recent call for the repeal of the unitary tax on multinational corporations based in Alaska, and his proposal for a new state system of mediation and arbitration that avoids the traditional time-consuming litigation, are examples of the liberal stance that the state government in Alaska has exhibited to attract foreign investors.

Geographic Proximity of Anchorage to International Capital Markets

Geographic location is one of the determinants for establishing any business activity, let alone setting up an IFC. Location economics is pervasive, not only in industrial management, business and agriculture, but also in banking and finance. To be viable, IFCs should be located near the suppliers and users of funds. Anchorage meets this requirement as it is equidistant from Europe, Scandinavia, the Pacific Rim, and the Untied States. For a viable IFC in Anchorage, there is great need for more frequently scheduled flights between Anchorage and IFCs in these other locations. The demand on the services of the proposed IFC in Anchorage can be from the Asian Pacific countries. The economies of these countries are expanding, and demand for capital to sustain growth in these places has been very high. This is why some multinational banks in Hong Kong, Singapore, and Bahrain were paying premiums above the Eurodollar market rate, so that they could attract foreign funds to be used in ASEAN and other neighboring countries. The People's Republic of China can also be a great prospective user of capital. The States, including Alaska, are also prospective users of capital. Surpluses in Japan, Taiwan, Korea, and some OPEC countries are relied upon to meet the demand.

Economic Stability

Like political stability, economic stability is an important component of a competitive and surviving IFC. Compared to the economies of Hong Kong, Singapore, and Panama, Alaska is endowed with a huge wealth of natural resources, but lacks a manufacturing base. In addition to oil, coal, fish, timber, and tungsten, Alaska has a massive amount of unexploited antimony, silver, tin, gas, zinc, copper, lead, asbestos, uranium, molybdenum, mercury, and platinum. The main barriers to utilization of these resources are the lack of a highly developed infrastructure (which is very costly to develop) and the need for adequate capital to finance the tapping of these natural resources. Therefore, the establishment of an IFC in Anchorage can benefit Alaska with the access to international capital needed to develop its rich resources. Another contributing factor to the economic stability of Alaska is its association with the biggest and richest of the democratic capitalist nations. This entails two immense economic assets: Alaska is not only in the United States, but is also one of the "sovereign" states. Tussing (1984) points out that to be part of the greatest of social and monetary unions, and subject to its laws and business practices, is an awesome economic advantage, particularly for the huge reservoir of skilled labor, technology, information and ideas, communications, media, entrepreneurship and financial capital such an association provides. These riches are readily abundant in Alaska or instantly accessible for any enterprise that has a promise of economic success.

Unique Services

An important way to bolster the competitive edge of a financial center is to provide a unique service or offer a niche. Some examples are: financial futures in Chicago and currency options in Philadelphia. To avoid unrealistic approaches, Anchorage financial institutions must develop financial services and products that create a demand or meet a need and they must be able to deliver these services in an efficient and effective manner to a highly competitive market place. Possible services are insurance and co-insurance, lumber futures and flotation of commodity-indexed financing instruments, but these ideas still need thorough investigation, with considerable emphasis on the relevant federal and state laws. This does not mean that the services of the proposed IFC must be confined to these specialties; rather, the IFC should additionally offer all types of Eurocurrency borrowing and lending.

Role of the Alaska Permanent Fund

The potential role of the Permanent Fund can be crucial in establishing an IFC in Anchorage. With assets of approximately $9 billion as of June 1986, and an estimated $30 billion by the next decade, the Fund may be able to help create the center, provided the idea is feasible and the legislators vote, first, in favor of international investment, and, second, for the Fund's being the nucleus of the proposed center.

Ease of Restrictions

For a country to host a successful IFC, there should be liberal government regulations on foreign banking, foreign exchange transactions, taxation, securities, and work permits for expatriate staff. Ease of restrictions can also be developed through the International Banking Facilities (IBFs). U.S. financial depository institutions, Edge Act corporations, Agreement corporations, and U.S. branches or agencies of foreign banks authorized to engage in business activities in the U.S. qualify as IBFs. Should the idea of opening IBFs in Alaskan banks be feasible in terms of cost/benefit analysis, then the role of state government would be negligible, since the existing favorable regulations governing IBFs are already in force. Moreover, IBFs could offer all services now provided by offshore banking centers. However, the question is whether Anchorage, with its constraints, can compete with the 550 other IBFs in the lower 48 states, especially those in the western states and Canada.

No city in the U.S. has been declared a full-fledged offshore banking center like those of Bahrain, Bahamas, Hong Kong, Panama and Singapore. Many years ago, New York City tried unsuccessfully to obtain that status, but the Federal Reserve Board was not receptive, reasoning that such a center in the city with the largest flow of capital in the world might curtail the effectiveness of the Fed's monetary policy tools, since the center would be outside its jurisdiction. Given the attitude of the Fed, setting up an offshore banking hub in other states, including Alaska, would encounter obstinate resistance. The idea of establishing an IFC has also been considered by Hawaii. Despite several advantages--its tourist fascination, its geographic proximity to the capital markets in the Asian Pacific countries, its time zone, and its developed financial and banking infrastructure--Hawaii still has far to go in trying to be an IFC.

Although the absence of a personal income tax in Alaska is advantageous, establishing a full-fledged IFC in Anchorage demands even more liberalization. The governor's recent call for the repeal of the unitary tax on multinational corporations and the idea of establishing a time-saving legal mediation and arbitration system are positive steps in this direction. To set up a center in Anchorage that functions along the lines of those in Bahrain, Hong Kong, and Singapore, state and federal laws and regulations already in force should be eased. And that process requires tremendous political clout, maneuverability, and endurance on the part of Alaska's representatives and senators, at both the state and federal levels.

Anchorage's Free Trade Zone

A free trade zone is an area generally located near a seaport or airport in which firms can import goods duty-free, if they are to be re-exported or used in the manufacture of goods for export. A free trade zone is regarded as a phenomenon parallel to offshore banking centers.

> "They serve to articulate the commercial and industrial process on a world scale just as the IFCs serve for the financial articulation of that same global market. Free zones and IFCs respond to the same phenomenon of internationalization of production and capital, and to the new forms of integration of the periphery with the center of the capitalist system." (Gorostiaga 1984, p. 93).

Currently, the Municipality of Anchorage is considering establishing a foreign trade zone at Anchorage International Airport and the Port of Anchorage. It is expected that an application will be submitted thereafter to the federal government for possible approval in a year. It should be mentioned that in 1984, the federal government approved a foreign trade zone for Valdez, a port city in Southcentral Alaska. The zone is currently inactive due to a lack of local interest! While the demand for a foreign trade zone in Anchorage is uncertain yet, according to the Director of the Port of Anchorage, interest has been expressed by several firms.

Secrecy

Banking secrecy and confidentiality of financial transactions are the most important attractions of some international banking centers, like Switzerland and Panama. The 1934 Banking Law of Switzerland provides for banking secrecy. Although not unique to Switzerland, bank secrecy is more thorough there than in most other countries. Like Swiss laws, Panama's Banking Law of 1959 requires financial institutions to observe secrecy with respect to the existence of and amounts in accounts, as well as the identities of the owners. In recent years there has been friction between Swiss authorities and the U.S.Securities and Exchange Commission, and between the Panamanian and U.S. authorities, about interpretation of secrecy because of litigation related either to insider trading or drug smuggling. Setting up an IFC in Anchorage could be promising if state banking laws are enacted to provide for bank secrecy. The experience of existing IFCs can be emulated in this regard.

Image and Quality of Life

Many people overseas as well as in many areas of the lower 48 have negative, primitive perceptions about Alaska. They are still under the impression that all people in Alaska, including those in Anchorage, live in igloos and use dog sleds to commute to and from work. This stereotyping has hurt the state's image to a great extent, and there is a dire need to clarify some facts. Anchorage is a cosmopolitan city with all the amenities, facilities and ethnicity of any U.S. city. Warmed by the Pacific current, the weather in Anchorage is not as harsh as outsiders think. Summer temperatures in Anchorage average in the mid-60s and range upward to the mid-70s. Lows during winter average 20 degrees, with the weather overall approximating that of Montana. Normal annual precipitation measures 14.74 inches. In fact, Anchorage receives less snowfall than some cities in Ohio, Montana, Nebraska, and the Dakotas, and less probably than the international financial centers of Vancouver or Montreal.

SUMMARY

One approach to diversify Alaska's energy-based economy is to rally the financial sector, both local and state governments, around the idea of establishing an international financial center (IFC) in Anchorage. The proposed center would emulate the success stories of the offshore banking hubs in Bahrain, Hong Kong, Panama and Singapore. The main objective of this paper is, therefore, to investigate this possibility. In general, many factors jointly play a decisive role in developing a competitive and surviving IFC. Despite the multitude suggested by various scholars, these factors are complementary. The relative weight of each variable vis-a-vis others, nevertheless, is still debatable. The less controversial factors regarded by scholars and practitioners as prerequisite for a successful IFC are discussed here in terms of their relationship to Anchorage. In assessing the different factors, the author has found that some may contribute favorably to the idea of establishing an IFC in Anchorage. These factors are: sophisticated telecommunications; a well-developed international airport; political stability; an economic stability that is relatively stronger than that of Bahrain, Hong Kong, Panama and Singapore; a time zone advantage; and a relative geographic proximity to foreign IFCs in the Asian Pacific countries. The factors that are less favorable to the establishment of an IFC in Anchorage are: less frequently scheduled flights between Anchorage and other IFCs; a less than enthusiastic international investment policy on the part of Alaska's State Senate to allow the Permanent Fund to invest internationally; and the fact that Anchorage's free trade zone has a long way to go before it becomes operational. The unfortunate experience of Valdez' free trade zone can be discouraging for the Municipality of Anchorage--local businesses in Valdez, Alaska were not interested in utilizing its facility. Furthermore, the idea of setting up an IFC in Anchorage would be seriously hampered by four significant factors. First, there is the problem of tough competition from other North American, European, and Asian IFCs, which is bolstered by the unique services they render to the world. The absence of a possible financial niche, that Anchorage could capitalize on in pursuing the idea of establishing an IFC, can be detrimental to its future prospects. Second, the city is faced by a lack of international financial and banking expertise by Anchorage's shaky financial institutions who have been adversely affected by the present Alaskan recession. Third, there is a need for more competitive tax rates and more liberal government regulations that can attract multinational enterprises to Anchorage. And fourth, Alaska's political clout with the federal government is questionable and it would be, therefore, extremely difficult to secure a special status for Anchorage as a full-fledged offshore banking center that is free of the direct control of the U.S. Federal Reserve System.

REFERENCES

Alaska Department of Labor. *Alaska economic trends.* Various monthly issues, 1986-1987.

Alaska Department of Revenue. 1987. *Revenue sources*, January.

Alaska Pacific Bank. 1986. *Alaska business trends: 1987 preliminary forecast.*

Alaska Statute. Title 36: Public Contracts, Sections 36.10.005, 36.10.006, and 36.10.990 on employment preferences and local hire.

Aliber, Robert. 1976. Towards a theory of international banking. *Economic Review.* Federal Reserve Bank of San Francisco, Spring:5-8.

Anchorage Chamber of Commerce. 1987. *Anchorage, 1987.*

Cheng, Hang-Sheng. 1976. The U.S. West Coast as an international financial center. *Economic Review*, Spring:9-19.

Conninx, Raymond. 1987. A letter sent to the author, June 1987. DIBC, London, UK

Dufey, Gunter, and Ian Giddy. 1978. *The international money market.* Englewood Cliffs, N.J.: Prentice-Hall.

Giddy, Ian H. 1983. The theory and industrial organization of international banking. In Robert G. Hawkins, et al., ed., *The internationalization of financial markets and national economic policy.* Research in international business and finance. Greenwich, CT: JAI Press.

Gorostiaga, Xavier. 1984. *The role of international financial centers in underdeveloped countries.* New York: St. Martin's Press.

Haegele, Monroe J. 1975. Iran's potential as a finance center. *International Finance.* New York: Chase Manhattan Bank. February:7.

Johnson, Harry G. 1976. Panama as a regional financial center. *Economic Development and Cultural Change*, January 24(2):261-286.

Kindleberger, Charles P. 1974. *The Formation of Financial Centers: A Study in Comparative Economic History.* Princeton: Princeton Studies in International Finance, Princeton University, 36:6.

Laws of Alaska. Chapter No. 69. An act relating to preferential hire of Alaskans, approved by the Governor: May 31, 1986.

Lessard, Donald R. and Adrian E. Tschoegl. 1985. Panama's international banking center: Where does it stand and what can be done to insure its continued viability and increase its contributions to the Panamanian economy? Discussion Paper 85-2, Miami: International Business and Banking Institute, University of Miami.

McCarthy, Ian. 1979. Hosting offshore banks: Benefits and costs. *Finance and Development*, December:45-48.

Moffett, Michael, and Arthur Stonehill. 1987. *International Banking Facilities revisited*. A paper presented at the International Banking and Finance Conference, Anchorage: University of Alaska.

Nadler, Marcus, et al. 1955. *The money market and its institutions*. New York: Roland Press.

Nicholas, Ted. 1978. *How to form your own corporation without a lawyer for under $50.00*. Wilmington, Delaware: Enterprise Publishing Company.

Park, Yoon S. 1982. The economics of offshore financial centers. *Columbia Journal of World Business*, 17(4):31-35.

Price Waterhouse. 1986. *Foreign exchange information: A worldwide summary*. New York: Price Waterhouse.

Reed, Howard Curtis. 1980. The ascent of Tokyo as an international financial center. *Journal of International Business Studies*, 11(33):19-35.

Reed, Howard Curtis. 1981. *The preeminence of international financial centers*. New York: Praeger.

Sheshunoff & Company, Inc. 1987. *The banks of the Pacific Northwest*. Austin, Texas.

State of Alaska, Department of Commerce and Economic Development, Division of Banking and Securities. 1987. *Comparative statement of assets, liabilities and capital accounts of Alaska state banks*. Year-End 1981-1986. Juneau, Alaska.

State of Alaska, Department of Transportation and Public Facilities, Division of Planning and Programming. 1981. *Master plan study: Anchorage International Airport.*

State of Alaska, Department of Transportation and Public Facilities. 1985. *The economic impact of the Anchorage International Airport.*

State of Alaska, Department of Transportation and Public Facilities. 1986. *Analysis of airline rates, fees, and charges: Anchorage and Fairbanks International Airports.*

Tussing, Arlon R. Alaska's petroleum-based economy. In Morehouse, Thomas A., ed. 1984. *Alaska resources development: Issues of the 1980s.* Boulder, Colorado: Westview Press.

Vernon, Raymond. 1960. *Metropolis 1985.* Cambridge: Harvard University Press.

Wasserman, Max J., et. al. 1963. *International finance.* New York: Simmons-Boardman.

3. THE PREREQUISITES FOR AN INTERNATIONAL FINANCIAL CENTER

Michael A. Goldberg
Robert Helsley
Maurice D. Levi
University of British Columbia

INTRODUCTION

With the dramatic increase in the importance of the Asia-Pacific region as a source of international trade, there has been an explosion of interest in where the financial activity generated by that trade will be located. Those cities which have dominated the international financial marketplace and which are located in the European-Atlantic Region, such as New York and London, seem too detached to service the new center of gravity of international trade. For more political than economic-geographical reasons, there is also doubt about the prospects of Hong Kong and even of Singapore in capturing the new financial business derived from trade emanating in the Pacific Rim. It is for this reason that attention has been turned to cities such as Anchorage and Vancouver to determine if they might stake a position in this arena.

If we are to assess whether there is prospect for a particular city to emerge as a center of international finance, it is useful to examine the attributes of those cities which are currently international financial centers. This can be done casually, but since there are multiple attributes, and because these can potentially interact, it is preferable to use statistical analysis. Unfortunately, it is difficult to find readily available measures of many candidate attributes, and there is no obvious way of even measuring the size of international financial centers. However, this is not a reason to abandon an effort to apply statistical technology to the problem. A conscientious effort to discover sources of data can be successful and throw considerable light on what it takes for a city to emerge as a center of international financial activity.

In an effort to determine if the city of Vancouver has the "right stuff" to grow as an international financial center, we have conducted an intensive search for measures which can be used to perform an econometric analysis to determine what has given rise to international financial centers (Goldberg, Helsley and Levi, 1987a, 1987b). The results we have obtained

---

The authors are Professor, Assistant Professor, and Professor in the Faculty of Commerce and Business Administration, University of British Columbia. Computer assistance was provided by Doug Maclean. Financial support was provided by the Ministry of Finance and Corporate Relations of British Columbia. The authors are, however, responsible for all views expressed and any errors that may remain.

can be used to examine the prospects of any city, and it is our purpose to do so here for the case of Anchorage, Alaska. Before doing so, we should describe the bases of data and the methodologies employed. We should also look at the general implications which are not specific to any city. The outcome of the study can then be related to what Anchorage has, or does not have, to offer.

DATA USED

In order to ensure that any conclusions we are able to reach are robust to the method employed, it was decided to proceed on five different levels of analysis. These are:

1) An analysis that explains variations in the size of international financial activity over different countries. This involves a cross-sectional analysis using data measured at the national level.

2) An analysis that explains variations in the size of international activity in a given country over time. This involves a time-series analysis, again using data measured at the national level.

3) A pooled cross-sectional, time-series analysis explaining variations in financial activity between countries and over time. This also uses national-level data.

4) An analysis that explains variations in financial activity between the 50 states of the United States. This is a cross-sectional analysis that uses state-level data.

5) An analysis that explains variations in international financial activity between different cities. This is a cross-sectional analysis that uses city-level data.

In all five different bases of analysis, it is of course necessary to measure the size of financial activity. It was decided to use two different bases for this measure:

i) from the balance sheets of banks, and
ii) from the fraction of the total workforce employed in the financial sector.

The balance sheet data of banks use variously total assets, total liabilities, and the size of foreign assets and liabilities. The fraction of employment in the financial sector measures the percentage of the workforce that is in banking, insurance, and real estate. These data were obtained from a number of different sources, some international and some national. A summary of the sources of data is given in the Appendix.

EMPIRICAL RESULTS

The cross-sectional, national level analysis

The cross-sectional, national level analysis is based upon a cross section of 42 countries.[1] These are the 42 countries for which consistent measures of the explanatory and dependent variables are available. The base year for the analysis is 1984. The choice of variables employed in this study is clear from Table 1, but it is useful to give a brief account of the reasons for including these particular variables.

The GDP per capita serves as a measure of economic development in a country. This variable is included to determine whether or not the financial sector grows with the level of real income. The significantly positive coefficient on this variable suggests that indeed, countries with higher income do have larger banking sectors judged by foreign assets. As Table II shows, they also have a larger fraction of the workforce employed in the financial sector.

Imports are included in both Tables 1 and 2 to see whether or not there is a separate impact of imports on the demand for financial services. Such an outcome would be reasonable since there is a considerable amount of financial paperwork involved in an import. For example, there is a need to purchase foreign exchange and generally also letters of credit. In comparison, domestic transactions frequently involve no more than the transfer of bank accounts via checks. As the results of both Table I and Table II demonstrate, imports do exert a positive effect on the size of financial activity in different countries, most particularly when activity is measured by the size of foreign assets.

The next variable that we note in both Tables 1 and 2 is exports. We find here that an increase in exports as we go from one country to another results in a smaller financial sector as judged by both foreign assets and employment. This result might appear surprising. It is therefore useful for us to consider why such an outcome may occur. One possible explanation of the negative impact of exports on the size of financial sectors is that in those countries where commodity or manufacturing exports are important, wage rates might be bid to such a level that it is difficult for them to compete in the financial service sector. For example, it might be that in countries where there are economic rents to be enjoyed in selling oil or other natural resources, wage rates might be such that banks find it unprofitable to locate there. An alternative is that exporters might borrow in those countries where they sell their products. They might do this in order to denominate their payables in the same currency as their receivables. This provides a form of long-term foreign exchange hedging. Of course, with the development of offshore currency markets, it is possible to borrow in foreign currency terms at home, but for many of the countries in this cross sectional study, the possibility of borrowing large amounts at home in foreign currency terms is not present.

TABLE 1
Cross-Sectional Results For 42 Countries

Dependent Variable: Foreign Assets (all variables in logs)

Variable Name	Coeff.	Std. Err	T-Ratio	Std. Coeff.
GDP per capita	.583	.303	1.937	.288
Imports	2.729	.691	3.946*	1.815
Exports	-1.587	.655	-2.442**	-1.106
Saving Rate	- .710	.906	- .784	- .091
Total debt	- .127	.224	- .570	- .110
Foreign debt	.121	.096	1.268	.159
Investment				
abroad	.015	.181	.084	.019
foreign	- .232	.197	-1.178	.159
Reserve ratio	.158	.257	.257	.075
Offshore dummy	2.328	.809	2.878*	.357
Constant	-5.846	3.858	-1.515	.0

R-Squared adjusted:	.7620	Std. Err of estimate:	1.1288
Log likelihood function:	-362.41	Durbin Watson:	2.1448

* Significant at the 1 % level.
** Significant at the 5 % level.

TABLE 2
Cross-Sectional Results For 42 Countries

Dependent Variable: Percent of labor force in financial sector

Variable Name	Coeff.	Std. Err	T-Ratio	Std. Coeff.
GDP per capita	.356E-05	.101E-05	3.538*	.628
Imports	.928E-06	.498E.06	1.863	2.206
Exports	-.959E-06	.469E-06	-2.048**	-1.905
Saving Rate	-.845E-01	.498E-01	-1.698	- .226
Total debt	-.124E-06	.667E-07	-1.858	-1.108
Foreign debt	.201E-06	.225E-06	.893	.265
Investment				
abroad	.131E-04	.701E-05	1.876	.801
foreign	.646E-07	.104E-05	.062	- .013
portfolio	-.892E-06	.111E.05	- .802	- .213
Reserve ratio	.817E-02	.258E-01	.317	.046
Offshore dummy	.196E-01	.947E-02	2.068**	.262
Constant	.516E-01	.124E-01	4.145	.0

R-Squared adjusted	.5700	Std. Err of estimate:	0.01742
Log likelihood function:	99.43	Durbin Watson:	1.8448

* Significant at the 1 % level.
** Significant at the 5 % level.

The savings rate is included in the national-level, cross sectional analysis to see whether or not there is more financial activity where there is more financial intermediation between savers and borrowers. We find from the results in both Tables 1 and 2 that there is no such effect. Indeed, while not statistically significant, the direction of effect appears to be negative. Total debt is also included to see whether the countries with more debt have bigger financial sectors to intermediate with this debt, and again it appears to be unimportant. Foreign debt also appears to have no significant effect, as is also the case for different measures of foreign investment.

In order to see whether there is an impact of commercial bank reserve ratios or other attributes of different countries' banks that are relevant for their degree of regulation, a couple of measures were included to try to take care of different regulatory regimes. This was achieved by including the average bank reserve ratio in each country, and for the case of the "tax havens", a dummy variable to recognize this fact.[2] It is clear that the size of the financial sectors in the tax havens is larger than would be suggested by the other variables. However, it would appear that reserve ratios have no effect on the size of financial sectors.

The Time-series, National Level Analysis

Time-series analyses were performed for the United States, the United Kingdom, and Canada. These results are summarized in Tables 3, 4, and 5. As much as possible, we retained the same measures as were used in the cross-sectional analysis of 42 countries. However, in the case of the United States, it was also necessary to consider the lagged dependent variable as there was significant serial correlation in the error term. In the case of the United Kingdom, this did not appear to be a problem, and in the case of Canada, the serial correlation appeared to disappear with the inclusion of the unemployment rate.

An examination of Tables 3-5 shows very similar results to those reported from the cross-sectional level of study. We find a positive impact of GDP per capita over time. That is, as people in these countries have become richer over time, we find a larger and larger fraction of the workforce employed in the financial sector. We also find for the case of the United States and Canada that growth in imports gives rise to a growth in the size of the financial sector, confirming the results from the cross-sectional study. We also find confirmation of the negative impact of exports on the size of the financial sectors in these countries over time.

The intermediation variables--savings rate, debt, foreign debt, and investment--are insignificant in general in the time-series studies, just as they were in the cross-sectional national level analysis. Hence, we find confirmation that intermediation appears to be less important than does the level of economic activity judged both by GNP and by foreign trade. The commercial bank reserve ratio appears to have a negative impact for the United States and Canada. This is the way one would expect the results to be, since countries with high reserve ratios would be expected to lose business to other countries.

What is most notable perhaps in the results in Tables 3-5 is the incredibly high R^2s. We find that we are explaining approximately 99% of the variation of the size of the workforce in the financial sector during the twentieth century. This is a very substantial result, and suggests that we have included most of the important variables. Indeed, we note that even on the cross-sectional analysis, we have explained a fairly substantial fraction of variation with R^2s of 0.76 in the case of measuring financial activity by foreign assets and 0.57 in the case of using the labor force.

Pooled Cross-sectional, Time-series National Analysis

The combined use of cross-sectional and time-series data is possible for a subset of the 42 countries, namely, only for 16 OECD nations. Using the technology of pooled regressions, and bank assets and labor force as measures of financial activity, we obtain the results shown in Tables 6 and 7. An examination of the t-ratios in these regressions confirms the results obtained earlier. We find, for example, that imports appear to be significant when measuring financial activity by foreign assets, although they do not appear significant when judged by the labor force. Exports retain their negative impact in both tables. Other results are not as convincing as in the other studies, and we note that the R^2s are not as substantial.

The Analysis of 50 U.S. States

The next base of analysis uses data for the different states in the United States. When this is done, we are able to see whether or not the effect of income and foreign trade carries over to the more micro-based information that is available within a country. The results of our state-level data are shown on Tables 8-10. We see that whether we measure financial activity by financial assets in the state or by employment in the state, there is a significantly positive effect of personal income on the size of financial activity. There is an incrementally positive effect of imports, and negative effect of exports. These results confirm our earlier results. The results on Table 10 show that the conclusions are unchanged when we include near banks and foreign banks along with domestic banks when computing financial assets.

TABLE 3
Time-Series Study of United States, 1900-84

Dependent Variable: Percent of labor force in financial sector

Variable Name	Coeff.	Std. Err	T-Ratio	Std. Coeff.
GNP per capita	.325E-02	.114E-02	2.858*	.189
Lagged dep. var.	.862	.344E-01	25.046*	.834
Imports	.911E-07	.504E-07	1.809	.104
Exports	-.104E-06	.502E-07	-2.074**	- .108
Saving Rate	-.803E-02	.620E-01	-1.296	- .017
Total debt	-.558E-05	.353E-05	1.581	.043
Foreign debt	.201E-06	.225E-06	.893	.265
Investment				
abroad	-.932E-07	.165E-06	- .563	- .012
foreign	-.215E-06	.308E-06	- .698	- .018
portfolio	-.120E-05	.164E-06	-.732	- .012
Reserve ratio	-.140E-01	.561E-02	-2.503**	- .038
Unemp. rate	.214E-03	.660E-04	3.242*	.060
No. banks	.190E-06	.556E-07	3.424*	.059
Constant	-.211E-02	.217E-02	- .975	.0

R-Squared adjusted: .9935 Std. Err of estimate: 0.00154
Log likelihood function: 431.69 Durbin Watson: 1.4053

* Significant at the 1% level.
**Significant at the 5% level.

TABLE 4
Time-Series Study of United Kingdom, 1960-84

Dependent Variable: Percent of labor force in financial sector

Variable Name	Coeff.	Std. Err	T-Ratio	Std. Coeff.
GNP per capita	.462E-04	.510E-05	9.058*	1.076
Imports	.141E-06	.208E-06	.676	.090
Exports	-.462E-06	.244E-06	-1.890	- .266
Saving Rate	.677E-01	.242E-01	2.790*	.111
Total debt	-.498E-07	.422E-07	-1.181	- .059
Investment				
abroad	-.164E-05	.625E-06	-0.26206	- .147
foreign	-.542E-06	.967E-06	- .560	- .034
portfolio	.297E-l0	.580E-06	5.127*	.326
Reserve ratio	.498E-01	.351E-01	1.419	.083
Constant	-.888E-01	.161E-01	-5.507*	.0

R-Squared adjusted: .9877 Std. Err of estimate: 0.00217
Log likelihood function 124.19 Durbin Watson: 1.9526

* Significant at the 1% level.

TABLE 5
Times-Series Study of Canada, 1946-84

Dependent Variable: Percent of labor force in financial center

Variable Name	Coeff.	Std. Err	T-Ratio	Std. Coeff.
GDP per capita	.419E-02	.696E-03	6.028*	1.718
Imports	.569E-06	.202E-06	2.815*	1.976
Exports	-.618E-06	.214E-06	-2.883*	-1.714
Saving Rate	.122E-01	.109E-01	1.034	0.022
Total debt	-.178E-06	.426E-07	-3.851*	- 0.569
Investment				
abroad	-.106E-05	.719E-06	-1.470	- 0.131
foreign	.101E-05	.497E-06	2.032**	.079
portfolio	.183E-06	.547E-06	0.355	.021
Reserve ratio	-.548E-01	.251E-01	-2.187**	- .104
Unemp. rate	.558E-03	.204E-03	2.731*	.131
Constant	.251E-01	.389E-02	6.452*	.000

R-Squared adjusted: .9886 Std. Err of estimate: 0.00119
Log likelihood function: 213.70 Durbin Watson: 2.0626

* Significant at the 1% level.
**Significant at the 5% level.

TABLE 6
Pooled Cross-Sectional, Time-Series Study of 16 OECD Countries, 1975-84

Dependent Variable: Foreign Assets (all variables in logs)

Variable	Coeff.	Std. Err	T-Ratio	Std. Coeff.
GDP per capita	- .694	.446	-1.557	- .132
Imports	3.306	.691	4.782*	2.343
Exports	-2.236	.680	-3.286*	-1.633
Saving Rate	1.058	.547	1.933	.114
Total debt	.095	.126	.757	.061
Investment				
abroad	.338	.088	3.852*	.323
foreign	- .106	.104	-1.023	- .079
Reserve ratio	.286	.118	2.419**	.133
Year 1975	-1.864	1.342	-1.404	- .283
Year 1976	-1.858	1.392	-1.335	- .279
Year 1977	-1.629	1.429	-1.140	- .245
Year 1978	-1.277	1.468	- .869	- .192
Year 1979	-1.345	1.517	- .887	- .202
Year 1980	-1.209	1.563	- .774	- .182
Year 1981	- .921	1.561	- .590	- .138
Year 1982	- .757	1.552	- .488	- .113
Year 1983	- .594	1.550	- .383	- .089
Year 1984	- .555	1.542	- .360	- .083

R-Squared adjusted: .6353 Std. Err of estimate: 1.2083
Log likelihood function: -1858.3 Durbin Watson: .3266

* Significant at the 1% level.
**Significant at the 5% level.

TABLE 7
Pooled Cross-Sectional, Time-Series Study of 16 OECD Countries, 1975-84

Dependent Variable: Percent of labor force in financial center

Variable	Coeff.	Std. Err	T-Ratio	Std. Coeff.
GDP per capita	.572E-02	.541E-03	10.596*	.888
Imports	.332E-07	.139E-06	.238	.099
Exports	-.955E.07	.119E-06	- .806	- .267
Saving Rate	.670E-01	.308E-01	2.174**	.162
Total debt	-.209E-07	.107E.07	-1.960**	- .264
Investment				
abroad	.178E-05	.374E-06	4.773*	.345
foreign	.134E-05	.600E-06	2.232**	.242
portfolio	.685E-06	.328E-06	2.086**	.139
Reserve ratio	-.524E-01	.238E-01	-2.199**	- .123
Unemp. rate	.242E-02	.390E-03	6.192*	.523
Year 1975	-.151E-02	.106E-01	- .143	- .283
Year 1976	-.404E-02	.105E-01	- .386	- .279
Year 1977	-.697E-02	.105E-01	- .662	- .245
Year 1978	-.150E-01	.111E-01	-1.349	- .192
Year 1979	-.211E-01	.117E-01	-1.793	- .202
Year 1980	-.265E-01	.121E-01	-2.190**	- .182
Year 1981	-.234E-01	.119E-01	-1.963	- .138
Year 1982	-.176E-01	.119E-01	-1.485	- .113
Year 1983	-.194E-01	.122E-01	-1.588	- .089
Year 1984	-.188E-01	.124E-01	-1.509	- .083

R-Squared adjusted:	.5821	Std. Err of estimate:	.01272
Log likelihood function:	81.97	Durbin Watson:	.4004

* Significant at the 1% level.
**Significant at the 5% level.

When using U.S. state-level data, it is possible to examine the influence of the location of U.S. multinational corporations and of foreign corporations. These data are available from Dun and Bradstreet. The location of headquarters is important, since it might be believed that banks and other financial institutions congregate around the headquarters of companies which give rise to the demand for a large portion of their business. That is, the derived demand for financial services is probably more closely connected to the headquarters of the firms than it is to the location of other economic activity. The results in Tables 8-10 show that indeed the location of headquarters is a fundamental component of the overall explanation of the size of financial activity. The number of U.S. multinationals, and the number of foreign firms with headquarters in a state, have significant positive effects on the size of financial activity, however it is measured.

The corporate tax rate might influence both the decision of a bank over locating in a particular state and the decision of other firms to locate there. A crude measure of the corporate tax rate is obtained by dividing state corporate tax revenue by state level corporate income. This has no significant effect on the size of financial activity, however measured. In order to check a conjecture of Charles Kindleberger that some of the location of financial activity may be due to historical accident, a variable was included which measures the age of each state, based on the number of years since the state joined the Union. It would appear from our results that historical accident is not important for the location of financial activity.

It is notable in the U.S. state-level study that, as in our previous bases of analysis, the fraction of variation in financial activity that we are explaining is very high. We find that we are explaining virtually all the variation in financial activity, with R^2 values well up in the 0.95 and higher region. We can feel confident, therefore, that we have included the most important variables. It would seem that there is little else other than domestic income, foreign trade, and the location of corporate headquarters that is relevant for the development of financial centers.

The Analysis of International Cities

The final base of our study is on the level of international cities. These data on international cities were obtained in the following manner. By studying the location of the world's 750 largest banks, it was possible to determine the size of assets in each city, and the total number of employees. The world's largest 750 banks have their offices located in 31 cities.[3]

The city level results are summarized in Tables 11 and 12. We find that the average annual income in each city has a positive effect, although this is not statistically significant. What is significant, however, is the positive impact of imports through each city, and the negative impact of exports. (The value of exports is proxied by the percent of the city's economy which is involved in manufacturing. This is a crude proxy, but unfortunately there is no city level data for the number of goods sent to other countries.) When using city-based data, it is feasible to determine the importance of the concentration of assets within particular cities of a given country. (The measure of concentration that we use is the fraction of all bank assets found for a given country that are in the city of interest.) It appears that concentration is an important variable with strong t-statistics.

Another factor that we can test with the international city data is the importance of being in a busy time zone. This can be judged by the ratio of assets in a given city to the total number of assets within the time zone in which that city falls. We find that this has a strong positive effect on the financial activity in our 31 cities. Of course, there is some spuriousness to this result in that important cities will be important within their time zones. However, we do note that this indicates some value of being large. That is, being large is important for attracting financial business. The city level study also allows us to recheck the importance of age. This can be done from measuring the date of the initial habitation of the city as given by Webster's New Geographical Dictionary.[4] As in the case of the state level study, it appears that age is not important. Historical accident does not seem to be a determinant of financial activity.

A final variable that is included in the city level study is whether or not that city happens to be a capital. This can be achieved by using a dummy of 1 for capitals. Intuitively, it might seem reasonable that capital cities would emerge as major financial centers. We could cite the cases of London, Paris, Tokyo, Rome, and Madrid to support this conjecture. However, there are also many other cases of cities which are not capitals such as New York, Sydney, and so on. The results confirm what our mixed intuition would suggest, mainly that whether or not the city is a capital does not have a significant impact on the size of financial centers.

If anything stands out in our results, it is the importance of a large value of imports in generating financial activity. This result is not surprising in retrospect, if we consider the history of the growth of banks in such centers as London and Amsterdam. Historical accounts tell us of the movement of merchants from their commercial activity into the banking industry. This movement occurred because merchants were required to produce large sums of money at irregular intervals as ships arrived with goods from abroad. These same merchants were also frequently required to provide credit to the buyers of their products. The merchants therefore found themselves with regular needs for money both to finance their purchases and to finance their sales. As a result of this need, there grew in cities such as London and Amsterdam institutions that are to this day known as merchant banks. This evolution would suggest therefore that imports are an important variable.

Anchorage is unfortunately not a center of import activity. It would therefore be necessary for Anchorage to develop some import trade in order to develop the derived demand for financial activities that could propel the city into the international finance industry. This suggests that an effort to develop the financial sector of Anchorage would need to be accompanied by an effort to develop import trade through Alaska. Suggestions such as the establishment of duty free zones would therefore seem to be closely aligned with suggestions for developing Anchorage as a service sector assisting with international trade.

TABLE 8
Study of U.S. State Data

Dependent Variable, Total Financial Assets by State
(banks and near-banks, domestic and foreign)

Explanatory Variable	Coeff.	Std. Err	T-Ratio	Std. Coeff.
Personal income	423.7	133.8	3.166*	.431
Imports	6775.9	1101.1	6.154*	.864
Fxports	-5024.3	1497.9	-3.354*	-.405
Corporations				
multinationals	330.4	111.76	2.957*	.191
foreign	56.29	30.02	1.875**	.121
Corp. tax rate	-8271.1	32462.	- .254	-.006
Constant	-4026.4	4657.0	- .865	.0

R-Squared adjusted: .9691 Std. Err of Estimate: 19319
Log likelihood function: -571.91 Durbin Watson: 2.1459

* Significant at 1% level
** Significant at 5% level

TABLE 9
Study of U.S. State Data

Dependent Variable: Employment in the Financial Sector by State

Explanatory Variable	Coeff.	Std. Err	T-Ratio	Std. Coeff.
Personal income	.900	.100	9.024*	.420
Imports	4.810	.820	5.864*	.457
Exports	-4.442	1.116	-3.981*	-.267
Corporations				
multinationals	.482	.083	5.789*	.208
foreign	.150	.022	6.710*	.240
Corp. tax rate	3.230	24.18	.134	.002
Constant	-.511	3.469	-.147	.0

R-Squared adjusted: .9905 Std. Err of Estimate: 14.39
Log likelihood function: -204.60 Durbin Watson: 2.0034

* Significant at 1% level

TABLE 10
Study of U.S. State Data

Dependent Variable, Total Financial Assets by State
(banks and near-banks, domestic and foreign)

Explanatory Variable	Coeff.	Std. Err	T-Ratio	Std. Coeff.
Personal income	426.0	135.3	3.148*	.267
Imports	6774.9	1112.1	6.092*	.864
Exports	-5019.9	1513.0	-3.318*	-.405
Corporations				
multinationals	328.87	112.97	2.911*	.191
foreign	56.12	30.33	1.850**	.121
Corp. tax rate	-9018.3	32854.	-.274	-.007
Age	-3.79	10.58	-.359	.009
Constant	2814.6	19640.0	.143	.0

R-Squared adjusted:	.9684	Std. Err of Estimate:	19513
Log likelihood function:	-571.84	Durbin Watson:	2.1243

* Significant at 1% level
** Significant at 5% level

TABLE 11
Study of 31 International Cities

Dependent Variable: Total Employees in Banks (in logs)

Explanatory Variable	Coeff.	Std. Err	T-Ratio	Std. Coeff.
Avg. annual income	.070	.195	.360	.032
% imports through port	.584	.204	2.865*	.247
% manufacturing	-1.176	.323	-3.636*	-.299
Concentration				
country	.418	.086	4.862*	.459
time zone	.479	.078	6.126*	.499
Age	.016	.065	.252	-.020
Capital	-0.59	.232	-.255	-.024
Constant	12.920	1.747	7.396*	0.0

R-Squared adjusted:	.8568	Std. Err of Estimate:	.20161
Log likelihood function:	-343.950	Durbin Watson:	2.528

*Significant at 1% level

TABLE 12
Study of 31 International Cities

Dependent Variable: Total assets of banks

Explanatory Variable	Coeff.	Std. Err	T-Ratio	Std. Coeff.
Avg. annual income	.229	.158	1.450	.101
% imports through port	.650	.167	3.903*	.266
% manufacturing	-.879	.266	-3.298*	-.216
Concentration				
country	.335	.068	4.939*	.375
time zone	.561	.064	8.808*	.570
Productivity	-.641	.123	-5.215*	-.324
Age	-.025	.054	-.468	-.029
Capital	-.283	.196	-1.442	-.110
Constant	14.16	1.949	7.264*	.0

R-Squared adjusted:	.9113	Std. Err of Estimate:	.36507
Log likelihood function:	-357.00	Durbin Watson:	2.8757

* Significant at the 1% level.
** Significant at the 1% level.

In addition to the lack of imports dampening the prospects for Anchorage is the importance to Alaska of exports. The results that we have described in this paper suggest that export activities do not enhance the prospects of a city to develop as an international financial center, and indeed the results suggest that there is a negative impact of exports. The importance of exports to Alaska would therefore seem almost to preclude the development of a financial industry in the state. However, there is some reason for hope in this regard. In the case of Anchorage, there is no reason why banking is moved "offshore", by the need to denominate payables in the currency of receivables; Alaska does use the same currency as the lower 48 states. If, therefore, the negative effect of exports is due to the tendency to borrow in the currency of the country of sale, this may not serve as an important damper to the prospects of financial activities in Anchorage.

The relatively young age of Anchorage and its distance from the nation's capital would not appear to damage the potential of Anchorage as an international financial center. Furthermore, the prospects for a special status as a tax haven, if it is achieved,in promoting the growth of financial activity, would seem to be promising. That is, we find the dummy variable for tax havens being significantly positive, and so if it were feasible for Anchorage to have such status, it might well be able to play a role in this regard. Unfortunately, Alaska has no control over national tax rates, and it therefore seems unlikely that Anchorage can compete with such locations as the Netherlands Antilles and the Cayman Islands in deriving off-shore business.

All the same, an international financial center in Anchorage might have some potential. It would seem from the important role played by corporate headquarters that it would be useful to see what can be done to encourage the major oil companies with a role in Alaska to move more of their other activities to the state. This could give rise to a greater demand for financial services and thereby create a larger financial sector in Anchorage.

NOTES

1. They are: Argentina, Australia, Bahamas, Bahrain, Belgium, Brazil, Burma, Canada, Chile, Columbia, Denmark, Egypt, Finland, France, Germany, Indonesia, Italy, Japan, Korea, Malaysia, Mexico, Netherlands Antilles, New Zealand, Norway, Panama, Peru, Philippines, Portugal, Singapore, South Africa, Spain, Sweden, Switzerland, Thailand, United Kingdom, United States, Uruguay, Venezuela, Yugoslavia.

2. A dummy variable was included for Bahamas, Bahrain, Netherlands Antilles, Panama, and Singapore.

3. These cities are Tokyo, Paris, New York, London, Osaka, Frankfurt, Toronto, San Francisco, Montreal, Munich, Amsterdam, Milan, Rome, Zurich, Chicago, Los Angeles, Madrid, Dusseldorf, Nagoya, Hong Kong, Seoul, Kobe, Sydney, Melbourne, Luxembourg, Yokohama, Hamburg, Cairo, Singapore, West Berlin, and Vancouver.

4. See Webster's New Geographical Dictionary. 1977. Springfield, Massachusetts: G & C. Merrian Company.

REFERENCES

Goldberg, Michael A., Robert Helsley and Maurice Levi. 1987. Factors influencing the development of banking and finance: An international and historical evaluation. Unpublished manuscript, University of British Columbia.

______________. 1987. The geographical location of financial activity. Unpublished manuscript, University of British Columbia.

Kindleberger, Charles P. 1974. *The formation of financial centers: A study in comparative economic history*, Princeton Studies in International Finance, No. 36. Princeton: Princeton University Press.

_________. 1985. The functioning of financial centers: Britain in the 19th century, the United States since 1945. In Wilford Feaethier and Richard Marston, eds., *International Financial Markets and Capital Movements*. Princeton: Princeton University Press.

APPENDIX

Data Sources

Foreign assets of domestic banks: Obtained from various issues of *International Financial Statistics*, International Monetary Fund, Washington, D.C.

Fraction employed in financial sector: *Yearbook of Labor Statistics*, International Labor Office, Geneva, Switzerland. Data in pooled cross-sectional, time-series analysis from Organization of Economic Cooperation and Development, Department of Economics and Statistics, Paris, France.

Real GNP per capita, imports, exports, foreign investment, savings rate, reserve ratio, from *International Financial Statistics*, International Monetary Fund, Washington, D.C.

Foreign debt from various national accounts, converted into U.S. dollars at year-end exchange rates.

Bank balances in U.S. states: *The Annual Statistical Digest*, U.S. Department of Commerce, Bureau of the Census.

Financial employment, personal income, imports and exports, in U.S. states: *Statistical Abstract of the United States*, Department of Commerce, Bureau of the Census.

Location of U.S. multinational headquarters: *Who Owns What: North America*, Dun and Bradstreet.

Location of foreign non-bank corporations in the U.S.: *Foreign Direct Investment in the United States: Operations of U.S. Affiliates - 1983 Estimates*, U.S. Department of Commerce, Bureau of Economic Analysis.

Tax rates in U.S. states: *Tax Capacity of the Fifty States*, U.S. Department of Commerce, Bureau of the Census.

Age of U.S. States: *Webster's New Geographical Dictionary*, G. & C. Merrian Company, Springfield, Mass., 1977).

Tonnage of Imports by city: *Lloyd's Ports of the World*, (Lloyd's Press, London, 1986), *Lloyd's Register of Shipping*, (Lloyd's Press, London, 1985), and *The World in Figures*, (The Economist, London, 1982).
Fraction employed in manufacturing by city: Ness and Marlin's *Book of World City Rankings*. (1986)

Financial employment by city, *The Banker*, (Financial Times, London, June 1986).

4. THE INTERNATIONAL FINANCIAL CENTERS: DEVELOPING THE COMPETITIVE EDGE

Sarkis J. Khoury
University of California, Riverside

INTRODUCTION

The evolution of major international financial markets represents a captivating study in politics and economics. Some international financial markets assumed prominent roles in the world economy by careful designs capitalizing on some natural advantages which were political, geographic and/or economic. Other financial centers achieved prominence slowly over time without identifiable, explicit policy measures to which the realized success can be, on the whole, directly attributed. Historical developments and sheer economic and political weight brought prominence to certain financial centers.

The objectives of this study are to compare and contrast the evolutions of different major international financial markets and to examine the nature of the competitive advantage of each. The study draws lessons from these developments as they relate to the efforts being made by many cities to become major international financial centers.

The explosive growth of international financial centers brought about an avalanche of products to accommodate speculators, investors and hedgers, no matter their risk profiles.

The international financial centers are more international than ever before. They have become quite contagious as domestic markets are beginning to acquire a more international character. They have also become more technology and information driven than ever before. Today, the asset base of a financial institution must incorporate explicitly the human resource factor for without it, coping with the complexities of the new markets and being able to compete internationally becomes impossible. The lesson here is no city or national market can ever aspire to become an international financial center without the appropriate technology and human resource base or a clear and effective mechanism for acquiring it.

The second reality in the world financial markets is the direct transformation of certain financial markets, like Japan's and Singapore's, and to a considerable extent Los Angeles' and Vancouver's, as a result of: the changing trade patterns in the world, the tremendous financial resources accumulated by Japan, and the emergence of China. The rise of the Pacific

Basin countries to prominence in manufacturing and trade brought on a revolution in their financial markets.

The Pacific Rim has nations which comprise 60 percent of the world's total population and whose economic growth over the past two decades has averaged about 7.5 percent. International trade among Pacific Basin nations and North America exceeded U.S. $200 billion in 1986 and surpassed the combined trade between North America and all of Europe, Africa and the Middle East. The dominant force in the Pacific reform is Japan, which is currently liberalizing its financial markets and which has become the world's lending leader of financial resources, replacing the United States during the period 1970-1982 and earlier Britain (see Edmunds and Khoury 1986). The increased activity in the Pacific Rim financial centers did not come at the expense of London or New York. The activity in the New York market and in the Eurodollar markets continued at a fast pace, as shown in Table 1. Increased internationalism is benefiting all markets.

The above suggests the development in the financial markets are produced by the internal dynamics of the markets or can be induced by outside factors, such as trade and level of economic activity within the national market.

THE FORMATION OF FINANCIAL CENTERS

There is less than unanimity among scholars and practitioners as to what constitutes an international financial center. We prefer to define it as a location where the sustainable level of financial transactions, both investment and borrowing, far exceed that justified by domestic economic and trade activities.

The competitiveness of an international financial center generally depends on those factors which influence the supply of financial intermediation services in a global economy. Keeping the competitive edge is, therefore, a necessary condition for maintaining the economic viability of a financial center as the nature of business activity changes, as alliances shift, as new entrants come into the market and as new products and concepts are introduced in the market place.

The payoffs from becoming an international financial center are significant indeed. The road towards that goal may be fraught with peril, however, and may be very costly even if it led somewhere else. The benefits reaped from such an endeavor may be temporary unless a well-conceived and well-financed dynamic strategy is adopted from the outset. The typical benefits which accrue from achieving an international financial status are:

TABLE 1
Foreign Bonds Issued in the United States

Full credit to lead manager; debt on a net proceeds base

Rank 1986	Rank 1985	Bank	1986 Amount $m	1986 No. of issues	1986 Share %	1985 Amount $m	1985 No. of issues	1985 Share %
1	3	Merrill Lynch Capital Mkts	2,519.3	18	32.5	808.5	3	16.0
2	2	First Boston	1,725.1	9	22.3	996.5	6	19.8
3	1	Salomon Brothers	1,284.1	6	16.6	2,072.3	10	41.1
4	6	Morgan Stanley	1,139.2	6	14.7	298.1	1	5.9
5	8	Drexel Burnham Lambert	629.6	3	8.1	111.5	3	1.8
6	4	Goldman, Sachs	248.0	2	3.2	339.0	2	6.7
7	5	Kidder, Peabody	148.9	1	1.9	299.6	2	5.9
8	-	LF Rothschild, Unterberg, Town	50.0	1	0.6	-	-	-

Foreign Equity Issues sold in the United States

Full credit to lead manager

Rank 1986	Rank 1985	Bank	1986 Amount $m	1986 No. of issues	1986 Share %	1985 Amount $m	1985 No. of issues	1985 Share %
1	1	Goldman, Sachs	503.1	5	39.3	161.9	1	36.6
2	-	Merrill Lynch Capital Mkts	271.7	3	21.2	-	-	-
3	2	Morgan Stanley	167.0	2	13.1	70.5	2	16.0
4	-	Wertheim	83.2	1	6.5	-	-	-
5	-	Bear, Stearns	48.0	1	3.8	-	-	-
6	-	Alex, Brown & Sons	47.0	1	3.7	-	-	-
7	5	Salomon Brothers	41.7	1	3.3	19.5	1	4.4
8	3	First Boston	31.2	1	2.4	52.0	1	11.8
9	6	Hambrecht & Quist	25.8	1	2.0	19.4	1	4.4
10	11	Prescott Ball & Turben	24.0	1	1.9	7.4	1	1.7

Source: **Annual Financing Report, Euromoney**, March 1987. p. 84

(1) Higher level of employment (consider the case of the Bahamas) and consequently higher tax revenues, better schools and infrastructure and other externalities, such as higher skills for the labor force.

(2) The development of additional financial services industries and of a string of small cottage industries.

(3) Increased success to new technologies which could benefit the service, the commercial, and the manufacturing sectors.

(4) Prestige for the nation and a higher profile for the domestic firms, allowing them better access to other financial markets and perhaps better access to their product and input (factor) markets.

(5) Possibly better macroeconomic policy as the nation learns to become sensitive to international issues and influences and to insulate to the extent possible, the domestic economy from the international effects.

(6) A mechanism for diversifying the economic base of a nation so that the cyclical effects are smoothed out.

The above benefits could come at a very heavy price as local inflation may soar, foreign competition may be destructive. The net benefits may be negative indeed. Therefore, a given nation or state within a nation cannot start with the assumption that becoming an international financial center is *per se* desirable. The viability of establishing an international financial center therefore, would hinge on the possibility of success and on the potential net benefits.

We now look at how certain financial centers have evolved over time to achieve their current status.

European Centers and New York

Charles Kindleberger (1974) revealed much about the development of European financial markets by his careful examination of their history. As interpreted by Kindleberger, the primary economic function of a capital market is the elimination of regional or sectoral monopolies and monopsonies by providing a central clearing place where suppliers of funds and demanders of funds engage in transactions that result in realistic market-determined prices. The efficiency of the allocative function of these markets is determined by the degree of competition in the market.

The evaluation of major financial centers throughout Europe shows that they had various implements which were largely uniform across countries. Banking prospered with trade and the increased industrialization that brought prosperity to Europe and to the banking/investment banking sector. So profitable were banking activities that many merchants switched partially or totally from trading goods to trading money. The Bank of England itself was founded by merchants.

The common denominators in the rise of European financial centers were the central locations of the cities for transportation and communication purposes; the needs to finance agriculture, commerce and industry, and to serve the owners of capital; and the political role of the seat of government. Berlin, Rome, Zurich and other financial centers, however, were able to prosper with government activities centered in other localities, as did New York. Government interference in the activities of the banking sector also played a role. The Bank of France, for example, was established in Paris by Napoleon and became a magnet for major banks outside Paris, such as Credit Lyonnais, which moved from Lyons to Paris in the 1850s.

One can conclude from the above that the sheer economic weight of commercial transactions, the centrality of a city for economic and political activity, the lack of viable alternatives at the time, government policy which focused on one city or one region, the entrepreneurship of the residents of a city can produce a financial center.

The story of New York follows the above script. New York, located strategically for purposes of national and international trade, became the principal center of finance. So successful became New York that some states enacted laws to stop the flow of funds to the big city. Foreign industrialists and bankers established themselves in this burgeoning center, and New York became a challenge to the leadership of London.

New York City early was the principal port for arrivals from and departures to Europe, and was central with respect to rapidly developing domestic economic activities along the Atlantic coast. Once established as the principal center in the United States, New York City continued to develop as a center because of interacting economic, demographic, geographic, institutional, and legal factors. In the case of the latter, for example, until recently, New York was the only state to permit branch banking by foreign banks. Despite the rapid growth of the Sunbelt states after World War II, New York City's preeminence as the financial center of the United States is still evident. Its lesser significance in agricultural loans, business services, wholesale trade, and import and export trade today also is evident as well.

Foreign governments and institutions did not fail to realize the attractiveness of New York. From World War I to the present, with minor interruptions, there were substantial foreign bond issues and other foreign borrowings in the United States. Investment banking firms picked up interest in foreign transactions because U.S. banks were forbidden by the Banking Act of 1933 from undertaking investment banking activities.

Immediately after World War II, the position of the United States as the only strong economy with no physical destruction of any of its productive capacities and a large capital surplus, helped put New York in the forefront of world financial markets. The U.S. government encouraged the issuance of foreign bonds in the U.S. market as a means of easing the dollar shortage abroad. Similarly, financial and banking services associated with the Marshall Plan, Point Four-Program, United Nations Relief and Rehabilitation Administration (UNRRA), and Economic Cooperation Administration (ECA) stimulated development of New York City as a world financial center.

Federal laws also were partly stimulative to New York's growth as a financial center, most notably the Edge Act, which gave the opportunity to many banks, particularly regional banks, to involve themselves in international banking. Many regional banks flocked to New York as a consequence. New York increasingly was becoming an exporter of banking services rather than of capital. The 1963 interest equalization tax, which effectively barred foreigners from raising funds by bond issues in New York, brought a flood of supplicants to New York banks.

The 1966 Foreign Investors Tax Act was no less helpful to New York. It removed many obstacles that prevented foreigners from investing in U.S. securities. The increased interest in the U.S. capital market that is centered in New York is manifested by the substantial rise in net purchases by foreigners of U.S. corporate securities. Those purchases increased from $703 million in 1965 to $5,435 million in 1975. The interest in U.S. government bonds was no less feverish, going from a net sales position of 4.76 million in 1965 to a net purchase position of $1,994 million in 1975. Most of these transactions were consummated in New York, where the New York and American stock exchanges are located. The mutual funds industry growth and the interest of Europeans in mutual funds further enhanced New York's position.

The growing internationalization of the banking institutions that thrived in New York also helped the city to gain its international character. Most banking business is done on the basis of reciprocal arrangements.

Citibank, which is firmly established in over 100 countries, and other banks like it, invited many foreign banks to this country, reciprocity being one way of maintaining market positions overseas.

Further help came from New York's key role in shipping and insurance and from the international population of the city. Almost every ethnic group is represented in the New York market, which is one of the reasons why Israeli, Puerto Rican, South Korean, and Pakistani banks established branches there.

The desires of foreign banks to diversity by regions, and particularly to enter the U.S. market through its biggest door, New York, and the imperfections of European capital markets with high issue costs, highly volatile share prices, and inability to absorb large issues with any regularity, helped the city get a firm hold on major financial transactions in the United States. New York City's market insures what James Tobin called "reversibility, liquidity, and predictability" because of its size, frequency of buy and sell orders, lower transaction costs, and the relative importance of the U.S. economy. All this led Richard Cooper to argue that New York is more likely to provide integration for European capital markets, than is any European market.

Finally, New York City is the home of the Federal Reserve Bank of New York, which is the only Reserve Bank authorized to have foreign accounts, operate internationally, and to act as a fiscal agent in both gold and foreign currency operations. The roles of the New York Federal Reserve Bank and of the dollar, held in the world as a reserve and trade currency, are highly significant. As a result, close relationships grew between New York underwriters and those of other financial centers, particularly those in England.

New York City's rise would have been even faster if it were not for various regulations by the Federal Reserve, including Regulation Q banning the payment of interest on money at call; various barriers to capital flows imposed by the U.S. government (for example, the Voluntary Foreign Credit Restraint Act) and the belatedness of the permission (1961) granting foreign banks the right to enter the New York market. Despite these hindrances (now removed), New York today is the major center for foreign banking activities in the United States.

Although prosperous and pacesetting, the New York market has yet to show the flexibility and the ingenuity of the London market. The greatest achievement of the latter is its ability to remain essentially self-regulating and to come up occasionally with brilliant financial innovations. Thus, after World War II, while U.S. bankers were treating the mounting Eurodollar balances with benign neglect, the Eurodollar bond issue was devised by Samuel Montagu of Warburgs. The Eurodollar market grew from about $20 billion in 1963 to $2,700 billion by the end of 1986, making it the most interesting and dynamic market.

The above discussion suggests that the development of New York as a financial center is due to economic, demographic, geographic, institutional, legal, governmental and political factors.

We now discuss the development of three cities as financial centers: Hong Kong, Singapore, and Vancouver, Canada. The lessons from their experiences are more relevant to any would-be centers because of the size and the "newness" factor.

Hong Kong

The major reason Singapore and Hong Kong have become important financial centers is the Communist revolution in 1949. Many Chinese who were non-Communist were forced to leave China and flee to its bordering countries. The people who left China were nationalist Chinese and they were considered to be very wealthy. All the money they brought with them was invested into these countries and that was the beginning of their financial and economic prominence.

Hong Kong is geographically the closest financial center to China. Many of the nationalist Chinese fled to Hong Kong for refuge. From 1949 to 1964, an estimated one million refugees fled into Hong Kong, and the flood continues as we write. With this aggressive population and the help of a great natural harbor, Hong Kong evolved from a naval station to one of the greatest trading and financial center in the Pacific. Hong Kong's rank went from 24th in exports in 1974 to 11th in the world in 1986. Three-quarter of total exports are attributed to textiles and electrical goods. Both of these exports account for 57% of total employment.

Financially, Hong Kong Banking and Mercantile Business Houses have branches all over the world. Hong Kong is considered to be the third largest financial center in the world. It has very close and large trading ties with China. Presently, 40% of China's foreign exchange comes from Hong Kong. More than 300 Chinese enterprises are in Hong Kong, including many joint ventures between the two. To avoid any slumps in the Hong Kong economy, China has guaranteed that private property and foreign investment would be protected by law, and the Hong Kong dollar would remain a convertible currency.

Hong Kong is expected to remain Asia's hottest equity market through 1987-1988. A broker on the Hang Seng Stock Exchange points out that it is the sheer weight of money flowing from abroad that continues to fuel Hong Kong's rise. The higher than expected economic growth is due principally to the private sector. Millions of dollars continue to flow into Hong Kong from outside investors. Hong Kong's dollar loans and advances have increased 10% from last year's 6%. Many believe Hong Kong will continue to be an important financial center and they also believe that the Hang Seng will pierce the 3,000 mark.

The issue of reverting Hong Kong's ownership to mainland China in 1997 seems to divide the analysts to the promise of Hong Kong as a political entity under the control of the vast Communist country. We believe that the optimists will prevail, for China needs a free and prosperous Hong Kong financial market, as does the rest of Asia. Low taxes, minimum regulation, and a very enterprising people will continue to fuel the growth of Hong Kong as a conduit between east and west, and China and the rest of Asia.

Singapore

Singapore presently has the potential to become the financial leader in the Pacific Basin. The background of Singapore is important to understand how their financial and economic systems work. Singapore relies heavily on imports. 70% of trade is based on entrepot imports (chiefly in crude rubber, timber, pepper, and petroleum products). Not only does Singapore have the busiest port in the world, but it has a strong currency which is 100% backed by gold. Foreign reserves currently stand at $24,400 million. In 1978, CDs were introduced and this helped Singapore financially. Beginning in 1980, Singapore became very active in the foreign exchange market. In 1983, the Singapore International Monetary Exchange (SIMEX) was formed. In 1984, they started trading futures.

There is one authority that controls any institution whose operations may affect Singapore's monetary stability, credit and exchange conditions, and the Republic's development as a major financial center. It is called the Monetary Authority of Singapore (MAS). In 1981, Herman Hochstadt of the MAS said that the MAS will come down hard on those who can not or will not maintain self-regulation. Some financial institutions didn't take this warning seriously and suffered as a result. Several big banks, local as well, were fined heavily in 1982 for circumventing reserve requirements in the Banking Act. Institutions that gave out loans over the official limit of $55,000 were fined if they were not approved by the MAS. Overseas Union Finance (OUF) was fined, like many others, as a result. Eventually, after the MAS appealed to the highest court, OUF was soon closed down. Other institutions began to take notice.

The MAS felt these extremes were necessary because deposits are a family's livelihood and they need to be protected. In 1984, the Banking Bill and the MAS Bill was passed by Parliament and this gave the MAS even tighter control over the Republic's commercial banks and financial institutions. Even foreign banks would have to deal with the MAS if they wanted to swap foreign currencies for Singapore dollars. It gave MAS some form of security for placing surplus Singapore dollars with these foreign banks; this was something that the commercial banks weren't able to do. Currently, leasing companies as well as credit card companies are being controlled by MAS.

On December 2, 1985, triggered by the Pan-Electric crisis over its defaults on loan repayments and the collapse of the forward contract pyramid involving its shares, the Stock Exchange of Singapore closed its doors in a humiliating three-day closure of business, and in the days that followed, most share prices tumbled to almost 35% below their net asset backing. Since that time, the government has tried with much success to turn the economy around.

A Central Provident Fund (CPF), which used to require 50% of income, was reduced to 25% in 1986 and is presently at 20%. Even government charges have been reduced and tax concessions to corporations have been given. The corporate tax went from 40% to 33% and in some cases even reduced to as low as 23%. There is presently no more payroll tax of 20%. Port dues for import vessels has decreased by 25%. Airport costs have even been reduced by 10% to increase tourism.

The government sees the greatest potential for future growth in the area of international services, especially banking and financial services. Singapore offers a 10% tax break to companies setting up large operational bases. Singapore is also trying to further develop countertrade. The government decided in 1986 that any company using Singapore for countertrade will get a 5-year tax holiday. Singapore also expects a large amount of financial operations to be attracted to it because of the strong yen; therefore, the Japanese are looking for cheaper locations to base their regional operations. Costs have come down and both quality and competitiveness has increased.

The growth of the Singapore market can be attributed largely to an enlightened and consistent government policy which allowed for tax incentives and liberalized regulations, and created and supported new financial markets, such as the Asian Dollar Market and SIMEX. Singapore's location, its enterprising people, and its strong diversified industrial base also helped.

Vancouver, Canada

While not in Singapore's class, Vancouver is one of the most important financial centers in Canada.[1] Vancouver gained its status by capitalizing on its location (halfway between London and Tokyo), the importance of its port (the largest in Canada), its time zone advantage (it overlaps the second shift on the London Stock Exchange), its enterprising population, and its excellent communication system and infrastructure. Thirty-three foreign banks are now represented in Vancouver. Vancouver is the hub for venture capital activity and the finance resources industries in Canada's west. Its exchange is now "one of the busiest exchanges in North America in terms of the number of shares traded, second only to the New York Stock Exchange" (see Tan and Vertinski 1987, p. 12). The exchange is particularly valuable, for there exists no unlisted market in British Columbia. The other contributing factors to Vancouver's growth are: reasonable (initially) regulatory environment; introduction of many innovations such as commodity and equity options and linkage to a 24-hour option clearing network; and generally good business environment.

While the government of Singapore showed the road to further internationalization of its financial markets, the Canadian federal government was an obstacle to growth, as it controls the banking sector through rather rigid banking laws. Thus, the ability of Vancouver to further its image as a financial center is tied to legal and political considerations which are well beyond its control.

We now look at what Anchorage can hope to achieve, based on the experiences of other centers and their current competitive standing.

Anchorage Potential as a New Financial Center

The discussion of the various financial centers has shown thus far that the common threads in their development are: locational advantage, trade, industry, and in some cases, government policy specifically designed to project a market on the international scene.

There is ample evidence in the literature that wherever trade and direct investment flow, so do banking facilities (see Khoury 1978). Mr. Peter Drucker observed, however, in an editorial published in the May 26, 1987 issue of *The Wall Street Journal* that:

> International investment is booming as never before. It has now become the dominant factor in the world economy. Most of it is investment in securities, of course. But the growing portion--by now a third or more--is permanent investment in manufacturing

and financial services. Traditionally, investment has followed trade, but trade is increasingly becoming more dependent on investment.

The Alaska case would, in Drucker's scenario, require a large influx of foreign direct investments, typically in oil, minerals, timber, and fisheries, which produces a significant trade activity and, consequently, a commensurate, at a minimum, banking activity in order to become a financial center.

With depressed oil prices and largely unexplored mineral resources, Alaska's development, whether domestically or foreign driven, seems a distance away. The current banking and international banking activity in Alaska is slim when compared with those of Los Angeles county and the State of Hawaii, two potential competitors (Table 2). Total assets of Alaska commercial banks amounted to $5.03 billion in 1986, one-half those of Hawaii and one-twentieth of those of Los Angeles county. Thus, based on size alone, foreign banks, like the Japanese and the British, who enter the United States intending to compete with their U.S. counterparts in all areas of banking, are unlikely to be interested in the Alaska market, unless their trading and manufacturing companies invest in Alaska substantially enough to make the delivery of banking services economically feasible. The Alaskan economy is expected to shrink dramatically in Fiscal 1987 from Fiscal 1986. Alaska's GNP in Fiscal 1986 was $3.075 billion, down from $3.26 billion in 1985. Expected GNP for fiscal 1987 is $1.4 billion and that for 1988 is $1.716 billion. The dramatic drop in economic activity in Alaska is due to the slump in the oil sector which accounts for about 80 percent of total output.

Table 2 also shows that the international activities of Alaska commercial banks were nonexistent in 1986. No foreign securities were purchased; no loans to banks in foreign countries, governments and official institutions were made; and no commercial, industrial loans and leases to non U.S. addresses were booked. The international activity by Hawaiian banks is substantial by contrast, as is the activity of commercial banks in Los Angeles county. The latter is small, however, when compared with the international activity of major New York banks.

It can be safely said, therefore, that Alaska's commercial banks have had little desire or incentive to reach overseas and foreign banks have not rushed into Alaska, because the payoffs are simply not there at this time.

TABLE 2
International Banking Statistics

	Alaska			Hawaii			Los Angeles County		
	Total	Non-Interest Bearing (NIB)	Interest Bearing (IB)	Total	Non-Interest Bearing (NIB)	Interest Bearing (IB)	Total	Non-Interest Bearing (NIB)	Interest Bearing (IB)
TOTAL ASSETS									
1986	5.03b			10.41b			104.2		
1984	4.44b			8.15b			88.2		
TOTAL DEPOSITS									
1986	4.07	1.3m	0.1m	9.27b	96m	399m	82.4	0.2	8.3
1984	3.58	0.9m	0.1m	7.18b	74m	476m	69.5	0.3	9.7
Balances Due From Banks in Foreign Countries and from Foreign Banks									
1986	35.3m			1.16b			1.7		
1984	4.1m			913m			2.3		
Foreign Securities									
1986	0			1.7m			0.8		
1984	.7m			.9m			0.1		
Loans to Banks in Foreign Countries									
1986	0			29m			1.5		
1984	0			37m			2.1		
Commercial/industrial Loans and Leases to non-U.S. Addresses									
1986	0			222m			3.9		
1984	0			150m			3.4		
Loans to Foreign Government & Official Institutions									
1986	0			33m			1.8		
1984	0			34m			1.8		

The current impediments to Alaska becoming a major financial center are numerous:

(1) Weather. Except for a few months of the year, most of Alaska can be forbiddingly cold.

(2) Size and skill of the population. By the end of this century, the most optimistic forecast pegs Alaska's population at 600,000, the lowest population count among the fifty states. There exist no banking schools or leading finance departments in Alaska to train the indigenous population to play a leading role in a dynamic financial global market.

(3) Size of the economy. The total value of goods produced in Alaska was only $1.4 billion in Fiscal 1987, 80% of which came from the oil sector. The size of economic activity does not warrant an influx of foreign banks.

(4) Difficulty of relaxing federal laws. A state which does not control all banking regulations, monetary policy, foreign exchange rates and income tax laws cannot compete effectively with nations that do, unless history and economic and political realities are working in its favor. The emergence of offshore banking centers, of the tax-haven variety like Nassau or the Bahamas, was largely due to liberal banking regulations and largely to the absence of any corporate tax. Alaska cannot compete with these centers, for it does not enjoy the political independence and flexibility to do so.

(5) Geographic impediment. While Alaska lies on the Pacific, it is far enough north to reduce its value as a trade route. Its proximity to the Soviet Union is not an advantage which can be explored commercially. Vancouver and Los Angeles remain very tough competitors. Also, Alaska is far removed from America's economic and political center. It cannot tread on this.

(6) Time zone problem. The location of Alaska in relation to Honolulu, Vancouver, and Los Angeles does not give it any special advantage in terms of time zone or access or infrastructure. None of the other cities, including Los Angeles, has become a true international financial center. Why should or how could Alaska?

(7) Oil dependence. The oil crisis will continue to haunt Alaska until the crisis disappears, and/or the Alaskan economic base becomes more diversified.

The economic boom still expected in America's last frontier is the only way one can rationalize the development of Alaska as an international financial center. Greater economic growth and a larger population must occur first before Alaska can aspire to be a financial center. Meanwhile, Alaska can attempt to capitalize on either or both of the following:

(1) Specialize in a small, but promising sub-sector of the banking industry. South Dakota has managed to become America's credit card capital. Alaska can find a niche in the financial sector worthy of its commitment.

(2) Develop a banking study and research center capable of attracting top bankers from all over the world to rest, contemplate, reflect and learn about the latest developments in banking. The University of Alaska Anchorage can play a pivotal role in this regard. Few such centers exist now. Another one should be welcome. UA Anchorage can start the process by hosting, for example, the next Western Financial Association meeting. The education side of banking could constitute a promising start for Alaska on its way to become a genuine financial center.

CONCLUSIONS

The translation of dreams of states and countries into reality is a long-term, tedious process. Anchorage has promise if it starts immediately on a course that will allow it to carve a niche in the banking sector. Banking education and research is a good start. The lessons from other nations or states which have attempted to become financial centers could be very valuable for Alaska. The experiences of Miami and Houston may also be worth examining, although location and the ethnic distribution of the indigenous population could be the overriding factors.

NOTES:

1. For an extensive discussion on Vancouver and its rival Singapore, see S.J. Tan and Ilan Vertinski (1987). D.C.

REFERENCES

Annual Financing Report. 1987. London: Euromoney.

Edmunds, Stahrl W. & Sarkis J. Khoury. 1986. Changing patterns of exports by Pacific Basin countries to the United States. *Business Forum*, Spring:12-18

Kindleberger, Charles P. 1974. *The formation of financial centers: A study in comparative economic history*. Princeton Studies in International Finance, No. 36. Princeton, Princeton University Press.

Khoury, Sarkis J. 1978. *Dynamics of international banking*. New York: Praeger Publishers.

Tan, S.J. & Ilan Vertinski. 1987. Strategic management of international financial centers. In S. Khoury and A. Ghosh, eds. *Recent Development in International Banking and Finance*. Lexington: Lexington Books.

Wall Street Journal. 1987. Drucker, Peter. May 26.

5. HONG KONG AS AN INTERNATIONAL FINANCIAL CENTER: A HONG KONG BANKER'S PERSPECTIVE

David K.P. Li, JP
Director and CEO
The Bank of East Asia Limited, Hong Kong

INTRODUCTION

This paper discusses three intertwined questions. First, what makes Hong Kong an international financial center? Second, how should a prospective borrower approach Hong Kong banks for financing? And, third, to what extent are Hong Kong banks involved in financing energy and natural resources projects?

Hong Kong is not only an international financial center of some magnitude, but also a cosmopolitan city. Hong Kong draws bankers and businessmen from virtually every corner of the world and Hong Kong people are enthusiastic world travelers. Although Hong Kong is not a funding center on the level of Tokyo, New York, or London, it is an important source for international capital. In 1986, Hong Kong was the world's fourth largest center for loan syndication, after London, New York, and Paris. Hong Kong's banking sector's net external assets at the end of 1986 exceeded those of the United States by almost U.S.$2 billion. To understand the Hong Kong capital market and put the services you may seek to tap in perspective, it might be useful to consider how and why Hong Kong became an international financial center.

REASONS FOR PROMINENCE OF HONG KONG AS AN IFC

Looking quite superficially at the Hong Kong experience, I can identify ten reasons why Hong Kong emerged as an important world market:

(1) History. Over the last 140 years, Hong Kong has evolved into a major regional trading center. In the '50s, '60s, and '70s, Hong Kong was one of the few places in Asia with an open economy.

(2) Political stability. During the '50s and '60s when Asia was often called the "region of revolt," Hong Kong offered security and stability. Under the terms of the 1984 Sino-British Joint Declaration Hong Kong's future stability is guaranteed by international treaty.

(3) A vibrant domestic economy. Over the last twenty years real GDP growth has averaged 7.8% annually. Exports have done even better, averaging a 20% yearly gain.

(4) A positive tax environment. While no tax haven, a prudent attitude toward government spending has kept tax rates low. The corporate rate is just 18%; the personal rate only 16.5%.

(5) A sound legal system. Under British administration the traditions of judicial independence and the Common Law have been transplanted and are well-entrenched in Hong Kong. Again, the 1984 Sino-British Joint Declaration on Hong Kong's future assures the present legal system will continue.

(6) An efficient physical infrastructure. From port facilities to air transport, computer services, and telecommunications, Hong Kong has kept pace with the leading edge of world technology.

(7) Trained manpower. At every stage in its development as a financial center, Hong Kong has been able to supply skilled, sophisticated, English-speaking personnel.

(8) An advantageous location. Hong Kong has as its hinterland the fastest growing part of the world economy. In addition, it holds a favorable time zone position between American and European markets -- though the advent of electronic banking technology must eventually have an impact on 24-hour trading.

(9) Reasonable living conditions and operating costs. Not only is Hong Kong a pleasant place to live, with good housing, schools, and recreation facilities, it is not as expensive as London, New York, or Tokyo.

(10) Credibility. This is an intangible quality. It reflects Hong Kong's role as a center both for regional business and the worldwide overseas Chinese community.

SOME TIPS ON TAPPING HONG KONG CAPITAL MARKET

To utilize Hong Kong capital market successfully, we need to identify three things: major participants, their service priorities, and the scope and direction of capital markets.

First, there is a need to identify the major participants in this market. On the banking side, there are four main categories:

* There are the Hong Kong-based British banks, of which the Hongkong & Shanghai Banking Corporation is by far and away the largest.

* There are the Hong Kong-based Chinese banks. Of these, I am happy to say my own bank, The Bank of East Asia, is the biggest.

* There are the Hong Kong branches of banks from the People's Republic of China. These are led by the Bank of China, which is now building Hong Kong's tallest skyscraper.

* Next, there are more than 100 licensed branches of foreign banks, including such well known names as Citibank, Chase Manhattan, and Bank of America.

In addition, there are other more specialized financial institutions, including merchant banks, deposit-taking companies, investment companies, securities companies, investment funds management companies, investment advisor firms and venture capital companies. Beyond these, there are companies that service or are closely related to the financial industry. Almost 40 law firms from the United States now have offices in Hong Kong. Moreover, IBM has just moved its Asia-Pacific Group operations to Hong Kong from Tokyo -- a transfer that may become quite familiar news, even for units of Japanese financial institutions, if operation costs in Tokyo continue their upward spiral.

Moreover, mention should be made of Hong Kong-based business. Hutchison Whampoa's investment in Canada's Husky Oil is only one example of the way Hong Kong companies are willing to go abroad, either for expansion or diversification.

Second, in tapping international capital markets in Hong Kong, prospective borrowing firms should also identify these organizations priorities. If we take just the banks, we can make the following generalizations:

* Foreign banks tend to think regionally. Sitting in Hong Kong, a foreign bank will most likely want to concentrate on Hong Kong itself, China, Taiwan, Korea, and perhaps Southeast Asia.

* The mainland Chinese banks generally have an even sharper focus -- Hong Kong and China.

* The Hong Kong-based Chinese banks are strongly retail and customer-oriented. Insofar as they can, they will try to go where their clients go and supply the services their clients need.

* The Hong Kong-based British banks also tend toward a regional orientation -- although the Hongkong & Shanghai Banking Corporation has near global capabilities.

Other financial institutions tend to slot into these categories, largely on the basis of country of origin or field of specialization.

The one problem with this kind of typology, however, is that it overlooks the give-and-take which occurs in a financial center. Priorities get shuffled as opportunities open.

Every day in Hong Kong, bankers, businessmen, lawyers all meet, talk and exchange ideas. It sounds simple. It is simple. But it is the consequence of Hong Kong's financial sector having achieved the necessary critical mass to generate business on its own--both for itself and other financial centers. From personal experience I can tell you the results are often surprising and exciting.

Third, firms should identify the scope and direction of the Hong Kong capital market. In other words, firms should know the different kinds of services that have been rendered by the Hong Kong market. Hong Kong is the world's fifth largest foreign exchange trading center. In 1986, the daily volume traded hit U.S.$20 billion. Hong Kong is the world's third largest gold trading center with a total daily turnover exceeding one million ounces in 1986. In stock market futures trading, Hong Kong also ranks third in the world, after Chicago and New York. The Hong Kong stock market is Asia's largest outside Japan. Moreover, Hong Kong is a major center for funds management. More than 200 unit trusts, worth over U.S.$9 billion, are directed from the Territory.

Hong Kong has never seen itself as a center for energy and natural resources finance. The one exception is China, for which Hong Kong has developed an extensive service and finance capability. In 1986, for example, a U.S.$75 million syndication was arranged through Hong Kong for a joint venture between the U.S. Occidental Group and the Bank of China Trust and Consultancy to develop the Pingshuo coal mine in China's Shanxi province. This does not mean that Hong Kong capital market is not interested in energy or resource projects outside China. In 1986, one of the larger Hong Kong companies, Hutchison Whampoa, purchased a major stake in Canada's Husky Oil. But it is important to understand that businessmen and bankers in Hong Kong are not beating the bushes for energy and resource-based deals. The major reason is lack of knowledge in these fields. When Hong Kong-based bankers and businessmen look beyond China and other Asian countries, they naturally are drawn to the places they know best and industries they understand well. In this regard, it is interesting to note, however, that the last two or three years have seen an increase in the number and variety of deals brought from the United States for funding through Hong Kong. To a great extent, these deals are on a private placement basis.

Hong Kong and China

Then there is the People's Republic of China. Hong Kong has always placed an important role as a gateway to China, and today over one-fifth of China's external trade is with Hong Kong. Increasingly, however, Hong Kong has come to play an even more important role as a financial center for China. In terms of capital and financial know-how, China's requirements are enormous. In the first half of 1987 alone, banks in Hong Kong concluded syndications worth more than U.S.$1 billion for China projects. It is estimated that China will require more than U.S.$15 billion in new commercial borrowing by 1990.

Hong Kong banks, financial institutions, and businesses also play a vitally important role in the establishment of joint ventures in China. It is now almost ten years since the Bank of East Asia helped establish China's first joint venture--a project, I am happy to say, that continues to prosper. Today, no other financial center can rival Hong Kong's experience and connections for matching partners and opportunities in China.

6. ARAB BANKS ADAPTING TO NEW TRENDS IN THE INTERNATIONAL FINANCIAL CENTERS

Hikmat Nashashibi
Chairman
Arab Bankers Association, London

INTRODUCTION

It started in New York with the abolishing of the fixed commissions in 1975. They called it "May Day." It later moved to London, and by October 27, 1986, the "fixed commission-single function era" came to an end. They called it "Big Bang." This has obviously put pressures on other countries and markets in Europe, leading to what can be called "European Bang." These pressures are being felt increasingly worldwide at present as financial authorities face the choice of either matching the liberal terms elsewhere or seeing business move away, leading to what can be termed as "Global Bang."

What about an "Arab Bang" or at least a "mini Arab Bang"?

Today, there is no excuse for bankers, financiers and corporate treasurers *of all nationalities* to be unaware of the depth and pace of international change. For it is a financial revolution springing from successive rapid-fire advances in communications technology, and their money business is at the heart of it. Let me start by discussing the origin and development of Arab involvement in the international capital markets.

ARAB INVOLVEMENT IN THE INTERNATIONAL CAPITAL MARKETS

Arab banking's involvement in the international capital markets is a relatively new development. It started with the creation of European Arab consortia banks in the late 1960s on a very limited scale, as the principal function of these banks, based in Paris and Brussels, was trade finance and Eurodeposit activities. After the oil price increases in 1973/74, the three big Kuwaiti investment companies became active in the international financial markets, making their way mostly in the underwriting and management of Eurobond issues. The distinct contribution by these companies has been their lead-management of Eurobond issues denominated in Kuwaiti Dinars, particularly to developing countries. In 1977, other Gulf-based banks entered the international capital markets. They centered their activities on Eurocredits or Euroloans. And like other banks operating in international finance, lending to developing countries was their most important activity.

Since 1979, many Gulf oil producing states decided to direct some of their longer-term investments towards the setting up of new, well-capitalized Arab banks or towards increasing the capital of existing banks. Other Arab banks operating in the international capital markets from within the region or abroad decided to increase their capital. New privately-owned banks were also created with large initial capitals. This new wave of capital injections has given Arab international bank lending a sound equity base, estimated at over ten billion dollars, upon which it can buy risks *directly*. As many of the Arab banks are new, or newly-international, without big commitments, most have room for relatively large lending to most countries.

In fact, as relatively new entrants to the international market, Arab banks had the tendency to take a longer-term view of profitability and were prepared in the short run to write loans at aggressive margins with a view to develop international asset growth strategies rather than concentrate on immediate profitability.

The sharper profile of Arab international banking emerged, in fact, in the last few years only. Ironically, it coincided with the declining oil financial surpluses, which stimulated the very creation and growth of these institutions. Clearly, this indicates that Arab international banking has an established base and a momentum in its own right.

In 1977, Arab banks accounted for less than 2 percent of the international bank lending market (Euroloans or Eurocredits) when they lead-managed one billion dollars of Euroloans and the market's size for the year was $42 billion. In 1982, Arab banks' involvement increased to 11 percent, when they lead-managed $10 billion of Euroloans, whereas the market's size for the year was $85 billion. In 1983, Arab banks accounted for 11.42 percent of the entire international loans market. In 1984 and 1985, this ratio dropped to 6 percent.

It is important to note that approximately half of the volume of Euroloans lead-managed by Arab banks in the last seven years was channeled for the Arab borrowers *themselves*. Therefore, the international markets, *in addition* to being the most important outlet for the deployment of Arab financial surpluses, have in fact contributed to:

(a) transforming the region's liquidity into longer-term Arab loans.

(b) integrating indirectly the underdeveloped Arab capital markets themselves.

(c) Intermediating between the region's supply and demand for loanable funds efficiently in terms of: amounts, currencies, maturities and prices.

In describing Arab Eurolending, it is very important to emphasize the commitments of Arab banking to regional lending and to promoting integration of Arab financial markets. There are, in fact, strong organic interactions between the regional and international activities of Arab financial intermediation.

The shortcomings of financial markets in many Arab countries are not due to a lack of overall savings, but rather to an *imbalance* between the supply and demand for capital at different maturity levels. The markets being undeveloped and small, investors' liquidity preference is high, whereas the demand for funds is of a longer-term nature and sometimes needs a concessional component, due to the low internal rate of return on the average product.

INTEGRATION OF ARAB FINANCIAL MARKETS

The prospect of integrating Arab financial markets, therefore, raises the question of the possible disparities in the saving rates between different countries, and in the types of institutions needed to transform short money into long money and to effect transfer of capital between high and low saving areas. The way in which financing requirements are met depends to a large extent on the composition of the funds available, and although there is a supply of long-term money in the aid sector, most funds (including government funds) are short-term deposits. Arab Eurobanking based in the region and abroad is needed to effect this "maturity transformation."

It is difficult to assess the actual degree of integration among Arab financial markets. Linkages with the international financial markets are large, compared to those between Arab markets themselves. This naturally is a direct reflection of the prevailing pattern of trade and economic relations between Arab countries and the rest of the world. With intra-Arab trade not exceeding 10 percent of total Arab exports and imports, and with the absence of a pan-Arab policy aiming at economic integration, plans for *direct* integration of Arab financial markets appear to be "Utopian" in nature at present, and not obviously linked to real economic relationships. The concept of a regional Arab financial market is in essence an economic "super-structure" providing liquidity for more fundamental (or what one might term "infra-structural") trade and economic relationships. And as is always the case, the infra-structure should determine the nature of the super-structure. To a large extent, therefore, the promotion of regional trade and the coordination of development programs will shape what happens to a regional Arab financial market.

From what I have mentioned, therefore, one is forced to conclude that it is premature to seek direct integration as the means of achieving free flow of capital between Arab countries. Indirect integration via Arab Eurobanking, however, has actually been occurring.

Though integration represents the fulfillment of complete elimination of all impediments to the free flow of capital among Arab countries, financial surpluses can also, therefore, escape national boundaries to the extent permitted by restrictions on direct integration of Arab financial markets, by entering the international financial markets.

Though an integrated Arab financial market ought to be the result of natural economic development, it will nonetheless require constructive input from Arab governments and financial institutions. The adjustments which the government will have to make are concerned primarily with closer coordination of their national economic policies and in the importance attached to the financial instruments they use. Their overall objectives, however, need not necessarily be drastically altered to make progress in this direction. As these adjustments are carried out, the Arab financial institutions that are currently more active in the Eurolending will be able to set the pace for the rest of the market. A more integrated Arab financial market, that stems from all that, will take the form of a network of transactions which, if at first limited, will gradually be extended to cover all categories of financial flows. And at every step of its gradual growth, an Arab market has to be efficient enough to offer comparative advantages to borrowers, in terms of amounts, maturities, types of finance, and costs of funding, as well as investment attractions to lenders.

ARAB BANKS AND EUROLENDING

While increasing their exposure to international loans, Arab banks have had a limited profile in the underwriting of bond issues and international securities in general. Bonds lead-managed by these banks have been largely confined to Kuwaiti Dinar denominated issues.

The biggest single year for the Kuwaiti Dinar bond market was in fact 1978 when 15 issues were completed for international borrowers. The first public issue came in 1974, and the volume has started to increase since then, with some innovations. KD Certificates of Deposit appeared, FRCDs, and later DK floating rate bonds with warrants attached. Furthermore, the quality of foreign borrowers tapping the market started to improve. Foreign borrowers included prestigious names like OKB, Finland, City of Oslo, BNP, CCCE, Norges Kommunal Bank, Credit Lyonnais, Eurofima, SEK, Credit Nationale, Asian Development Bank and Charbonnages de France.

Talking about KD international bonds in 1987 may appear somewhat arcane. The market remains effectively closed at present, but its educational benefits have been enormous. Its success compared with other Arab currency bonds has been considerable and it may yet be revitalized and flourish as a permanent feature of the international market.

U.S. dollar new issues have been the other most important component of Arab banks' international bond activity. Within that sector, the main presence has been in the floating rate notes (FRNs) area. The interest in FRNs is quite natural for banks attempting to break into the bond market for the first time, as the techniques of Euroloan finance are very similar to FRNs. Arab involvement in U.S. dollar straight issues has been confined largely to co-management and underwriting of issues. A similar level of Arab activity is observable in the U.S. dollar convertible issues.

Arab presence in the DM international bonds was, and still is, consistent, though largely limited to co-managements and underwritings.

Arab banks have occasionally lead-managed "currency" bond issues in the last few years.

Let me mention some of the reasons that, I believe, have contributed to the lack of success of Arab banks in the international bond market and securities in general. Briefly:

(1) The complex nature of the market itself. Unlike the syndicated loan market, international bond issues have remained the preserve of the select group of securities houses who pioneered the instruments two decades ago. Mandates for international bond issues have tended to be awarded to either this club of houses or to houses having historical ties with issue.

(2) The lack of real experience in the securities business in general. Arab financial intermediaries have been predominantly confined to 'deposit and loan' activity and the mentality associated with it. In this respect, they are largely oriented to spread lending and to "on-balance sheet" income. This explains the relative lack of investment banking mentality in terms of risk-taking in new issues underwriting.

(3) The shortage of Arab investment bankers with sufficient experience, professionalism, and connections. Related to that is the shortage of systems, procedures and limits enabling prompt decisions and risk management in the firm.

(4) Lack of real capability to down-stream securities to final takers. Arab banks have been limiting their scope of placement, largely to their own governments or to buying securities for their own account.

So far, I have talked about the Arab involvement in international securities as underwriters. In recent years, we have seen the Arab involvement in the market as borrowers. The issuers were primarily banks, such as ABC, Alahli Bank of Kuwait, Frab, B.A.I.I., and the N.C.B. of Jeddah. This is a natural development, as the international bond market is becoming increasingly "the banker to banks."

The potentials are excellent, in my opinion, for Arab banks to lead-manage bond issues for Middle East sovereign, corporate and bank names in the future. This will, nevertheless, require that these banks exhibit a much greater degree of professionalism, innovation, placement ability and track record to convince their own borrowers to be taken to the Eurocapital market by them.

NEW TRENDS IN INTERNATIONAL FINANCIAL CENTERS

Let me discuss, now, how Arab banks can adapt to the new trends in the international capital markets. Globalization, deregulation, and securitization of markets, institutions and products are the basic changes shaping a new era for the financial services industry. These terms have been the industry's buzzwords for a couple of years, pushing the frontiers of domestic financial marketplaces as far as the telephone lines can stretch. Such thoughts used to come from forecasters. Today, they are urgent nuts and bolts issues that are permanently altering the financial map. There has never been a truly global financial services industry aiming at the retail and institutional client like today. And financial institutions throughout the world are throwing more money, people and physical facilities at it than at any time before. In all the major world financial centers, particularly New York, London and Tokyo, hardly a day passes now without one of the major firms opening a new office abroad, raiding top talent to beef up overseas operations or acquiring a foreign financial company.

Wall Street firms, for example, are increasingly looking upon New York as one of three legs, including London and Tokyo that will form the foundation for their future. Not only are American corporations increasingly raising capital abroad, but foreign governments also have been lowering barriers to the flow of capital in and out of their countries. When a deal is done, it is no more from Massachusetts to Illinois, it is all the way around the Horn to Tokyo and London. And the time is not far away when the American market will be a "region" for the mega Wall Street firms. In most instances, opportunities to make investments in overseas business exceed firms' ability to retain earnings. If anything, it appears that most firms underestimated the growth of international transactions.

Indeed, international transactions are fast becoming a big chunk of Wall Street business. Expansion overseas is no longer an option. The global market is a reality. And you can't deliberate for long whether you will be a factor in it or not. Previously, overseas business of a Wall Street firm was rather narrow in scope. Firms had to focus on selling American securities to wealthy foreign investors. Today, Wall Street firms are doing almost the same mixture of business abroad as at home. They are structuring and underwriting securities aimed specifically at foreign investors; they are making markets in foreign and United States securities for overseas investors; they are providing financial advice, including merger and acquisition counseling and global portfolio management. They are "Americanizing" the securities industry worldwide.

The impetus for this change is coming from two principal sources: the increasingly slippery nature of capital and blurring of domestic and international markets because of the electronic technology which allows cheaper transfer of information, and computing, to anyone anywhere if he has a simple "electrical socket"; and financial deregulation leading to what we termed earlier as a "Global Bank." As far as banks are concerned, the changes could hardly be more timely, because they coincide with the trend towards investment banking: the business of bringing together investors (individuals and institutions) and capital users, rather than depositors and borrowers, and making tradeable financial products out of virtually everything from mortgages to car loans. All this cuts out the traditional banker. He has no longer much to sell except, perhaps, his underwriting, trading, distribution and positioning capability, as well as the "unbundled" risk varieties of his traditional asset and liability products tied up to the bank loan business, i.e., the credit, maturity, interest risks, and foreign exchange exposure. He is being constantly disintermediated, unable to continue to survive on traditional customer loyalties or protected markets, and gradually pushed to reshape his institution.

The globalization, deregulation, and securitization of the financial services to the wholesale, as well as the retail, client *imply* a lot of things to market participants, including Arab Gulf participants:

(1) Lending is moving very rapidly away from the bank loan form to the securities form. Eurobonds volume of new issues amounted in 1986 to $180 billion. In 1987, in all likelihood, they will surpass the $200 billion mark. Euroloans may very well become a source of bridge finance *only*, until market conditions allow borrowers to tap the securities markets.

(2) A market for cross-boarder equity issues is rapidly developing. It will follow the same footsteps of Eurocredits and Eurobonds in evolution, but much, much faster.

(3) Customers of whatever nationality or geographic location are becoming very sophisticated and up-to-date. Bankers, therefore, can earn their fees only if they provide a value-added financial service that is *both* expeditious and efficient in terms of amounts, maturities, currencies and costs.

(4) Financial products offered have to be competitive "anywhere under the sun," irrespective of the nationality of the firm producing them. They should have at least a comparative advantage over similar products produced outside their domestic or national domain.

(5) Human faculties loom very high in importance among the other factors of production leading to a financial services industry. Other factors of production such as capital or physical facilities are of much less importance. The industry is basically a people's industry where the factory goes home at the end of the working day. To put it differently, "our real capital is our staff. When they go down in the lift at night, our capital goes down too!"

(6) To succeed in such an era, market participants have to be either everything to everybody, i.e., a "full-line firm", or a "special niche firm," i.e., producing very few specialized financial products in which the firm has a real competitive edge.

(7) Strategic planning is the heart of the new game, that is, to produce the right products, simple or packaged, at the right time and place. Top management, therefore, do not deserve their fat salaries by playing the role of sheer runners of shows, but by being strategic planners.

(8) Off-balance sheet fees should be a main source of income complementing spread lending. This income should be stable in character.

These implications are forcing all the bankers of the world to look beyond their next deal and ask some awkward questions about what their business is and what it should be.

Arab bankers are no exception. They have to adapt successfully to the new era of international finance. This requires, first and foremost, a basic shift in their mentality from commercial bankers working with credit risk only to investment bankers working with market risk. It requires, also, that a major thrust be directed at the investor, particularly the "Arab dentist", and a particular franchise built on quality people and adequate capital. In finding their niche, Arab houses will concentrate first on products which are difficult to "unbundle". There are still many products which are not suitable for global trading, for example, equity and debt issues for medium size and small companies.

Furthermore, relationships between Arab financial institutions and Arab borrowers are very strong in the domestic markets. This means it is harder for big global securities firms to penetrate purely domestic business. Let me draw a historical analogy here. During the period 1978-1986, Arab banks lead-managed Euroloans for various borrowers of the world, to the tune of $48 billion. Of this figure, interestingly enough, $21 billion were Euroloans lead-managed for Arab borrowers, or 43 percent of the total. The progress of this "Arab-to-Arab Euroloans activity" was noticeable in the last few years and will continue to grow steadily in the future.

Arab borrowers, like all the borrowers of the world, are getting "security conscious." A special niche for Arab banks is therefore to concentrate successfully on "Arab-to-Arab Eurosecurities activity" based on *cost effectiveness*. The niche business needs strategic thinking. Arab bankers need to ask themselves what business they are in. They need to identify which of those businesses have comparative advantages, and whether those advantages can be improved upon. Discovering niches and filling them demands imagination. For the unimaginative Arab banker, the future can be bleak.

7. INTERNATIONAL BANKING CENTERS IN ASIA

Francis P. Sing
President

INTRODUCTION

In general, international banking activities may be classified into five areas:

(1) foreign trade financing, such as issuance of letters of credit for import

(2) currency exchange, such as buying and selling of foreign currencies -- foreign exchange trading

(3) transfer of funds across national boundary, and foreign currency deposits fall under this heading

(4) foreign borrowing and lending and,

(5) foreign investment.

To be an international banking center, bankers in the location should be able to perform all the functions mentioned above.

International banking center, as used in this paper, refers to a place where banking activities related to international business are concentrated. The essential aspect of the concept is then the concentration of those banking activities which, in one way or another, are related to international business operations. It is the key word, *concentration*, which separates New York City from Boston or Atlanta, for example. No doubt, banks in Boston and Atlanta can and do perform anyone of the five categories of international banking activities listed above, but neither of them has the breadth and depth of banking services New York City has to offer.

Judging by the type of services performed, an international banking center may assume any of the following characteristics (Dale, 1984): (1) a city through which domestic capital-flow to outside world takes place, such as London and New York City, two prime examples in this class; (2) a city which, by virtue of its geographical location and facilities, serves as a center where foreign lending and trading of foreign currencies take place, such as Hong Kong and Singapore, and (3) a place where, because of its favorable banking regulations and tax laws, foreign lending and borrowing occur, such as the Bahamas, Channel Islands and Cayman Islands. The last group is often referred to as "offshore" banking center. (See, for example, Dale 1984, p. 16)

Of the first type of international banking center, London is the best example, for it has been a banking center of the world well over one hundred years. During the reign of Queen Victoria, the pound sterling was the international currency par excellence. It was used in international trade and payments all over the globe, and was the envy of the rest of the world. The reasons for such a success were many and among them were industrial and commercial power, as well as military might, of the Great Britain, financial resources and services, including insurance and large volumes of capital export, the City of London had offered. Even though the British economy is no longer the strongest in the world today, London still enjoys, partly because of its glorious history of the 19th and the early 20th Centuries, its preeminent position as the world financial center, not so much as the major net capital exporter, but rather as an entrepot and the hub of Eurocurrency market. Other major international banking centers falling under this heading include New York City and Zurich.

The second type of international banking center is a city which serves as an intermediary or entrepot in that both foreign borrowers and lenders utilize the banking facilities of the city to consummate their deals. Evidently, in order to be able to establish itself as an intermediary financial center, a city must have, not only an extensive banking network with the outside world, but also favorable banking regulations and tax laws. Hong Kong and Singapore are two good examples in this category.

The third kind of international banking center is the so-called "offshore" center which "has been brought into being by the 'new' international bank lending based on the Euromarket." (Dale 1984, p. 16) As Dale points out in his cited work, the distinctive characteristic of the offshore banking center is that it provides an intermediary service to foreign borrowers and lenders, not so much on the basis of local banking facilities, but rather on the favorable tax laws or its lack of banking regulations. Even though some offshore centers do have banking facilities where deposit-taking and lending actually take place, due mainly to their geographical location or to the availability of local expertise, others serve merely as shell centers. In the latter case, which came into being purely as tax havens, foreign lending and borrowing are booked there, but actual transactions occur elsewhere. Therefore, there is no need for banking facilities in an offshore shell center. Well-known offshore shell centers are the Bahamas, Cayman Islands in the Caribbean Sea, and the Channel Islands off the French west coast.

Conceptually, it is rather easy to classify an international banking center into one of the three categories, but in reality it is often difficult to do since several major international financial centers have been performing two of the three types of services, namely, net exporter of capital and an intermediary role of matching lenders and borrowers at the same time.

In discussing the feasibility of developing Anchorage into an international banking center, one is inclined to judge the potential of Anchorage in comparison to two regional international banking centers:

Hong Kong and Singapore. The reason for choosing the two as examples for Anchorage to emulate is that both centers are of entrepot in nature, and that is what the City of Anchorage is going to be once it decides to establish itself as an international banking center.

HONG KONG

An island off the southeast China coast, together with Kowloon peninsula and a large stretch of land on Mainland China just north of Kowloon and known as the New Territory, form the crown colony of Hong Kong. It has 391 square miles and a population of five and a half millions, approximately. To serve these people and many millions more in China and other parts of the world, there are 151 licensed banks with 1,533 branches in Hong Kong at the end of 1986. In addition, there were 255 Registered Deposits Taking Companies (RDTC) with 359 branches, and 33 Licensed Deposits Taking Companies (LDTC) with 49 branches in the same period. Altogether there were 444 authorized financial institutions with 1,941 branches in Hong Kong. (In a way, Hong Kong is over-banked). Of the 151 licensed banks, 15 belong to China, 37 to Europe, 25 to Japan, 22 to the United States, 20 to Hong Kong and 32 to other countries. From such a diversified group of banks, one can see how cosmopolitan the City of Hong Kong is.

From the analysis of the data attached herewith, (see Tables 1 and 2), we realize that commercial banks in Hong Kong have utilized to a great extent funds obtained offshore, and at the same time, have made a substantial amount of loans overseas. In other words, Hong Kong has demonstrated its characteristic as an intermediary center for international lending.

Table 1 shows that of all the loans and advances made by all banks in 1980 and 1986, the proportion for domestic use declined slightly over the six-year period, but it still accounts for slightly over one half of total loans. On the other hand, the proportion of loans for international business rose from 46.6% of total loans in 1980 to 47.5% in 1986. The item of special interest is that of other offshore loans which almost tripled in six years, and by far the largest single item of all loans and advances in both 1980 and 1986.

Judging from the sources of funds as shown in Table 2, the increasing importance of foreign currency deposits during the period was extraordinary. In 1980, domestic currency deposits accounted to 85.2% of total deposits, but by 1986 the proportion dropped to 43.2%. On the other hand, foreign currency deposits, which in 1980 amounted to only 14.8% of the total, rose to account for 56.8% in 1986. In terms of rate of increase over the six-year period, domestic currency deposits rose only by 2.4 times, while foreign currency deposits increased by 17.9 times. Since total customers' deposits in 1980 were less than the amount needed to fund all loans, the short-fall was made up by money market borrowing and stockholders' equity as indicated in Table 3.

Table 1

Banking Statistics of Hong Kong (All Banks)

(Figures in billions of Hong Kong Dollars)

Classification of Loans	1980	%	1986	%	% Change
Manufacturing	$10.5	5.5	$25.1	4.9	+139.0
Transportation & Util.	$10.3	5.4	$22.8	4.4	+121.4
Building & Construction	$19.4	10.2	$34.8	6.7	+79.4
Retail & Wholesale Trade	$14.5	7.6	$33.7	6.5	+132.4
Housing Mortgages	$11.6	6.1	$49.2	9.5	+324.1
Financial Concerns	$ 7.7	4.1	$26.4	5.1	+242.9
Personal Loans	$12.3	6.5	$29.4	5.7	+139.0
Other Loans	$15.2	8.0	$49.3	9.6	+224.3
Total Loans For Use In Hong Kong	$101.5	53.4	$270.7	52.5	+166.7
Trading Financing	$ 22.9	12.1	$ 55.2	10.7	+141.1
Shipping Loans	$ 11.4	6.0	$ 31.1	6.0	+172.8
Other Offshore Loans	$ 54.2	28.5	$158.7	30.8	+192.8
TOTAL LOANS	$190.0	100	$515.7	100	+171.4

Source: James Capel (Far East) Limited. 1987. *The banking industry of Hong Kong*. Hong Kong.

TABLE 2

Sources of Funds (All Banks)

(Figures in billions of Hong Kong dollars)

	1980	%	1986	%	% Change
Total Hong Kong Currency Deposits	$101.8	85.2	$241.3	43.2	+137.0
Total Foreign Currency Deposits	$17.7	14.8	$317.4	56.8	+1,693.2
TOTAL DEPOSITS	$119.5	100	$558.7	100	+367.5
FOREIGN CURRENCY DEPOSITS					
Demand	$ 1.1	6.2	$ 4.5	1.4	+309.1
Savings	$ 2.8	15.8	$27.5	8.7	+882.1
Time (unsecuritized)	$ 2.2	12.4	$151.1	47.6	+6,768.2
Time (securitized)	$11.6	65.6	$134.3	42.3	+1,057.8
TOTAL	$17.7	100	$317.4	100	+1,693.2

Source: James Capel (Far East) Limited. 1987. *The banking industry of Hong Kong*. Hong Kong.

In 1986, total deposits of domestic and foreign currencies were large enough to meet the loan demand of domestic and foreign clients. But due to the fact that a large portion of foreign currency time deposits was invested in securities, commercial banks had to tap money market funds and stockholders' equity to make up the difference as indicated in Tables 1 and 2.

From Table 4 and Table 5 presented on the following two pages, we can see how extensively Hong Kong commercial banks engaged in international banking activities. From Table 4, one notices that of all external sources of money market funds in 1986, three major ones were from Europe, mainly London, Tokyo and Singapore. Altogether they accounted for 76% of the total. On the other hand, the three major suppliers borrowed 73% of all money market funds from Hong Kong, leaving a balance of 27% for other countries as shown in Table 5. In addition to telling us the extent of Hong Kong banks' participation in international banking operations, both tables show two significant developments in Hong Kong offshore banking activities: first is the rapid growth of Tokyo as a source and use of Hong Kong money market funds, and second is the extensive use of offshore islands as shell centers for international operations.

Now the question is what makes Hong Kong into such an important international banking center? The answer may be found in the following considerations:

(1) As a crown colony of Great Britain, Hong Kong has enjoyed political and social stability and security which are essential to economic development and well-being.

(2) A laissez-faire economic system which unleashes the full energy and entrepreneurial spirit of the populace, thus making Hong Kong one of the most prosperous and modern cities on earth.

(3) A well-developed infrastructure for commerce and industry. Hong Kong is a free port. It has rail and highway connections with Mainland China and air links with all major countries in the world. Its telecommunication facilities are one of the best the world over. Its power supply is more than adequate in meeting the need of its industry.

TABLE 3
Sources of Funds

(Figures in billions of Hong Kong dollars)

	1980	%	1986	%	% Change
HONG KONG CURRENCY					
Demand Deposits	$14.7	7.7	$32.3	6.3	+119.7
Savings Deposits	$40.0	21.1	$97.9	19.0	+144.8
Time Deposits	$56.4	29.7	$114.9	22.3	+103.7
Net Money Market Liab.	$67.4	35.5	$59.0	11.4	- 12.5
Shareholders' Funds	$ 5.4	2.8	$28.5	5.5	+427.8
Total, domestic	$183.9	96.8	$332.6	64.5	+ 80.9
FOREIGN CURRENCY					
Demand Deposits	$ 1.1	0.5	$ 4.5	0.9	+309.1
Saving Deposits	$ 2.8	1.5	$ 27.5	5.3	+882.1
Time Deposits*	$ 2.2	1.2	$151.1	29.3	+6,768.2
TOTAL CURRENCY	$190.0	100	$515.	100	+171.4

* Not securitized. Foreign currency deposits which had been securitized were
HK$11.6 billion in 1980 and HK$134.3 billion in 1986.

Source: James Capel (Far East) Limited. 1987. *The banking industry of Hong Kong*. Hong Kong, p.30.

TABLE 4

The Geographical Analysis of Money Market Operations -- The Funding Sources

(Figures in billions of Hong Kong dollars)

MONEY MARKET LIAB. DUE TO BANKS ABROAD	1980	%	1986	%	% Change
Europe (mainly London)	$64.2	39.3	$287.8	29.8	+348.3
Tokyo	$ 9.1	5.6	$258.0	26.8	+2,735.2
Singapore	$41.0	25.1	$186.5	19.3	+354.9
United States	$10.9	6.7	$ 67.7	7.0	+521.1
Middle East	$ 8.6	5.3	$ 27.0	28.0	+214.0
China	$ 0.8	0.5	$ 19.2	2.0	+2,300.0
Taiwan, Indonesia & South Korea	$ 4.8	2.9	$ 11.0	1.1	+129.2
Offshore Banking Centers:					
Bahamas	$ 4.7	2.9	$ 55.1	5.7	+1,072.3
Vanuatu	$ 3.6	2.2	$ 10.9	1.1	+302.8
Cayman Islands	$ 3.5	2.1	$ 4.9	0.5	+ 40.0
Others	$12.4	7.6	$ 33.6	3.5	+171.0
Classification Differences*	-$0.2		$ 2.4		
TOTAL	$163.5	100	$964.1	100	+490.0

* Classification differences arise because the statistics on the external liabilities to banks outside Hong Kong are compiled on the basis of *the location* of the funding sources and thus include funds remitted from the overseas branches of the locally incorporated banks.

Source: James Capel (Far East) Limited. 1987. *The banking industry of Hong Kong*. Hong Kong.

TABLE 5

The Geographical Analysis of Money Market Operations -- The Fund Receivers

(Figures in billions of Hong Kong dollars)

MONEY MARKET CLAIMS ON EXTERNAL BANKS	1980	%	1986	%	% Change
Europe	$34.3	30.7	$240.5	23.9	+601.2
Tokyo	$ 8.1	7.3	$354.4	35.3	+4,275.3
Singapore	$16.6	14.8	$137.6	13.7	+728.9
United States	$ 9.9	8.9	$ 61.0	6.1	+516.2
Middle East	$ 3.6	3.2	$ 7.7	0.8	+113.9
China	$ 2.4	2.1	$ 11.1	1.1	+362.5
Taiwan	$ 2.3	2.1	$ 13.9	1.4	+504.3
Indonesia	$ 0.6	0.5	$ 0.7	0.1	+ 16.7
South Korea	$ 8.3	7.4	$ 41.2	4.1	+396.4
Offshore Banking Centers:					
Bahamas	$ 1.3	1.2	$ 54.7	5.4	+4,107.7
Vanuatu	$ 9.3	8.3	$ 0.6	0.1	- 93.5
Cayman Islands	$ 1.1	1.0	$ 18.4	1.8	+1,572.7
Others	$14.0	12.5	$ 63.0	6.2	+350.0
TOTAL	$111.8	100	$1,004.8	100	+798.7

* The table above shows the geographical spread of total claims on banks abroad. These statistics are compiled on the basis of the *location* of the receiving banks and thus include funds deposits by the locally incorporated banks in their overseas branches.

Source: James Capel (Far East) Limited. 1987. *The banking industry of Hong Kong.* Hong Kong.

(4) A well-developed and relatively free banking system. The fact is clearly indicated by the number of banks Hong Kong currently has and the volume of business conducted by all of them in 1986. Hong Kong imposes no foreign exchange control.

(5) Favorable tax laws which exempt non-residents' foreign currency deposits from withholding tax and offshore banking profit from its local corporate income tax.

SINGAPORE

Singapore, located at the southern tip of Malay peninsula, is a cosmopolitan city-state with a population close to 2,700,000. It has been a crown colony of Great Britain for a long time, and from 1963 to 1965 it was a state in the Federation of Malaysia. Since 1965, it has been an independent republic in the British Commonwealth. Its territory is only 225 square miles. But because of its strategic location and its people's energy and hard work, Singapore has evolved from a British trading post in the 19th Century to a commercial and industrial center in Southeast Asia in the post World War II period. In recent years, it has become an international banking center. The immediate cause of this latest development was the establishment of a special international department by the Singapore branch of the Bank of America to handle, under license, transactions of non-residents in the Asian currency market. Subsequently, a special unit of account called Asian Currency Unit (ACU), denominated principally in U.S. dollars, was introduced in 1968, thus creating two separate banking structures, one for local banking business and the other for offshore operations. As pointed out by Dale (1984) "this dual structure enables the authorities to promote Singapore's role as an international financial center while avoiding excessive competition in the domestic market." (Dale 1984, p. 121) In general, foreign-owned banks are prohibited from conducting business in the local currency market. However, any commercial bank may apply for an Asian Currency Unit license which permits the bank to engage in the Asian market activities.

Like the Eurocurrency market, the Asian currency market is dominated by interbank transaction. For example, of the $200.6 billion (in U.S. dollar) total assets, in Asian dollar accounts, of Singapore banks at the end of 1986, as shown in Table 6, $146.6 billion, or 73.1% of the total, is for interbank funds, as compared to $38.7 billion, or 19.3% of the total, loans to non-bank customers. A breakdown of the interbank funds shows that $111.1 billion, or 75.8% of the total, were either lent to or deposited at financial institutions outside Singapore. As far as the liabilities are concerned, the interbank transactions of $159.4 billion represent 79.5% of the total liabilities of $200.6 billion. Of the interbank funds, $123.9 billion, or 77.7%, were deposits from offshore sources. What these figures suggest is that "Singapore may be regarded as a staging post for interbank funds rather than a center intermediating between final borrowers and lenders." (Dale 1984, p. 45)

TABLE 6

Asian Dollar Market

(Figures in billions of U.S. dollars)

ASSETS	1982	%	1986	%	% Change
Loans for Non-Bank Customers	$27.6	26.7	$38.7	19.3	+ 40.2
Interbank Funds					
In Singapore	$ 1.8	1.7	$ 4.9	2.4	+172.2
Inter-Asian Currency Units*	$19.2	18.6	$30.6	15.3	+59.4
Outside Singapore	$48.6	47.1	$111.1	55.4	+128.6
Total	$69.6	67.4	$146.6	73.1	+110.6
Other Assets	$ 6.1	5.9	$15.3	7.6	+150.8
TOTAL ASSETS	$103.3	100	$200.6	100	+ 94.2
LIABILITIES					
Deposit of Non-Bank Customers	$17.6	17.0	$33.8	16.8	+ 92.1
Interbank funds					
In Singapore	$ 1.5	1.5	$ 4.9	2.5	+226.7
Inter-Asian Currency Units	$19.2	18.6	$30.6	15.3	+ 59.4
Outside Singapore	$58.5	56.6	$123.9	61.8	+111.8
Total	$79.2	76.7	$159.4	79.5	+101.3
Other Liabilities	$ 6.5	6.3	$ 7.4	3.7	+ 13.8
TOTAL LIABILITIES	$103.3	100	$200.6	100	+ 94.2

* Asian Currency Unit is a separate accounting unit of banks and other financial institutions given approval to transact in the Asian dollar market.

Sources: *Monthly Statistical Bulletin*, April 1987. Monetary Authority of Singapore, pp. 33, 34.

One may attribute the phenomenal success of Singapore's effort to establish the city-state as an international financial center to the far-sightedness of the government in doing the right thing at the right time. Certainly, that is true. But there are other factors as well which have been responsible for the rapid growth of the Asian currency market in Singapore, and they are: (1) a well-developed banking industry which can support the activities of an international banking center; (2) a strategic location not only in terms of international commerce in a rapidly developing region of the world, but also in terms of its time zone which enables banks in Singapore to transact business with Western Europe, the Middle East, Hong Kong, Tokyo and Sydney on the same day; (3) a democratic form of government and a stable social environment which allow the free enterprise system to work and flourish, and (4) an excellent telecommunication network which enables messages to be transmitted instantaneously all over the world. Of course, the right thing the Singapore authorities did was to deregulate the offshore banking business and the subsequent support and encouragement given to the banking industry. The support and encouragement took the form of reducing the cost of doing offshore banking business in Singapore. In the period of 1967-1978, the government had abolished the 10% withholding tax on interest income from non-resident foreign currency deposits, exempted the 20% liquidity ratio applicable to foreign currency deposits, reduced corporate income tax rate from 40% to 10% on net income from offshore lending, (the 10% rate was scheduled to be entirely eliminated in 1987), permitted the issuance of Asian dollar certificates of deposits to non-residents, lifted foreign exchange controls and allowed Singapore residents to deal in Asian currency units.

The magnitude of growth in international banking business in Singapore can be seen by comparing the figures in Table 6 and Table 7. At the end of 1982, total assets of Asian dollar account were \$103.3 billion, 4.5 times of total assets in domestic currency account of S\$48.5 billion, (or \$22.9 billion in U.S. dollars) of all commercial banks. By the end of 1986, total assets of Asian dollar account grew to \$200.6 billion, or 5.5 times of total assets in domestic currency account of S\$76.8 billion, or \$36.2 billion in U.S. dollars. In terms of growth rate during the period, 1982-1986, the former grew at the rate of 94.2%, while the latter grew only at 58.4%. In fact, the total amount of Singapore's Asian Dollar Accounts in 1986 was much larger than that of foreign currency deposits, even allowing for interbank funds (money market operations), in Hong Kong, even though the total amount of domestic currency deposits of all banks in Singapore was smaller than that in Hong Kong. This testifies to the fact that Singapore, in a relatively short period of time (1968-1986), has emerged as a world-class international financial center.

Before leaving the scene of banking activities in Hong Kong and Singapore, it should be pointed out that there is a fundamental difference in terms of foreign currency deposits between the two cities, even though both centers impose no foreign exchange control. Accounts in Asian Currency Units are prohibited from engaging in any business in Singapore dollars, the same arrangement as the International Banking Facilities in

TABLE 7
Assets and Liabilities of All Banks

(Figures in billions of Singapore dollar)

ASSETS	1982	%	1986	%	% Change
Cash and dues From Banks	$10.1	20.8	$28.3	36.8	+180.2
Balance With MAS	$ 1.4	2.9	$ 1.9	2.5	+ 35.7
Securities and Equities	$ 3.7	7.6	$ 5.5	7.2	+ 48.6
Loans and Advances	$31.3	64.6	$38.1	49.6	+ 21.7
Others	$ 2.0	4.1	$ 3.0	3.9	+ 50.0
TOTAL ASSETS	$48.5	100	$76.8	100	+ 58.4
LIABILITIES					
Deposits of Non-Bank Customers**	$23.4	48.2	$30.6	39.8	+ 30.8
Amount due to Banks	$14.4	29.7	$33.3	43.4	+131.3
Others	$10.7	22.1	$12.9	16.8	+ 20.6
TOTAL LIABILITIES	$48.5	100	$76.8	100	+ 58.4

* Including money at call to discount houses and bills financing.

** Excluding non-bank customers' holdings of S$ NCDS.
Note: US$ 1.00 = S$ 2.12

Source: *Monthly Statistical Bulletin*. April 1987. Monetary Authority of Singapore, p. 9

United States. This regulation is to prevent the "round-tripping" of Singapore dollars. On the other hand, there is no such a proscription in Hong Kong with respect to foreign currency deposits. So one can conclude that the Hong Kong banking system is less stringent than that of Singapore.

Anchorage As International Financial Center

In analyzing the feasibility of Anchorage being developed into an international financial center, I have used Hong Kong and Singapore as two examples to illustrate what Anchorage should do in order to become an international financial center. As indicated at the beginning of this paper, there are three different types of international banking center, namely, net capital export center, entrepot, and shell center. Hong Kong and Singapore perform the function of an entrepot in that they channel funds from the sources of supply to the places where funds are used. In my opinion, that is, most likely, the role Anchorage is going to assume when and if the city decides to establish itself as an international banking center. I have come to this conclusion simply by means of elimination. First, Anchorage will in no way replace New York City as this nation's capital export center as far into the future as I can see. Anchorage does not, and will not in the foreseeable future, have the banking infrastructure New York City possesses. In addition to seven giant commercial banks and many banks of medium and small size, New York City has the largest Federal Reserve Bank of the Federal Reserve System. It also has the world's largest security market through which capital of this country flows abroad. Its extensive systems of transportation and telecommunication are the envy of the world, and its long history of being the financial center of the United States, like London to Great Britain, will no doubt continue to sustain New York City as one of the world's centers of finance. Moreover, the insurance industry has a very strong presence there. On top of all these, New York City is the cultural center of the United States. So it is not probable, to put it mildly, for Anchorage to replace New York City as the capital export center of this country.

On the other hand, because of our federal tax laws and banking regulations, Anchorage can not become a shell center for international banking, like the Bahamas or Cayman Islands. It was just because of our tax laws and banking regulations that shell centers arose on those offshore islands. So what we have left, then, is the role of entrepot or intermediary Anchorage can assume.

The idea I wish to suggest for Anchorage is to set up International Banking Facilities (IBFs) here. In order to make International Banking facilities workable in Anchorage, the State of Alaska will have to enact legislation which will exempt operating profit derived by IBFs from both state and local income taxes. Even though Anchorage does not have the extensive banking facilities as New York City does, it already has possessed a good local banking network, and through modern telecommunication facilities, bankers in Anchorage can easily communicate with their peers in any part of the world. Furthermore, Anchorage has become a stop-over for trans-North Pacific air route and is easily accessible.

Anchorage, located at the tip of Cook Inlet and close to the Gulf of Alaska, has a relatively mild climate in comparison to most parts of the state. It has a cool and pleasant summer and a less severe winter than Fairbanks, the second largest city in Alaska, for example. The scenic view of the city, with its small population, enhances the quality of life here. The state government, supported by revenue derived from the production of oil and gas, as well as revenue from the multi-billion dollar Alaska Permanent Fund, has created a favorable climate for business development. Besides levying no personal income tax, the state government encourages the establishment of business in Alaska by helping employees obtain necessary mortgages for their homes. Through the Alaska Housing Finance Corporation, the state lends money to home buyers at the market rate of interest with terms up to 30 years. With the support of the state government, together with the rich human resources from the local banking community and the University of Alaska, the proposal to set up International Banking Facilities in Anchorage is feasible and desirable in view of the economic goal of the state to encourage and foster business formation and development. The major drawback is the lack of commercial and industrial bases to support a strong and global-in-scope banking structure.

CONCLUSION

In summary, to establish an international financial center, a city should have the following essential conditions:

(1) Social and political stability. It is clear to every banker that no normal business can be conducted in a country where social upheaval and political unrest are rampant. The best example is Beirut, once a beautiful city on the eastern Mediterranean Sea and a flourishing international banking center for the Middle East, which is now ruined by its sectarian strife.

(2) Banking regulations and tax laws. Favorable or less stringent banking regulations and taxation reduce the cost, both explicit and implicit, of doing business. This factor has been crucial to the establishments of offshore banking centers on the Bahamas and Cayman Islands. The introduction of Asian Currency Units in 1968 in Singapore and the subsequent expansion of the Asian dollar market testify to the positive impact this factor has on the origin and development of international financial centers.

(3) Geographic location. An international financial center, other than a shell center, should be easily accessible by regular means of transportation. Furthermore, it should be close to major population, industrial and commercial centers. for example, it is impossible to develop an international banking center deep in the Borneo jungle or in the Appalachian Mountains.

(4) Transportation facilities. In addition to a strategic location, such as Singapore, an international financial center should have modern and extensive transportation facilities. London and New York City are easily accessible by steamships, railroads and airlines, not to mention extensive networks of modern highways.

(5) Telecommunication facilities. In a world of 24-hour trading of foreign currencies and wire transfers of funds across national boundaries, it is imperative that a city which wants to become an international financial center must have state-of-the-art telecommunication equipment and facilities.

(6) Economic base. Commercial and industrial developments are needed to support banking activities. In other words, banks, be they commercial, merchant, or investment, are set up to serve commerce and industry. For international banking activities, local commercial banks have to be, relatively speaking, large enough to be able to employ highly talented and experienced bankers to take charge of those operations. A case in point was the establishment of International Banking Facilities by Dai-Ichi Kangyo Bank, the largest commercial bank in Japan, in New York and Los Angeles back in 1981. Recently, it opened two more IBFs, one in Chicago and the other in San Francisco. The reason for opening four IBFs instead of one, say in New York City only, is of course to serve, more conveniently and efficiently, the Bank's clients where they are located.

(7) Living conditions. In order to attract international bankers and high-caliber traders of foreign currencies, the location of an international financial center is a very important factor as far as living conditions are concerned. The city must be a nice place to live and work, and that means availability of good housing, schools, churches, cultural and recreational facilities. Furthermore, the climate should be mild and the scenery of the area be beautiful.

Measuring against the seven criteria discussed above, Anchorage is in a fairly good position to become an international financial center. The only major barrier to the development is the lack of a strong and well-diversified economy to support the kind of banking structure an international financial center requires, such as those in Hong Kong and Singapore.

REFERENCES

Capel, James. 1987. *The banking industry of Hong Kong.* Hong Kong: (Far East) Limited.

Dale, Richard. 1984. *The regulation of international banking.* New Jersey: Prentice-Hall, Inc.

8. CHINA'S FINANCIAL REFORM AND ITS IMPACT ON INTERNATIONAL FINANCIAL CENTERS

Hsiu-Kwang Wu
The University of Alabama

INTRODUCTION

It is accurate to say that before 1976 there were no financial institutions or markets in the People's Republic of China (PRC), as we understand them in the West. There was only one gigantic bank, the People's Bank of China (PBC), and numerous small rural credit cooperatives. The PBC served as both a bank for the government and a "commercial bank" for the country. The PBC was established on December 1, 1948, eleven months before the Communist Party came to power. It is, in fact, a ministry-level organization (see Byrd 1983, p. 13). By 1953, all private banks were nationalized, and the PBC became the only bank which had offices throughout the country. Because of government policy, the bank had little to do with the financial markets of the non-communist world. Since 1976, under the program of financial reform which was stimulated by the "four-modernization" policy, a variety of financial institutions and instruments have been gradually developed. However, the PRC's financial system, to date, still can be characterized as primitive according to western standards.

The purpose of this paper is to discuss the current financial system in the PRC, as the result of recent financial reform, and its effects on international financial centers.

At the outset, it is important to note that, in following the financial developments in PRC, accurate financial statistics are hard to obtain. For example, in the *Almanac of China's Economy 1981 With Economic Statistics for 1949-1980*, out of a total 1,144 pages in the volume, the section on economic data consists of only 38 pages, of which 8 pages are devoted to a Communique of the State Statistical Bureau of the PRC on Fulfillment of China's 1980 National Economic Plan. Only one page is devoted to monetary statistics which consists of three tables on receipts and payments of State Credit Funds, deposits and loans by rural credit cooperatives, and foreign exchange and Gold Reserves. The other economic data included are mostly production data. The chapter in the volume on China's financial system does not have a single table.[1] Since the volume is considered to be a semi-official publication, inference can be made that the Chinese government is reluctant to make its statistics available to the general public. From my personal experience, in a special three-hour briefing by the State Economic Commission in Beijing in December 1983, no absolute figures were provided; however, figures in percentages were mentioned.[2]

In addition, sometimes these published statistics are misleading if no attention is paid to the institutional and political aspects of the financial system. For example, according to official figures, in 1987, 6,000 companies have issued common shares, which amounted to $1.6 billion. Although the amount is only about one percent of the bank's annual loans, it is generally believed that the figure is too high. For one thing, Chinese shares, unlike shares in the West, have many unusual features. Some of the shares are really a debt instrument and have fixed maturities and fixed interest rates. They are not really comparable to our shares. Besides, we know that there are only a few stock exchanges in existence. They are at Shanghai, Beijing, Wuhan, Tianjin and Shenyang. In Beijing, only one stock is listed. Trading hours are Tuesday and Friday morning. Most of the time the stock has no trade for three or four weeks at a time. Shanghai is the largest and lists only four stocks and two bonds (see Yining 1986, p. 17).

Therefore, in this paper, emphasis will be given to institutional and operational aspects of China's financial system. In following academic tradition, however, selected economic and financial statistics are provided in the Appendixes A, B and C. These data, as well as the statistics quoted in this paper, should be interpreted with care.

FINANCIAL INSTITUTIONS

China's current financial system consists of two major administrative jurisdictions: the PBC and the Ministry of Finance (MOF). Both organizations are directly under the supervision of the State Council. A diagram on China's financial system is produced in Figure 1. As in any other country, MOF performs fiscal functions such as taxation, budgeting, managing revenue and expenditures, and long-term financial planning. All its funds are deposited in a treasury account in PBC. Although the banking system now is independent, the influence of MOF cannot be underestimated. Before 1976, PBC was directly under the control of MOF. Currently, MOF only has authority over People's Construction Bank of China which provides funds and other banking services to state construction projects. This function is important in a planned economy. The MOF, however, does have responsibility, through its Foreign Financial Affairs department, in managing non-trade foreign exchange revenue and expenditure and loans from international institutions and foreign governments.[3]

The PBC became a central bank only in January 1984. It divested itself of its commercial banking function totally. It has responsibility, like any other central bank, in managing money supply and monetary system, and it is the most important organization in China's financial system.[4]

From an international financial market point of view, three organizations are particularly important. They are Bank of China (BOC), China International Trust and Investment Corporation (CITIC), and State Administration Exchange Control (SAEC). The BOC had been in existence before 1949 and is a specialized bank in foreign exchange under the supervision of the State Council. For practical purposes, however, it is controlled by the PBC. It has 310 overseas subsidiaries and has a correspondent relationship with 1,235 foreign banks in 152 countries (see

FIGURE 1
Diagram of the Financial Institutions of China

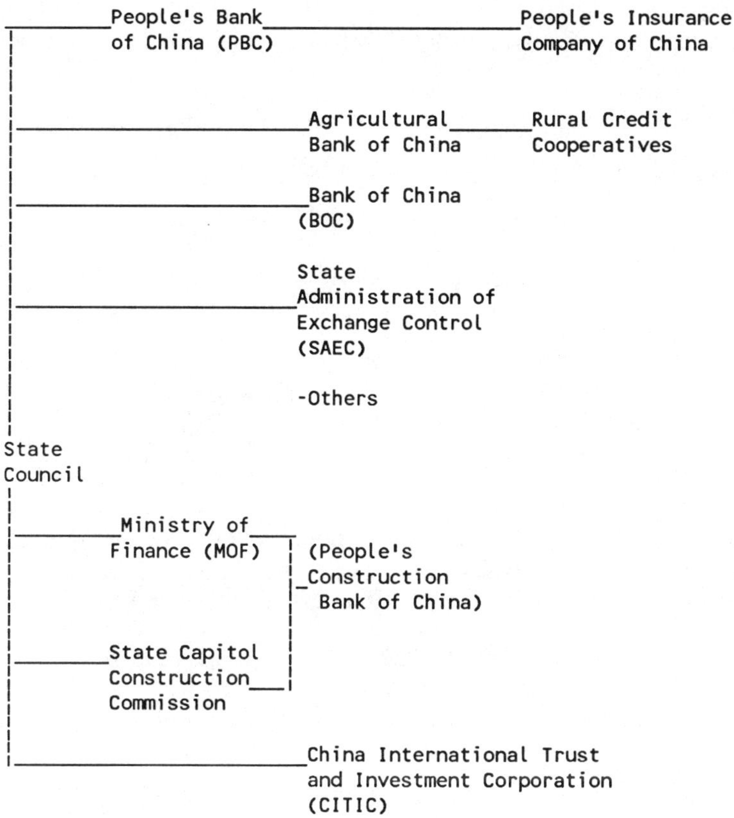

Sources: *China Official Annual Report, 1982/83*, Kingsway International Publications Ltd., Hong Kong, 1982, pp. 440-464, and China International Economic Consultants, Inc., *The China Investment Guide*, Longman, Hong Kong, 1984, pp. 233-301.

Ming 1987, p. 2). The main function of the bank is to engage in all types of business related to Renminbi's (RMB) i.e., foreign exchange transactions. According to foreign exchange regulations, all foreign exchange holdings of any organization and individual in China must be deposited with BOC. All foreign exchange transactions must be made through the BOC unless otherwise provided by state regulations. The sources of funds for the bank are:

(1) Foreign currency deposits by domestic organization and individuals

(2) Savings deposits by Chinese and foreign residents

(3) Deposits by overseas branches and foreign banks

(4) Loans from foreign banks

(5) Loans from governments and international institutions, and

(6) Bond issues abroad.

The bank has floated bonds for about U.S. $1 billion in Tokyo, Frankfurt, and Hong King since 1976 (see Debao 1987). In addition to these activities, BOC also supervises banks owned by China in Hong Kong. According to one estimate, 12 of 75 of Hong Kong banks are owned by China, and they account for about 17 percent of Hong Kong's deposits and 10 percent of total loans (see Byrd 1982, p. 20). Only recently, lBOC developed travelers checks and a credit card (Great Wall Debit Card). In 1986, credit card loans outstanding were about RMB 350 million yuan and the amount of travelers checks issued was about U.S. $130 million (see Debao 1987, p. 2).

The China International Trust and Investment Corporation (CITIC) was established by the State Council in October 1979. It is supposed to be a state-owned business enterprise and is accountable only to the State Council. According to the statute, CITIC's functions are:

> to introduce, absorb and apply foreign investment, advanced technology, and to import advanced equipment and to bring in advanced technology for purposes of China's national construction and promotion of socialist modernization of our country pursuant to the provisions of the Law of the People's Republic of China on Joint Ventures Using Chinese and Foreign Investment and other relevant laws and regulations.[5]

In short, it serves as an intermediary between Chinese and foreigners for investment purposes. The scope of its operation, however, is very broad. It includes:

(1) Making investments at home and abroad

(2) Organizing joint ventures

(3) Operating foreign exchange bank business

(4) Issuing bonds and other securities

(5) Operating domestic and international leasing business

(6) Providing consulting services, and

(7) Operating real estate and tourist business (see Jinzhong 1987, p. 1).

Since 1979, in seven years, CITIC has grown tremendously. Between 1984-86, its assets grew 400 percent, its loans 600 percent, its investments 300 percent, and its profits 150 percent (see de Rosario 1987, p. 118). CITIC's Income and Expenditure data from 1982 to 1986 are available and produced in Table 1. CITIC has been very active in the international financial markets. It has broken BOC's 30 year monopoly in dealing with foreign exchanges and in raising capital internationally. Since its existence, CITIC has raised capital by issuing three Japanese yen bonds, one U.S. dollar bond, one D.M. bond and two Hong Kong dollar bonds. The total amount raised by these overseas bonds is equivalent to about U.S. \$900 million. In fact, CITIC in 1982 was the first of China's institutions in the post-revolutionary era to float bonds overseas--a private placement of yen 10 billion (see de Rosario 1987, p. 119). CITIC during this period also has participated in currency and interest swaps in the amount of about U.S. \$150 million (see Jinzhong 1987, p. 1).

As of April 1987, CITIC's outstanding foreign currency deposit amounted to U.S. \$570 million, and its local currency deposits amounted to about RMB 100 million yuan. In 1986, CITIC also joined the international syndicated loan to Pakistan as a lead manager and joined the underwriting group of the syndicated loan to Turkey (see Jinzhong 1987, p. 1). In short, CITIC has been conducting commercial land investment banking business abroad.

CITIC also made substantial investments abroad. It invested about HK\$ 100 million in the second harbour tunnel project and real estate in Hong Kong. For U.S. \$45 million, it also acquired 95 percent of the common stock of Ka Wah Bank, which has 26 branches in Hong Kong and two branches in the U.S. (see Jinzhong 1987 and de Rosario 1987). In 1985, it also spent U.S. \$256.41 million to purchase the Hong Kong-based Cathay Pacific Airways. In addition to these investments in Hong Kong, CITIC also invested about RMB 2.64 billion yuan (about U.S. \$709 million) in more than one hundred projects worldwide, including an aluminum smelter in Australia, a pulp mill in Canada and timber in the U.S. (see Jinzhong 1987 and de Rosario 1987).

TABLE 1

CITIC's Income and Expenditures
1982 - 1986

(Rmb 000)	1982	1983	1984	1985	1986
Income	26,540	37,458	113,661	305,424	505,328
Interest	22,405	29,854	70,873	243,037	396,959
Commissions	696	850	3,541	7,287	20,084
Investment Income	156	2,389	26,578	51,549	49,127*
Gains on Exchange	3,262	4,332	12,650	-	-
Other**	21	32	19	3,551	39,159
Expenditure	18,430	26,061	66,064	198,128	384,812
Interest	15,728	23,196	60,376	180,225	361,346
Commissions	70	380	60	936	2,270
Operating Expense	1,208	630	1,986	6,942	1,771
Administration	1,332	1,674	3,272	6,435	10,478
Other	10	-	1	46	16
Depreciation	52	160	273	644	954
Amortisation	31	22	96	2,900	6,296
Tax	-	-	-	-	1,680
Profit	8,110	11,396	47,597	107,296	120,516

* Includes rental income (Rmb 24,574) and realized lease income (Rmb 3,478).
** Includes consulting fees, gains on foreign exchange and profit from securities trading.

Source: Louise de Rosario, "CITIC's Open Window and Methods Win Friends," *Far Eastern Economic Review*, May 7, 1987, p. 188.

Although CITIC is planning to establish a CITIC industrial bank, in comparison to BOC, CITIC is relatively small in size. At the end of 1986, BOC had assets of RMB 345 billion yuan, and CITIC has RMB 8 billion yuan. In China, CITIC has no branches; BOC has 369. In the Japanese bond market, BOC is given a triple "A" rating; CITIC is only given a double "A" rating (see de Rosario 1987, p. 123).

FINANCIAL MARKETS

Financial markets in China, as to date, are rudimentary. Some common financial instruments are only introduced recently. We shall discuss these new developments since 1979. Surprisingly, China, with exchange control and non-convertible currency, has some sort of a foreign exchange market (see Guantao 1987). This is a good example of practicing the PRC's principle of co-existence between the controlled markets and free markets. There were no foreign exchange regulations in China before 1979. The BOC, as we discussed, was the only financial institution which was allowed to deal with foreign exchanges. All imports and exports were conducted by the state foreign trade corporations, and there was no foreign capital. Due to financial reform, inflow of foreign capital, joint ventures, and the establishment of special economic zones, the State Council in 1979 established State Administration of Exchange Control (SAEC), and in December 1980 promulgated regulations and rules for exchange control. The purpose of the regulation, as stated by an official recently, is that:

> (In order) to attain its goal of modernization by the end of this century, an immense amount of foreign funds are needed. So, the problem of foreign exchange shortage would remain for long in the days to come. The limited foreign exchange must be kept under the state control in order to ensure a rational allocation and utilization (Zheti 1987, p. 1).

Under strict regulation, with a few exceptions, all foreign exchange must be deposited at BOC. Since November 1986, however, three types of corporations are allowed to trade foreign exchange in Shanghai for the purpose of remitting home their profits. They are joint ventures with foreigners, corporations with overseas Chinese capital and foreign capital.[6]

As for the domestic financial markets, instruments, to which we are accustomed, have developed only recently. The State Council on January 7, 1986, published regulations on bank administration which allows specialized banks to extend loans to each other and to negotiate interest rates for these loans. Commercial papers and bonds are now also allowed. In October 1986, CDs in the amount of RMB 30 million yuan were issued by the Bank of Communication of China in Shanghai for the first time. The maturities of corporate bonds are generally one year; very few have two years. They are all zero coupon bonds. Since 1981, MOF has issued treasury bills for RMB 4 to 6 billion yuan annually with a maturity from 5 to 10 years (Guantao 1987, p. 32).

As discussed above, stock markets have been established in recent years. They are, however, inactive. After the beginning of the campaign against "bourgeois liberalization" in January 1987, the State Council in recent months has ordered that state enterprise should stop issuing common shares. Some issues seem to have been postponed. The Everbright and Phoenix Bicycle issues have been held up by PBC. On the other hand, for the first time on April 1, 1987, stocks of Aishi Electronics Co. were allowed to be listed. In summary, China's financial markets are at infant stage. The future prospects depend a great deal on future political developments.

FINANCIAL REFORM AND CHINA'S PARTICIPATION IN INTERNATIONAL FINANCIAL MARKETS

One of the most important reasons for financial reform in China since 1979 is to obtain or "absorb" foreign capital for economic construction. Basically, there are five major sources of foreign exchange:

(1) Foreign direct investments, including overseas Chinese investments

(2) Net exports of goods and services

(3) Borrowing from international organizations and foreign governments

(4) Borrowing from international financial markets, and

(5) Arms sales abroad.

China has exploited all these sources. Although the data as usual are sketchy, according to a recent official estimate, the volume of direct foreign investment from 1979 to 1986 is about U.S. $20 billion. The investments were made by foreigners from more than 30 countries (see Ruogu 1987). China's net export decreased recently; in fact, its current account showed a deficit of U.S. $11.4 billion in 1985 (see Appendices A and C). Its total foreign exchange reserve was about $10.5 billion in 1986, and a substantial decrease from 1984 figure of U.S. $16.7 billion (see Appendix A). Recently, China has also been very active in arms sales abroad. Major sales were made to Iran, Thailand and Brazil. It is estimated that these sales probably contributed more than U.S. $2 billion to China's foreign exchange reserve (see Bonovia 1987, p. 33).

In addition to these sources which are so far limited, China has also borrowed in the international financial markets through BOC, CITIC and other organizations. Due to a budget deficit, the Chinese government reported recently that it plans to borrow a substantial amount under its own name from the Japanese financial markets.[7] It is estimated that China's total foreign debt has doubled from U.S. $9.6 billion in 1983 to about U.S. $20 billion in 1985.

Despite all these activities, China's foreign debt is relatively small and has little importance in international financial markets. Historically, China has had an aversion to foreign indebtedness. After the revolution, in the 1950s, China incurred a massive debt to the USSR. Since then, China has been completely without foreign debt until recent years. With the recent downfall of General Secretary Hu Yaobang and the slow down of financial reform, a large increase of foreign debt cannot be expected in the near future.

FUTURE PROSPECTS

The financial reform in China since 1979 can be summarized into two major areas:

(1) Developing new financial instruments and institutions in the domestic markets, and

(2) increasing participation internationally.

Domestic markets are generally closed to foreigners; consequently, they do not have a direct impact on international financial markets. Externally, China has been active since 1979; however, these activities are still very limited in scope and without much import. As for the future, China's financial reform depends a great deal on political developments. Specifically, from an international economic point of view, the future prospect of China as a financial power depends on the answers to the following three questions. First, can China practice effectively the principle of co-existence of controlled markets and free markets? Second, can China have one country with two systems? In other words, how would Hong Kong, with a capitalistic system, fit into China's political and economic framework in the 1990s? Third, can China have economic reform without political reform? These are difficult questions to answer, and only time will tell.

NOTES

1. The statistics are compiled by the Economic Research Center, The State Council of the P.R.C. and the Statistical Bureau (see Muqiao 1982).

2. Other important sources are the World Bank and International Monetary Fund. China recently also began to publish Statistical Year Books. Nevertheless, the useful financial data are still difficult to obtain. See State Statistical Bureau. 1987. *China: A Statistical Survey 1986*. Hong Kong: Longman.

3. See China International Economic Consultant, Inc. 1984. *The China Investment Guide, 1984/1985.* Hong Kong: Longman.

4. It is interesting to note that during the process of becoming a central bank only, the size of P.B.C. has decreased enormously. The total staff was reduced from 460,458 in 1984 to 130,744 in 1985, and its branches and other organizations also decreased from 23,166 in 1984 to 3,899 in 1985 (see Salem 1986).

5. See China International Economic Consultant Inc. 1984. *The China Investment Guide, 1984/1985.* Hong Kong: Longman.

6. See Guantao (1987).

7. See *United Journal*, April 18, 1987.

REFERENCES

Bonavia, David. 1987. Peking steps up cut-rate arms sales. *Far Eastern Economic Review*, May:33.

Byrd, William. 1983. *China's financial system: The changing role of banks*. Boulder: Westview Publishing Co.

China International Economic Consultant, Inc. 1984. *The China investment guide, 1984/1985.* Hong Kong: Longman.

China Official Annual Report. 1982/83. Hong Kong: Kingsway International Publications Ltd.:440-464.

Debao, Zhang. 1987. Efforts of diversification in the bank of China. *The People's Bank of China Financial Symposium*. New York: The People's Bank of China.

de Rosario, Louise. 1987. Open-window methods win friends. *Far Eastern Economic Review*. May:118.

Guantao, Yu. 1987. China's financial markets. *The People's Bank of China Financial Symposium*. New York: People's Bank of China.

Jinzhong, Dou. 1987. New developments in CITIC's financial operations. *People's Bank of China Financial Symposium*. New York: People's Bank of China.

Ming, Shang. 1987. Financial reform in China: Process, orientation and sequence. *The People's Bank of China Financial Symposium*. New York: The People's Bank of China.

Muqiao, Xue. 1982. *Almanac of China's economy for 1981 with economic statistics for 1949-1980*. Hong Kong: Modern Cultural Company.

Ruogo, Li. 1987. The new development of foreign investment in China. *The People's Bank of China Financial Symposium*. New York: People's Bank of China.

State Statistical Bureau. 1987. *China: A statistical survey for 1986*. Hong Kong: Longman.

The New York Times. 1987. A debate in China over stock trading. April 27.

United Journal. 1987. April 18.

Yining, Li. 1986. Possibilities for China's ownership reform. *Beijing Review*. December:17.

Zheti, Li. 1987. The New development of foreign investment in China. *The People's Bank of China Financial Symposium*. New York: People's Bank of China.

APPENDIX #A

Selected Economic and Financial Statistics of the People's Republic of China 1976-1986

Selected Economic Statistics

	1976	1977	1978	1979	1980	1981	1982	1983	1984	1985	1986
Consumer Prices (Period Averages) (Index Numbers: 1980=100)	-	73.51	76.45	93.32	100.00	105.81	108.20	113.00	117.50	127.60	-
Government Finance (Billions of Yuan; Year ending 12/31)											
Deficit (-) or Surplus	-	3.10	1.02	-17.06	-12.75	-2.54	-2.93	-4.35	-5.00	2.82	-
Revenue	-	87.45	112.11	110.33	108.52	106.43	112.40	124.90	146.50	185.41	-
Expenditure	-	84.35	111.09	127.39	121.57	108.97	115.33	129.25	151.50	182.59	-
National Accounts (Billions of Yuan)											
National Income	242.7	264.4	301.0	335.0	368.8	394.0	426.7	473.0	563.0	682.2	779.0
Natl. Income 1980 Prices	266.4	286.9	322.5	344.8	368.8	-	-	-	-	-	-
NI Deflator (1980=100)	91.1	92.2	93.3	97.2	100.0	-	-	-	-	-	-
Population (End of Year in Millions)	937.2	949.7	962.6	975.4	987.1	1000.7	1015.4	1025.0	1034.8	1045.3	1060.1
Balance of Payments (Millions of Dollars)											
Current Account	-	-	-	-	-	-	5823	4487	2509	-11,417	-
Direct Investment	-	-	-	-	-	-	386	543	1124	1,031	-

Source: International Monetary Fund

APPENDIX #B

Selected Economic and Financial Statistics of the People's Republic of China 1976-1986

Selected Financial Statistics

	1976	1977	1978	1979	1980	1981	1982	1983	1984	1985	1986
Exchange Rate (Official End of period $/yuan)	1.8803	1.7300	1.5771	1.4962	1.5303	1.7455	1.9227	1.9809	2.7957	3.2015	3.7221
Internat'l Liquidity (End of Period-Millions of U.S. Dollars)											
Total Reserves Minus Gold	-	2,345	1,557	2,154	2,545	5.058	11,349	14,987	17,366	12,728	11,453
SDRs	-	-	-	-	72	236	194	320	414	440	569
Reserve Position in the Fund	-	-	-	-	150	-	-	168	261	303	370
Foreign Exchange	-	2,345	1,557	2,154	2,262	4,783	11,135	14,476	16,705	11,913	10,514
Gold (Million Fine Troy Ounce)	-	12.8	12.8	12.8	12.8	12.7	12.7	12.7	12.7	12.7	12.7
(National Valuation)	-	544	584	590	571	516	491	464	435	486	541
U.S. Liabilities to China	48	53	67	50	53	190	204	250	1,156	1,867	1,873
U.S. Claims on China	5	12	5	45	242	129	236	317	727	705	-
Monetary Survey (Billions of Yuan; End of Period)											
Foreign Assets (Net)	-	2.41	.54	-1.64	-2.78	2.67	16.14	23.95	27.03	20.18	7.54
Money	-	58.01	58.04	73.66	91.93	107.04	115.70	137.05	212.59	248.32	386.16
of Which: Curr. in Circulation	-	19.54	21.20	26.77	34.62	39.63	43.91	52.98	79.21	98.78	121.84

Source: International Monetary Fund

APPENDIX #C
Selected Economic and Financial Statistics of the People's Republic of China 1976-1986

Selected Trade Statistics

	1976	1977	1978	1979	1980	1981	1982	1983	1984	1985	1986
International Transactions											
(Billions of Yuan)											
Exports	13.48	13.97	16.76	21.17	27.12	36.76	41.43	43.83	57.96	80.92	-
Imports, cif	12.93	13.28	18.74	24.29	29.88	36.77	35.77	42.18	61.44	125.97	-
Imports, fob	11.86	12.18	17.19	22.28	27.41	33.73	32.82	38.70	56.37	115.97	-
Direction of Trade(Exports)											
(Millions of U.S.Dollars)											
Industrial Countries	-	-	-	5,639	8,110	9,439	9,371	9,322	10,407	11,406	-
Developing Countries	-	-	-	5,664	8,838	11,252	11,596	11,729	13,159	13,877	-
Africa	-	-	-	90	482	677	760	525	543	421	-
Asia	-	-	-	4,360	6,530	7,430	7,222	7,655	9,347	10,704	-
Hong Kong	-	-	-	3,328	4,353	5,263	5,181	5,797	6,586	7,148	-
Singapore	-	-	-	297	421	658	648	567	1,209	2,063	-
Europe	-	-	-	600	629	491	361	375	385	488	-
Middle East	-	-	-	482	803	2,120	2,725	2,742	2,435	1,764	-
Western Hemisphere	-	-	-	132	395	535	528	432	449	501	-
USSR/Eastern Europe	-	-	-	1,211	1,191	782	894	1,032	1,251	2,031	-
Country or Area Not Specified	-	-	-	1,143	-	3	4	12	7	16	-
Direction of Trade(Imports)											
(Millions of U.S.Dollars)											
Industrial Countries	-	-	-	11,082	14,356	16,088	13,029	14,506	17,912	29,820	-
Developing Countries	-	-	-	2,624	3,840	4,197	4,265	5,150	6,274	10,501	-
Africa	-	-	-	159	285	227	261	311	310	285	-
Asia	-	-	-	731	1,700	2,364	2,540	2,710	4,140	7,096	-
Hong Kong	-	-	-	214	570	1,236	1,314	1,710	2,830	4,762	-
Singapore	-	-	-	105	190	113	103	114	141	241	-
Europe	-	-	-	735	796	668	595	546	657	1,101	-
Middle East	-	-	-	184	343	222	272	294	280	194	-
Western Hemisphere	-	-	-	815	716	715	597	1,290	888	1,825	-
USSR/Eastern Europe	-	-	-	1,338	1,310	811	1,251	1,360	1,535	2,144	-
Country or Area Not Specified	-	-	-	632	-	535	374	297	233	69	-

Source: International Monetary Fund

PART II

COST/BENEFIT ANALYSIS OF INTERNATIONAL FINANCIAL CENTERS

9. THE COSTS AND BENEFITS OF ESTABLISHING AN INTERNATIONAL BANKING CENTER

Anindya K. Bhattacharya
U.S. General Accounting Office, New York

INTRODUCTION

The purpose of this paper is to evaluate the costs and benefits of offshore banking operations. Specifically the objective of the paper is to assess the impact of offshore banking on the economic development of primary international banking centers such as New York, Montreal, and Vancouver, as well as secondary centers such as Singapore, Hong Kong, and Panama.

AN OVERVIEW OF OFFSHORE BANKING

Offshore banking generally refers to segregated transactions that are limited to non-resident accounts. It differs from onshore banking in that separate accounting records are kept for offshore transactions. Offshore banking is conducted out of both primary international financial centers such as London, New York, and Tokyo, and secondary centers such as those in the Caribbean and the Asia-Pacific region. The primary financial centers derive their role largely from a strong industrial base on which the financial requirements of their customers is based. By contrast, the secondary centers derive their role primarily from proximity to economies which are either the source of sizeable financial resources or have substantial requirements for financial services. A sub-category is tax-haven areas, which are used primarily as centers for booking foreign loans and deposits, and where little actual financial business (e.g. syndication, management) is conducted. Virtually all these offshore centers owe their existence to the absence, or a low level, of direct taxation on net profits of banks, the absence of exchange controls on offshore banking transactions, and minimal government regulations.

The gross size of the Eurocurrency market, as measured by offshore transactions including interbank positions, reached $3.2 trillion at the end of 1986. London's share in this market is around 25 percent, followed by New York's 15 percent, Hong Kong and Singapore 5 percent each, the Bahamas and Cayman Islands 2 percent, Bahrain 2 percent, and Panama 1 percent.

The views expressed in this paper are the author's and do not reflect those of the U.S. General Accounting Office.

In December 1986 Tokyo became an offshore banking center, followed by Montreal and Vancouver in January 1987. At the end of 1986, the size of the Japanese offshore market reached $93 billion.

THE ECONOMIC DEVELOPMENT IMPACT OF OFFSHORE BANKING IN PRIMARY CENTERS

In assessing the economic development impact of offshore banking on host countries, it is useful to differentiate between the primary and secondary centers of international finance. In the primary centers, the basic reasons for establishing offshore banking centers are:

(1) Competition from other centers and desire to establish the preeminence of one center over another

(2) Return of jobs from other offshore centers, and

(3) Generation of additional government revenue.

When the International Banking Facilities (IBFs) were established in New York in December 1981, the idea was to bring back business from other offshore centers, particularly London and the Caribbean. In the late 1970's, London had more U.S. banks than New York City, more foreign banks than any other center, and had the largest number of overseas bank branches. U.S. banks moved to London in those days to get around domestic regulatory restrictions on competition (e.g. the Glass-Steagall Act), bypass regulation Q on interest rate limits and regulation D on non-earning reserves, and lower the tax costs (62.3% in New York as against 52% in London). However, because of the differential between the overall tax rate in London (52%) and the U.S. federal income tax rate (48%), the U.S. banks could only claim 48% as foreign tax credit. Therefore, some banks moved to the Caribbean and established "shell" branches. However, New York State tax auditors questioned whether a portion of bank income ostensibly produced in the shell branches was in fact generated in New York, in which case they would have faced state and city taxes (over and above their 48% federal tax). Thus, the New York Clearing House Association of banks came up with the proposal to establish IBFs in the U.S. The IBF proposal allowed U.S. banks to make loans to and accept deposits from non-residents, free from state and local taxes as well as from state and federal reserve requirements and interest rate limits.

When the IBFs were founded, the New York Clearing House Association estimated that they would create about 5,000 direct and indirect jobs and generate $90 million in annual state tax revenue. The issue of a possible loss in local revenue did not arise, because the offshore business was being done outside New York anyway. To the extent that foreign branch activities were shifted to the U.S., taxes formerly paid abroad and credited against federal income tax would flow to the U.S. Treasury (an estimated $500 million).

Among the costs of IBFs were the possibility of leakage of resident U.S. deposits into IBFs through foreign subsidiaries of U.S. corporations. However, it was felt that the potential impact of such leakage to IBFs was small and could be taken care of by appropriate regulatory restrictions (e.g. setting minimum maturities on IBFs, prohibiting foreign subsidiaries from holding deposits in the U.S., subjecting IBFs to regulatory reporting and examination requirements).

More recently, in January 1987, Canada approved the establishment of International Banking Centers (IBCs) in Montreal and Vancouver. Again, the purpose was to bring new, incremental banking business back to Canada, not to leave it in other offshore centers. Proponents argued that IBCs would maximize "synergistic" forces in selected cities, create new jobs, and generate additional tax revenue. They argued that more than three quarters of international banking activity carried out by Canadian banks is conducted outside the country because of the high interest-withholding tax (15%) and the treatment of foreign tax credits in Canada (unlike the U.S., Canada does not have reciprocal tax treaties with other countries).

Opponents of the proposal argued that it is questionable whether much new employment or economic activity would be generated by the IBCs. Since the IBC proposal exempts only certain income taxes on nonresident transactions, the transfer of assets from abroad will be small, since banks will not transfer those assets that bear a withholding tax. Only high quality loans booked in overseas offshore centers without the tax would be transferred to IBCs. The impact on employment creation in Canada will be minimal, since the banks will probably only transfer existing jobs and not create many new ones. Only senior level management jobs will be in Canada--as at present. But the actual loan solicitation and negotiation will probably continue to take place abroad.

THE ECONOMIC DEVELOPMENT IMPACT OF OFFSHORE BANKING IN SECONDARY CENTERS

In assessing the economic development impact of offshore banking in secondary centers, it is useful to differentiate between tax-haven areas such as the Bahamas and Cayman Islands and regional financing centers such as Singapore and Panama. Since the former are essentially booking centers noted, among other attractions, for their zero tax rates, low operating costs and tight bank secrecy laws, offshore banking operations have economic significance for these islands to the extent that they generate local employment and government revenue. In terms of direct effects, the banking sector employs 10 percent and 3 percent of the local labor force in the Bahamas and Cayman Islands respectively, and bank and trust company license fees generate 6 percent and 13 percent of local government revenue respectively. In addition, there are certain indirect benefits such as taxation of employee income in banking and related businesses, generation of local support services (for example, printing, office equipment, law and accounting), and local investment (for example, in construction and telecommunications). On the cost side, the laissez-faire policy of these islands has led to an unduly heavy reliance on indirect taxes and has jeopardized their ability to marshal sufficient resources for development.

The case of Panama and Singapore, however, is different. Since they are regional financing centers, there are real banks that are housed in real buildings and that employ real people. Although offshore banking is largely exempt from national taxation and exchange control, foreign banks in these centers are subject to much greater local government supervision than in tax-haven areas. Due to the deliberate policy of local governments to utilize offshore funds for internal development purposes, foreign banks play an important internal role in both Panama and Singapore.

In Panama, foreign banks provide a major source of external financing for the local public sector, both in capital projects expenditure and in automatic adjustment of balance-of-payments deficit. The presence of offshore banks in Panama helps reduce the traditionally high dependence of the country on domestic monetary policies in the USA, the U.S. dollar being the legal tender in Panama. In the local private sector, the foreign banks provide not only commercial credits but also longer-term finance for agriculture (especially cattle raising and sugar), industry (especially in the Colon Free Trade Zone), construction (banks in Panama are encouraged to own their buildings rather than simply rent them), and personal credits. Also, the presence of major international banks is conductive to fostering the prestige of the country as a regional financing center, as evidenced particularly by the decision to establish the Latin American Exportation Bank (BLADEX) in Panama. Indeed, offshore banking developed local banking in Panama, which was accepted by the Government of Panama.

Similarly, Singapore has gained handsomely from the presence of offshore banks. Foreign banks have improved the balance of payments of resource-poor Singapore by providing valuable financial services and by attracting net capital inflow into the country. The existence of the Asian Dollar Market in Singapore has certainly contributed, though not exclusively, to the comfortable surplus in the country's overall balance of payments. Also, the contribution of the banking sector to Singapore's GDP is substantial, ranking as the third key growth sector in the economy after manufacturing and construction. Gross earnings from international banking operations contribute about 1 percent of Singapore's GDP. While it is difficult to establish a direct relationship between offshore banking and foreign investment in Singapore, there is no question that the presence of a large number of international banks has helped induce substantial MNC investment in the island. Also, external skills in banking and finance have been transmitted to Singapore, making the country a leading financial center in Asia, that trains citizens of neighboring countries in such skills.

More importantly, the existence of offshore banking in Singapore makes available to local borrowers a pool of hard currency funds that have historically been used for industrialization or development purposes. Aside from trade credits financed through offshore loans, local entities have made substantial use of the longer-term Asian dollar bond market. Chief among the local users of Asian dollar bonds are Singapore Airlines, Keppel Shipyard, the United Overseas Bank, the Development Bank of Singapore, and the Government of the Republic of Singapore. Indeed, very few Asian dollar bonds have been issued to non-Singapore developing countries of the Asia-Pacific region.

Extensive onshore utilization of offshore funds sets Singapore apart from its Caribbean counterparts, excluding Panama. In the Caribbean basin, much of offshore lending is concentrated in the short-term trade financing area, especially commodity export financing. There is very little longer-term loan syndication done directly out of the area, and there are no offshore bond market activities, both of which are arranged in primary centers of Eurocurrency finance. Unlike Singapore, this phenomenon deprives the Caribbean area of loan management and agency functions, which are crucial to the financial development of secondary centers of international finance.

Even in the Asia-Pacific region, the relative underdevelopment of the capital market component of offshore banking is a constraint on the development impact of the Asian Dollar Market on the region. While Singapore is a clear beneficiary of longer-term offshore funds, the same cannot be said of the other developing countries in the region. In the Caribbean and in the Asia-Pacific region, the problems that stand in the way of the development of offshore capital markets are basically the same: namely, the high debt-to-equity ratio of regional borrowers, the absence of an active secondary market in the regions, the relative unfamiliarity of regional borrowers in international capital markets, and the unwillingness of regional private investors to channel long-term savings directly into the regional centers. The lesser developed countries in the region find it difficult to qualify for Asian dollar bonds. Both the Asian dollar bond market and the secondary market in US dollar-denominated Negotiable Certificates of Deposits are dominated by Singaporean, Japanese and non-Asian entities. The concentrated nature of Asian dollar bonds limits the potential contribution of the Asian Dollar Market to the economic development of the region, although the possibilities of secondary-recycling exist, as evidenced by the floating of Euro-Asian bonds by the Asian Development Bank.

Offshore banking on the whole has brought net economic benefits to the Asia-Pacific region (the region has historically absorbed three-quarters of offshore funds, while providing less than half of total offshore liabilities), but not without certain costs to the host countries. On occasions, offshore banking operations have exercised a destabilizing influence on domestic inflation and management of monetary policy by local authorities. Between 1972 and 1975, for example, both Hong Kong and Singapore were deluged with a massive influx of foreign currencies, which were later swapped for investment in local stock and real estate markets. The resultant excess liquidity and imported inflation threatened the islands' vital exports and led to the imposition of a "Special Deposit Ratio" on interbank swap arrangements in Singapore and the enactment of the Deposit-Taking Companies Ordinance and the Securities Ordinance in Hong Kong.

Probably the most significant cost associated with offshore banking operations in secondary centers of international finance in the developing world is that of "capital leakage" from the domestic to the offshore sector. Since, in the typical circumstances, the same bank conducts both onshore and offshore transactions, there is a real risk of capital leakage from one to the other, especially when local conditions are difficult. All offshore banking centers in the developing countries have faced potential problems of tax evasion and exchange control evasion. Thus, it is of vital importance to insulate the domestic sector from the possible disruptions caused by the offshore sector.

In Panama, for example, there have been several examples of controversies regarding the "source" of offshore income. The same problem plagued Singapore in the early years when capital transfers among countries in the "Scheduled Territories" (or the "Sterling Area") were unrestricted. Unlike Panama, which has no exchange control regulations, the Monetary Authority of Singapore (MAS) coped with the problem of potential leakage of domestic savings by both strict licensing rules and exchange control regulations. For purposes of exchange control, the MAS distinguished not simply between residents and non-residents, but, among Singapore residents, between non-residents in Scheduled Territories and other non-residents, in so far as Asian Currency Unit (ACU) funding and lending were concerned. Initially, the MAS imposed a total ban on resident deposits in ACUs, which was progressively relaxed over the years in order to stimulate exports by using resident deposits as collateral for ACU loans as well as to promote the growth of the Asian dollar market. Still, the MAS maintained for a number of years a quantitative ceiling on the amount that could be deposited by resident individuals, corporations, and institutional investors, such as provident funds and pension funds. Finally, of course, the MAS continues to maintain strict supervisory control over all ACU banks, receives monthly and quarterly reports from each ACU bank, and reserves the right to revoke the ACU license in the event of non-compliance with Singapore's regulations.

The original two-tier system of Singapore, based on separate licensing, exchange control (which was eliminated in June 1978), and tax treatment for the domestic and offshore sectors, has proved its value in insulating to the extent possible, the domestic economy from offshore disruptions, while maximizing the benefits from offshore banking operations. There is, however, a high supervisory cost involved in this process in that it takes great technical skill to monitor the separation of offshore from onshore transactions. There is also a paradox involved in that if the distinction between onshore and offshore transactions is pressed too hard, the offshore market may not grow; on the other hand, if it is not pressed, then there is the potential problem of leakage. A partial de-regulation of money is hard to control and manage, especially in view of the fact that banks and money managers are supposed to be self-disciplined.

THE FEASIBILITY OF ESTABLISHING OFFSHORE BANKING IN ANCHORAGE

The issue in setting up offshore banking facilities in Anchorage is not technical feasibility but economic cost-benefit analysis. Since offshore banking refers to a separate accounting unit of banks and other financial institutions authorized to transact in the offshore market, there is no technical reason why it cannot be opened up in Anchorage. As long as the banks and financial institutions are there (Alaska has 11 banks, two of which engage in export-import financing), offshore banking facilities can be established in Anchorage, provided that a package of "minimal regulations/maximum incentives" is offered to the banks dealing in the offshore market. The key question to examine is the net economic benefit of offshore banking after subtracting the costs such as the initial cost of investment on infrastructure facilities, and waiver of taxes, exchange control (this point does not apply to Alaska, since the U.S. has no exchange control), and selected monetary regulation. A related issue to analyze for Alaska is keen competition from neighboring offshore centers such as Seattle, San Francisco, and Los Angeles (all of which have IBFs), Vancouver (which recently established an IBC), Tokyo, Singapore and Hong Kong.

On the economic cost-benefit front, the preceding analysis of the primary financial centers such as New York showed that important benefits (new jobs, tax revenues) could be obtained from offshore banking operations, and that the costs (capital leakage) could be minimized by proper supervisory control. Similarly, the experience of Singapore and Panama showed that offshore banking tied to onshore lending helped fulfil several host-country objectives such as local access to foreign skills and markets, and generation of local employment and government revenue. The most significant cost of offshore banking to the secondary centers appears to be disruptions in the domestic economy caused by speculative inflows of foreign capital and outflows of domestic capital through the offshore banks. Although such capital leakages could be prevented by appropriate regulatory actions, the latter carry a high cost in differentiating between onshore and offshore transactions.

From the Alaskan viewpoint, the major significance of offshore banking out of Anchorage would lie in diversifying the economic base of the state away from oil and in generating new employment and government revenues in the face of the recession since 1986. An analysis of the current economic situation in Alaska underscores the importance of diversification as one of the key policy options. The impact of declining oil prices on Alaska has been profound. Alaska's economy is currently in a recession--its first since 1980. Oil revenues, which used to account for nearly 90 percent of state general revenues in the early 1980's, have been cut by one-third, resulting in reducing state general fund revenues by one-half. Nearly 50,000 oil-related jobs have been lost since 1986. The boom in state spending and large employment increases during 1980-83 have come to a halt. Anchorage has been particularly badly hurt. As the most important town for the oil industry and the state government, its employment decline has been sharper than the statewide average. The financial services industry (banking, insurance and real estate), which currently accounts for about 10-12 percent of total employment in Alaska, is expected to retrench during 1987-88, in line with the general decline in the services industry during the recession. Overall employment in the financial services industry in Alaska is expected to fall by between 4 and 6 percent during 1987-88, while in Anchorage it is expected to decline by 2 1/2 percent in 1987 and remain flat in 1988. Alaska's overall unemployment rate of 12 percent is well above the national average. In 1987, the Alaskan economy recovered a bit from 1986 due to higher oil prices, but the partial recovery is tenuous, since it is dependent on worldwide factors affecting the price of oil. The same comment holds for Alaska's other natural resources (such as timber), prices of which are exogenously determined.

In view of the foregoing, it is understandable that Alaska should be interested in exploring offshore banking as one of the options in diversifying its natural resource-based economy. However, several conditions must be met before offshore funds could be persuaded to move to Anchorage. While there is no empirical correlation between the degree of openness of a financial center and the size of offshore banking operations, historical experience of other centers tells us that, to be successful, an offshore banking center must possess at least the following characteristics: stable political environment, favorable tax treatment, free or little exchange control regulations, good telecommunications facilities, a trained labor force, and minimum government regulations on reserves, interest rate limitations, and bank insurance fees.

Specifically, the experience of established international financial centers showed that the following incentives must be provided to promote the growth of offshore banking in the host centers:

* the abolition of liquidity requirements for non-resident deposits

* the abolition of interest-withholding taxes on non-resident transactions

* the reduction of corporate income taxes on offshore profits of banks and financial institutions

* the exemption of stamp taxes and estate duties for non-resident transactions

* the relaxation of exchange control in such a way as to permit offshore profits to be remitted freely, and

* the development of the offshore bond market so as to foster the promotion of the capital market component of international banking.

On the regulation side, the experience of established centers shows that the maintenance of general banking regulations (e.g. submission of monthly and quarterly reports, on-site examinations, etc.) is essential in insulating the domestic economy from possible offshore market disruptions.

CONCLUSION

In view of the fact that the Pacific region has several offshore banking centers (Seattle, San Francisco, Los Angeles, Vancouver, Tokyo, Hong Kong, and Singapore), it would be difficult for additional centers such as Anchorage to attract multinational banks and offshore funds. Granted that Anchorage is essentially a service-oriented town, a number of conditions would still have to be met by Anchorage in order to attract large international banks. Anchorage would have to offer significant regulatory relief to offshore banks that is not currently available in New York or Tokyo. The IBF in New York imposes reserve requirements upon offshore fund inflows, but not on outflows. The Tokyo market has highly restrictive regulations governing both inflows and outflows. Unlike London, the New York and the Tokyo markets do not permit offshore banks to deal in securities or certificates of deposit. For international banks, regulatory relief can be just as important as tax consideration in their decision to move to a particular financial center.

Another factor to consider for Anchorage is the need for massive infrastructure spending on service systems and telecommunications to overcome its competitive position problem posed by geographical isolation, harsh climate, and high cost of living and doing business. The issue here is for Alaska to spend the subsidy money now as opposed to investing it for future income.

A final factor to consider is that a narrowly-focused offshore banking operation that is limited to accepting deposits from and making loans to non-residents (along the lines of IBFs and IBCs) is a shrinking part of international banking today. A recent development in the international financial markets is the rapid growth of securitized lending (bonds, note issuance facilities, etc.) and the relative decline in bank lending. Securitized lending now accounts for over 80 percent of gross new credit in international markets, compared with less than 50 percent in the early 1980's. The recent shift in international financial flows from bank credit to the securities market reflects a variety of developments: borrower preference for tradable, longer-term instruments, lower cost of borrowing in the securities markets due to decline in inflation and interest rates, concern with banks' financial stability in view of the external debt crisis and the slump in shipping, agriculture, and oil and other commodities, deregulation in major financial centers that makes access to the capital markets easier than before, and financial innovation and technological progress that allow tapping a number of products such as swaps, futures, options, and international commercial paper. In the long run, for any international financial center to succeed in attracting business, the capital markets must be developed. The issue of capital market development in Anchorage, however, is beyond the scope of this paper.

In conclusion, the establishment of offshore banking operations in Anchorage requires careful cost-benefit analysis as well as critical policy decisions on the part of Alaska. This paper has examined the key issues and problems associated with offshore banking and has outlined a set of measures relating to regulatory changes that will, hopefully, be of some value in weighing the pros and cons of offshore banking in Anchorage.

REFERENCES

Alaska Business Monthly. May 1987. Alaska Trends.

Alaska Department of Labor. 1987. *Alaska Economic Trends*, February, April.

Alaska Journal of Commerce. 1987. April 2(17).

Alaska Pacific Bank. 1986. *Alaska business trends: 1987 preliminary forecast*. Anchorage, Alaska.

Anchorage Chamber of Commerce. *Anchorage, 1987*.

Bank for International Settlements. 1987. *International banking and financial market development*. Basle: Switzerland.

Bhattacharya, Anindya K. 1977. *The Asian dollar market: International offshore financing*. New York: Praeger.

__________________. 1980. Offshore banking in the Caribbean by U.S. commercial banks: Implications for government-business interaction. *Journal of International Business Studies*, Winter 2(3):36-46.

______________. 1983. Offshore banking: Costs and benefits. In Philip D. Grub, et. al. (eds.), *East Asia Dimensions of International Business*. Englewood Cliffs: Prentice-Hall.

Board of Governors of the Federal Reserve System. 1978. International Banking Facilities: Staff Study.

Goldsmith, Scott. 1986. The impact of collapse of world oil market on the Alaska economy: Institute of Social and Economic Research (ISER). Working Paper 86.3, University of Alaska, Anchorage.

Institute of Social and Economic Research Summary. 1984. Alaska resources: What beyond Prudhoe Bay? University of Alaska, Anchorage.

Knapp, Gunnar and Steve Colt. 1985. The Alaska economy: Where we are and how we got here: Institute of Social and Economic Research (ISER). Working paper 85.8, University of Alaska, Anchorage.

New York Clearing House Association. 1978. *International Banking Facilities in the United States: An analysis of the economic policy issues*. New York, New York.

New York State, Office of the Governor. Economic Affairs Cabinet. 1978. A proposal to facilitate the creation of domestic International Banking Facilities in New York State.

Organization for Economic Cooperation and Development. 1987. *Financial market trends*. Paris: France.

Price Waterhouse. 1987. *Anchorage business attitude survey: fourth quarter, 1986*. Anchorage, Alaska.

Standing Committee on Finance and Economic Affairs, Canada House of Commons. 1987. *Sixth report*. Ottawa: Canada.

Statement by the Honorable Michael Wilson, Minister of Finance, on the establishment of International Banking Centers, Department of Finance, Canada. 1987. *Release*, Ottawa: Canada.

State of Alaska, Division of Banking and Securities, Comparative statement of assets, liabilities and capital accounts of Alaska state banks as of March 31, 1987. Juneau, Alaska.

10. THE ECONOMIC IMPACT OF OFFSHORE BANKING CENTERS ON THE HOST COUNTRIES

Soon Young Chang
Han Yang University
Seoul, Korea

INTRODUCTION

Offshore banking centers (OBCs) have developed during the last few decades to the point where they have come to play a major role in the innovative world of international finance. This phenomenal growth can be attributed to several factors: the restrictive policies and regulatory procedures in banking in some industrial developed countries, expansion of international trade, impact of the recycling of petrodollars and the borrowing requirements of developing countries. These phenomena, combined with a telecommunications revolution which enables banking institutions to access large quantities of current financial information and to disseminate it via a global network, have accelerated the growth of the OBCs. In turn, this OBC expansion has contributed to the development of world finance and the world economy in a number of ways.

First, the OBCs increase the liquidity of international capital allowing for the expansion of international funding and investment opportunities. The virtual absence of taxation, monetary regulation, and foreign exchange control of OBCs attract surplus capital seeking a high return, generating investment opportunities exempt from such restrictions. OBC's efficient interbank markets enable these investments to be placed worldwide.

Second, the OBCs reduce the cost of international capital and this makes more projects financially feasible; the OBC's economies of scale cause a decrease in overhead cost. The diversification of the unsystematic risk by OBCs lowers the cost of international capital, resulting in an increased number of feasible projects.

Third, OBCs promote innovation in international finance, thus boosting efficiency in international financial markets. Their economies of scale, reduced regulation and control, and increased competition between their member banks generate financial innovations which are disseminated very rapidly and utilized fully to enhance the efficiency of the international financial markets.

Fourth, OBCs eliminate time zone problems that otherwise would hinder the conduct of business between two parties situated in different time zones. The existence of an OBC in Bahrain and Singapore, for example, allows parent banks in London to conduct business in both the Middle and Far East during normal business hours, a situation which would be impossible if the transaction had to be conducted only through London.

As the OBCs have an impact on the global economy, they also have an impact on their host economies. Some countries have benefitted from hosting OBCs, while others have not. Some OBCs play an important role in their host economies while others do not. OBCs, therefore, exert different impacts on their host economies.

Experience with successful OBCs suggest several necessary preconditions for that success. These include political and economic stability, developed telecommunications facilities, availability of highly skilled manpower resources such as international lawyers and accountants, favorable tax treatment, and little or no government interference and regulation.

It is natural that a country possessing these attributes should have an interest in hosting an OBC. The decision for a country to host an OBC would depend primarily on its assessment of the OBC's economic impact. Despite the vital importance of such assessments, little attention has been paid to them in the recent past. The purpose of this study, therefore, is to probe in depth the economic impact of an OBC on the host economy.

DEFINITION AND CLASSIFICATION

Definition

The lack of a consistent definition for an OBC in the literature causes problems with the concept of an OBC and thus limits research on evaluating OBCs. The practice by the authors of using different terminology to refer to an OBC compounds the confusion. To minimize this confusion in terminology, a clear working definition of an OBC will be presented in this section. H. G. Johnson (1976) employs the term "regional centers," defining as "largely hosts to foreign financial institutions that find it convenient to locate offices there rather than magnets of financial power in their own right."[1]

T. F. Kelen (1977) uses the term "offshore financial center," defining "a place where international financial business can be carried out in a fiscally neutral way."[2]

Dufey and Giddy (1978) use the term "offshore centers" to indicate financial centers that host financial intermediation activities primarily for non-residents borrowers and depositors..[3]

I. McCarthy (1979) defines offshore banking centers as "cities, areas, or countries which have made a conscious effort to attract offshore banking business, i.e. nonresident foreign currency denominated business, by allowing relatively free entry and by adopting a flexible attitude where taxes, levies, and regulations are concerned.[4]

Mary Cooke (1981) defines an offshore financial center as "a place where the banking business is totally disproportionate to the needs of the domestic market."[5]

G. Dufey (1983) coins the term "aggressive center" to point out international financial centers that are created as a result of a government's deliberate effort to develop.[6]

R. A. Johns (1983) defines offshore financial centers as centers located in "economies which have a deliberate attempt to attract thereto international trade oriented activities by the minimization of taxes and the reduction or elimination of other restrictions on business operations, such that, within the jurisdiction of the center, aggregate economic activity is substantially geared to the special global invisible trade needs of external enterprises and investors."[7]

S. L. Choi (1984) makes an attempt to clarify the definition of an offshore center.[8] He claims that an "offshore financial center" is an international financial center that has the following three characteristics: First, these centers provide fiscal and regulatory incentives to attract foreign financial institutions to their centers. Second, the foreign financial institutions primarily serve nonresidents and only exceptionally deal with residents directly. Host governments frequently impose taxation and regulations regarding capital and foreign exchange transactions in order to insulate domestic markets from the offshore market. Therefore, the foreign financial institutions function rather as an "entrepot." Third, the host countries have significant economic size and their level of economic development has moved beyond the "traditional" stage. Choi maintains that only four centers qualify under his definition--Hong Kong, Singapore, Panama, and Bahrain.

For purposes of this study, an OBC is defined as a place where a deliberate attempt has been made to attract offshore banking business by minimization of taxes and/or other restrictions on operations.

This definition is directly correlated to that of McCarthy and qualifies twenty-five centers as OBCs: Anguilla, the Bahamas, Bahrain, Barbados, the Cayman Islands, Costa Rica, Guernsey, Hong Kong, Isle of Man, Japan (IBF), Jersey, Lebanon, Luxembourg, Macao, the Netherlands Antilles, New Hebrides, Nicaragua, Panama, the Philippines, St. Vincent, the Seychelles, Singapore, Taiwan, the United Arab Emirates, and the USA (IBF).

Classification

I. McCarthy (1979) identifies two types of offshore centers--"paper" and "functional centers." He defines "paper" centers as places where a transaction is recorded for tax purposes only with no physical deposits, withdrawals and loan services available. "Functional" centers, he defines as places where banks have a physical presence raising, investing, and lending funds of their own accord. He contends that whereas a "paper" center can be located virtually anywhere due to modern telecommunications, a functional center cannot because it is a product of its own environment.[9]

H. Poinacheck (1982) subdivides offshore centers into "shell" centers used as locations of record and "functional" centers where actual financial transactions are conducted.[10] Bhattacharya (1982) claims that offshore centers can be divided into two categories: primary centers having a strong industrial base on which the financial demands of customers are based, such as London and New York, and secondary centers in developing countries that derive their role primarily from geographical proximity to the economies either with substantial financial resources or with sizable financial demand, such as Panama and Singapore.[11] He views tax haven centers as a sub-category of the secondary centers, defining those as centers which are used mainly for booking foreign loans and deposits and where little actual financial business is conducted.

Y. S. Park (1982) provides important academic work on the classification of OBCs, classifying four types of offshore centers according to the sources and uses of funds for the market area being served:[12]

(1) Primary centers. A primary center is the most developed form of offshore center. Even though its sources and uses of funds are located worldwide, developed industrial countries that make up its major market area are predominant suppliers and users of funds. With its dominant financial intermediary role, a primary center serves as the hub of international banking and finance for its market area, offering a whole spectrum of offshore financial services, such as trading in Eurocurrencies and foreign exchange, international financial marketing, Eurocredit management and syndication, and Eurobond underwriting.

(2) Booking centers. A booking center, such as the Bahamas and the Cayman Islands, can be viewed as a financial entrepot where funds are channeled from the outside in the sense that its financial intermediation is mainly for and between nonresidents. A booking center has only to meet the minimal requirements for the financial infrastructure, as its primary attraction to banks lies in its highly favorable tax and other regulatory systems.

(3) Funding centers. A funding center, such as Singapore and Panama, channels offshore funds from outside its market area into local areas. For instance, the ASEAN countries as a group are the target net borrower in the Asian Dollar Market. In Panama, most local projects have been financed by offshore banks there.

(4) Collection centers. A collection center such as Bahrain contrasts sharply with a funding center in that it channels funds from its market area into areas outside its own area. Its market area, with excess savings resulting from the low absorptive capacity, accumulates the surplus funding in an efficient collection center. This efficiency generated by its economy of scale, positive external factors arising from specialization, joint facilities, and the services of support industries, enhances the economics of a collection center.

ECONOMIC IMPACT OF OBCS

This section contains a thorough discussion of the benefits and costs that are involved in hosting OBCs. Furthermore, these factors are divided into two major areas: direct benefits/costs and indirect benefits/costs.

BENEFITS

Benefits which host countries may derive from establishing OBCs can be classified into two categories: direct and indirect. Direct benefits can be further subdivided into taxes and levies as well as operating expenditures of offshore banks and employment.

Direct Benefits:

License Fees. The license fee is the most common form of levy. Most OBCs impose license fees on offshore banks. However, revenues from this source would have economic significance for only those booking centers with relatively small economies, for the amounts collected would likewise be small.

Capital and Liquidity Requirements. Although these requirements are imposed in order to ensure the solvency of the banking system, they may be considered as levies in cases where offshore banks are required to maintain deposits with the central bank or monetary authority of the host country. The direct contribution of these requirements will depend on the way the requirements are satisfied. Some OBCs require offshore banks to hold specified amounts of domestic, financial and/or capital assets.

For instance, in the Philippines, offshore banks are required to retain $1 million of the government's paper. In the case of Panama, international licensed banks are required to hold a minimum of $250,000, which can be held in the form of a deposit with the National Bank of Panama or in government securities of less than five-year's maturity issued by the National Banking Commission. In Singapore, offshore banks are required to maintain S$4 million in the form of government securities, Treasury bills and immovable properties.

The magnitude of benefit will depend on the difference between the market interest rate and the rate of return on these assets. In most cases, however, the latter tends to fluctuate with the former, diminishing the benefits.

Taxes. Taxes arising from hosting OBCs include withholding taxes, profit taxes, income taxes on local employees and stamp duties. Of these taxes, withholding taxes disappeared in the OBC when Hong Kong eliminated them in 1982. Since offshore banking consists mainly of interbank transactions, the profit margins are so relatively small that imposition of any withholding tax by an OBC that directly affects gross income would deter offshore banks from conducting business in such a center. For this reason, the absence of a withholding tax on interest income accruing to nonresidents is considered an essential precondition for the OBC. A tax on profits is likely to produce an adverse impact on offshore banking business to a lesser extent than a withholding tax, for the former is only imposed on net profits after expenses are subtracted. Chown and Keller contend:

> Taxes on gross interest are a far more serious deterrent to offshore business. A withholding tax, even at a modest rate of 5%, would kill any offshore business more surely than a 50% tax on net profits.[13]

However, due to increased competition, few OBCs are willing to introduce this tax. For example, the Philippines which commenced offshore banking with a 5 percent tax on profits, repealed it finally in 1981 to enhance its competitiveness as an OBC. Income taxes on local employees in the offshore banking sector may be also regarded as indirect benefits. Obviously, the magnitude of revenues from this source will depend on the number of employees and income tax rates in the country.

In general, stamp duties have been imposed as a percentage of the face value with a fixed maximum amount of financial instruments. As is the case with withholding taxes, however, they may have adverse impact on the development of high volume/low margin offshore banking. For this reason, there has been a tendency to eliminate stamp taxes, as is evidenced by Singapore's removal of stamp duties in 1980.[14]

Operating Expenditures. Operating expenditures of offshore banks consist mainly of salaries and wages, rent of offices, administrative expenditures and telecommunication expenses. Among these, salaries and wages are the largest component of operating expenditures.

The number of participants in the center has a significant impact on operating expenditures. The increase in number of offshore banks is directly related to employment, demand for office space and utilization of telecommunication facilities. But this may not be the case for the booking centers where most banks do not have a substantial functional presence. The scope of business carried out in the OBC will also have an impact on the employment level of offshore banks. If offshore banks conduct merely booking transactions, the number of employees will not be significant despite the relatively large volume of transactions recorded there.

The magnitude of operating expenditures will also depend on the cost of inputs. Local labor costs, telecommunication expense, and rent in the host country will all have a marked impact on the level of operating expenditures. It can be concluded, therefore, that onshore expenditures of offshore banks form the largest proportion of the total direct benefits in OBCs.

Employment. One of the significant direct benefits attributable to OBCs is the positive impact on employment. For instance, in Panama, employees in the offshore sector accounted for approximately 8 percent of the total local labor force in 1983. The magnitude of employment is closely related to that of operating expenditures, since salaries and wages of local employees constitute the largest part of operating expenditures. For OBCs with miniscule economies and local labor forces, this benefit will have great significance. But for OBCs with sizable labor forces, it will have little impact.

Indirect Benefits

Although it is difficult to make a discrete assessment of indirect benefits due to their intangible nature, they are generally regarded as considerable. Especially for countries contemplating establishing functional OBCs, these benefits will merit higher consideration than direct benefits when potential benefits are assessed. Major indirect benefits include capital inflows (onshore utilization of offshore funds), development of the domestic banking industry, internationalization of domestic banks, development of local expertise in international finance and accelerated growth of related industries such as insurance companies, money brokers, merchant banks and investment companies, international legal and accounting firms, hotels, printing plants and telecommunication companies. The enhancement of national prestige and security is also an important indirect benefit.

Capital Inflow. The problem that constrains most LDCs in implementing their economic development plans is a shortage of capital. For these countries, capital inflows via hosting the OBC, which could be the most effective method of resolving such a problem, would have a strong appeal. In this case, the establishment of an OBC should be considered as a supplementary element of the national economic development plan. In this regard, the Philippine OBC can serve as the best example. As set forth in the Presidential Decree 1034 on September 30, 1976, the primary policy objective of the OBC was to facilitate the inflows of foreign currency funds into the country. For this purpose, offshore banks in the Philippines were allowed to provide foreign currency loans to resident customers. Panama and Singapore also have extensively utilized offshore funds for internal development purposes. But the Bahamas has not realized this benefit due to its low capital absorptive capacity. On the whole, OBCs with sizable economies and considerable capital absorptive capacities are much better positioned to reap this kind of benefit than OBCs with very small economies, a miniscule industrial base and thus low capital absorptive capacity.

Development of the Domestic Banking Industry. It is widely acknowledged that the level of a country's economic development is closely linked with the level of development of its financial system, and thus a strong and efficient financial system is essential to the country's economic strength.[15] Patrick argues:

> Financial intermediaries have an important function in providing a market mechanism for the transference claims on real resources from source to the most efficient investors. The more perfect are financial markets, the more nearly optimum allocation of investment is achieved. In a way, the financial system accommodates economic growth; on the other hand, to the extent that the financial system is underdeveloped and/or inefficient, it restricts growth below what optionally could be achieved.[16]

Banks are the most important elements in the development of economic strength. Cameron points out that banks provide liquidity to the economy by creating money and promoting industrialization and thus economic development by assisting entrepreneurs or performing entrepreneurial functions themselves, as can be proven by the German and Japanese cases.[17] Presence of offshore banks should stimulate the banking industry of the host countries, although to varying degrees depending on the scope of business conducted by offshore banks. It seems obvious that there is very little impact on the domestic banking system in booking centers where offshore banks hardly conduct any substantive transactions. On the other hand, functional centers where the interface between offshore banks and domestic banks is generally considerable should stimulate the development of the domestic banking system.[18] In these centers, the presence of international banks would increase the efficiency of domestic banks by transferring sophisticated banking techniques, introducing up-to-date banking innovations and motivating more proficient management skills.[19] Domestic banks, with increased efficiency, would be able to provide far better services to their local customers, hence benefitting the entire economy.

Internationalization of Domestic Banks. Constant interface with international financial markets coupled with the establishment of extensive overseas channels of communication can be viewed as significant factors for effective offshore banking transactions. In OBCs whose domestic banks are permitted to conduct offshore banking transactions, local banks, to be competitive with international banks, will have to increase contacts with international banks. In this way, OBCs may be very conducive to the internationalization of domestic banks in the host country.

Development of Local Experts in International Finance. As is the case with other industries, qualified personnel are prerequisites for the development of the banking industry, which is essential for economic development. International banking operations, in particular, require a high level of expertise and experience which can be reached through intensive education, training and practice. Offshore banks provide valuable job-training opportunities for the local work force, hence serving as an effective vehicle for the development of local expertise in international banking. Being well aware of the importance of this benefit, authorities in most of the functional OBCs strive to maximize this benefit from hosting the OBCs.

For example, it is a requirement in the Philippines for offshore banks to train local employees and report their progress to the Central Bank.

Fostering local expertise in international banking may be to the benefit of offshore banks as well. In general, even if all the expenses for training local employees are taken into consideration, employing expert expatriates costs more than local hires. For these reasons, offshore banks tend to be very cooperative with the host countries in developing local experts in international banking, as is evidenced in Bahrain and Singapore.

Stimulation of the Development of Related Industries. The presence of offshore banks generates demands for international accounting firms, law firms, international money brokers, merchant banks, printing establishments, hotels, transportation and telecommunication. Obviously, real estate activities associated with this growth also increase. This progressive augmentation of trade and commerce would have positive effects on local employment and on the rest of the economy.[20]

Enhancement of National Prestige and Security. The existence of a successful OBC in a country serves as an outstanding indicator of that country's high level of social and political stability, heightening its credibility and prestige. The augmented credibility and prestige in turn promotes direct foreign investment in the country. The increased direct foreign investment, coupled with the existence of international banks, enables foreign investors to enjoy a greater stake in the country. Accordingly, any problem that will affect adversely the country's security will be of serious concern. Furthermore, in view of the fact that bankers usually enjoy marked political influence in the homeland, the establishment of an OBC will be instrumental in improving national security of the host country. The Taiwan OBC, for example, has this potential benefit very much in mind.[21]

COSTS

Costs associated with OBCs can be divided into direct and indirect costs, as is the case with benefits.

Direct Costs

In theory, expenditures on telecommunication networks, supervision and regulation, and education can be viewed as direct costs associated with hosting OBCs. In practice, however, these costs, in some cases, can also qualify as long-term benefits.

Expenditures on Telecommunication Infrastructures. As previously mentioned, well-developed telecommunication networks are necessary for successful OBCs. Major OBCs already possessed adequate telecommunications facilities prior to the establishment of the OBCs. Even if a country, aspiring to be a successful OBC, invested in new telecommunications facilities, their costs would be easily recouped by user's charges. The resulting improved efficiency of the basic economy thus transmutes the cost of this capital investment into a long-range benefit.

Supervisory Costs. Supervision and administration costs which mainly consist of salaries and government officials can be viewed as expenses to the host economy. They tend to be compensated, however, by charges to offshore banks (i.e., license fees, registration fees). Furthermore, supervision and administration costs incurred from hosting OBCs can be offset to a substantial degree by the improved supervision and administration capability which will contribute to the orderly growth of the entire banking industry in the country.

Education and Training Costs. Expenditures on education and training will be incurred when the host country wants to fill the job positions in the offshore banks from the local work force. However, these costs will be recovered to a great extent by increased employment and the development of local expertise in international banking.

In summary, the foregoing direct costs can be considered as expenses only in the short term but may be considered as benefits in the long run.

Indirect Costs

As is the case with indirect benefits, indirect costs generally have a greater impact on the host economy than direct costs. For countries planning to host functional OBCs, these costs will normally have a higher priority than direct costs in the decision making leading to the establishment of OBCs. Major indirect costs include the disrupting impact on monetary policy, inflationary effects, the adverse impact on domestic interest rates, adverse impact on domestic economic policy, capital leakage, the inflow of speculative offshore funds, and fiscal problems.

Disrupting Impact on Domestic Monetary Policy. Hosting OBCs may cause a disrupting impact on domestic monetary policy, especially in cases where there exists asymmetry between onshore and offshore markets. In this regard, the experience of Singapore can serve as an example. In Singapore, as domestic deposits are still subject to a 26 percent reserve requirement (minimum cash balance of 6 percent and two-tier liquid asset ratio of 20 percent), the effective cost of Singapore dollar deposits is higher than that of foreign currency deposits. The banks circumvent this reserve requirement by swapping Singapore dollars for foreign currencies (mainly U.S. dollars). By doing this, they can reduce the costs of deposits and thus provide more attractive rates to residents. Clearly, such practices cause an increase in the domestic deposit base, and a decrease in money supply, thereby placing upward pressure on domestic interest rates. Moreover, the erosion of the domestic liabilities base could damage the country's monetary and economic polity to a significant extent in the long term. These practices have been widely employed, especially between 1981 and 1982 (during this time, deposits of nonbank customers rose by 47 percent). Since the magnitude of these transactions has become larger, the MAS has deterred these activities by using moral suasion as well as imposing fines on the violators.

Inflationary Effect. The inflow of a substantial amount of offshore funds in the domestic market will have an inflationary effect on the price level of the host country, if its monetary system cannot absorb endogenous liquidity. McKinnon maintains that a burst of net credits by offshore banks to residents would lead to higher spending and thus cause inflationary pressures, unless these external credits resulted in a net inflow of imported goods.[22] Therefore, OBCs with small open economies whose domestic prices are primarily dominated by the flow of imports and exports would be better able to mitigate external inflationary pressures than OBCs with sizable economies where protectionism prevails.

Adverse Impact on Domestic Interest Rates. As the offshore market grows, it promotes the integration of the domestic market into the international financial market, causing domestic interest rates to follow closely those of offshore markets, especially in the absence of exchange control. Therefore, high and volatile interest rates of the offshore markets are reflected in the domestic rates and may cause difficulty to some local industries. This problem might reduce the competitiveness of the domestic export industry in the international market and even threaten the viability of smaller local businesses which cannot afford the high cost of financing. In this regard, the experiences of Panama and Singapore are very relevant.

Adverse Impact on Domestic Economic Policy. As noted earlier, in some OBCs, offshore funds have played a significant role in the host countries' economic development plans. The increased availability of offshore funds could cause the host countries to become unduly reliant on offshore funds in the formulation and implementation of economic policy. However, in case offshore funds are not provided as was expected, the economic planning will not succeed. If offshore banks curb local credits when the host country implements an expansionary economic policy, that policy will be doomed to failure. This scenario has been the experience of Panama.

Capital Leakage. One of the most significant costs associated with hosting OBCs is capital leakage from the domestic to the offshore market. This is especially true in cases where the same banks conduct both onshore and offshore business, thus blurring the distinction between the offshore and onshore sector. When this delineation becomes obscured, there exists a high risk of capital leakage. Capital leakage increases in consonance with the degree of destabilization of the country's social and political order. The Philippines' experience demonstrates that an OBC in a socially and politically unstable country may be abused as a vehicle for capital leakage.

Inflows of Speculative Offshore Funds. OBCs may be instrumental in stimulating the inflows of speculative offshore funds. In Singapore, for instance, speculative funds were exchanged into local currencies and invested in local stock and real estate markets between 1972-73.[23] Hong Kong also experienced this type of speculation during 1973-74 and once more in early January 1975. During those years, local deposit rates were adjusted 13 times. The ratio of advances and loans to deposits grew from 63 percent at the end of 1971 to 96.5 percent at the end of 1975. This sharp increase was due to the inflow of massive amounts of offshore speculative funds. The increased liquidity was invested in local stock and real estate markets, causing an imported inflation and thus threatening the competitiveness of export industries.[24]

Fiscal Problems. Offshore banking may cause some fiscal problems. In most OBCs, interest paid on offshore deposits is exempt from taxes, while interest paid on domestic deposits is subject to taxes. For this reason, the shifting of domestic deposits into the offshore sector has been encouraged in some OBCs, creating fiscal problems.

SUMMARY AND CONCLUSIONS

Our analysis in the previous section demonstrates that OBCs provide direct benefits such as employment, taxes and levies, operating expenditures as well as indirect benefits such as the development of the domestic banking industry, capital inflow, development of local expertise in international finance, internationalization of domestic banks and the development of related industries.

On the other hand, OBCs bring about both direct and indirect costs. Direct costs include expenditures on telecommunications, education and supervision. Indirect costs involve the disrupting impact on monetary policy, inflationary effect, capital leakage, inflow of speculative offshore funds, and adverse impacts on domestic economic policy and interest rates.

However, host countries do not derive the same set of benefits and costs from hosting OBCs. The economic impact of an OBC on the host country varies from country to country, depending on the characteristics of the country involved. Here, the characteristics of the country refer to economy, location, social and political stability, currency and foreign exchange control, regulatory and supervisory environment, and tax environment.

APPENDIX

The result of comparative analysis of the five OBCs with dissimilar characteristics shows that they have experienced different sets of benefits and costs. Specifically, the Bahamas have reaped significant direct benefits, such as employment and operating expenditures of offshore banks, from the OBC. In 1983, the number of Bahamian employees in the offshore banking sector totalled 2,719. Total operating expenditures of offshore banks reached $103.3 million, accounting for 6.2 percent of the GDP in 1983. However, significant indirect benefits have not been realized in the

Bahamas. On the other hand, there has been little indication that the OBC has generated significant costs to the Bahamas.

The major benefits that Bahrain has derived from hosting an OBC include direct as well as indirect benefits. Total employees in the offshore banking sector reached 2,539 in 1983, of which 1,499 were Bahrain nationals. Direct expenditures consisting of license fees and operating expenditures amounted to $170 million in 1983, accounting for 3.5 percent of GDP. Significant indirect benefits include development of related industries and development of local expertise in international finance. On the other hand, two significant costs have been incurred from hosting the OBC, namely, the disrupting impact on domestic monetary policy and the adverse impact on the relations between Bahrain and neighboring countries.

Panama has realized significant direct as well as indirect benefits from hosting the OBC. The number of the Panamanian employees totalled 5,292 in 1983, comprising approximately 8 percent of the total local labor force. Operating expenditures amounted to $194 million in 1983, accounting for 4.5 percent of GDP. Major indirect benefits arising from hosting the OBC involve capital inflow, stimulation of development of domestic banks and development of related industries. Significant costs incurred from the OBC include the disrupting impact on domestic economic policy and the adverse impact on domestic interest rates.

The Philippines has failed to realize significant benefits from the OBC, except capital inflow. The direct benefits have been negligible. The number of Filipino employees employed by offshore banks totalled 257 in 1983, representing merely 0.001 percent of the total local labor force (18,474,000 in 1982). Direct contributions such as taxes, levies and operating expenditures reached $27.6 million in 1983, constituting 0.0064 percent of GDP. The only significant benefit attributable to hosting the OBC has been capital inflow. Outstanding loans to non-bank residents amounted to $1.528 billion, equivalent to one-third of the total assets of the Philippine OBC, as of the end of 1983. On the cost side, capital flight has been substantial.

Singapore has enjoyed significant direct and indirect benefits from the OBC. It was estimated that the number of employees in the offshore banking sector totalled 22,999 in 1983, accounting for 2 percent of the total labor force (1,206,000 in 1983). The ACUs' contribution to GDP was estimated to reach 5.7 percent in 1983. Major indirect benefits associated with hosting the OBC consist of the development of local expertise in international finance, development of related industries and capital inflow. Significant costs which Singapore has experienced include inflow of speculative offshore funds, the disrupting impact on domestic monetary policy and adverse impact on domestic interest rates.

The above results, therefore, indicate that the economic impact of an OBC on the host country varies from country to country, depending on the characteristics of the country involved.

NOTES

1. H. G. Johnson. 1976. Panama as a regional financial center. *Economic Development and Cultural Change*. January:262.

2. T. Kelen. 1977. The World Offshore Finance. *The Banker*. April:75.

3. Gunter Dufey and Ian M. Giddy. 1978. *The International Money Market*. Englewood Cliffs, New Jersey: Prentice Hall, Inc., p. 24.

4. Ian McCarthy. 1979. Offshore banking centers, benefits and costs. *Finance & Development*. December:45.

5. Mary Cooke. 1979. *Offshore financial centers*. London: The Banker Research Unit, Financial Times Limited, p. 4.

6. Gunter Dufey. 1983. Banking in the Asian Pacific area. In R. Moxon, J. F. Trutt and T. Roehl (ed.), *Asia Pacific dynamics*. Greenwich, CT, p. 36.

7. R. A. Johns. 1983. *Tax havens and offshore finance*: A study of transnational economic development. New York: St. Martin's Press, p. 35.

8. Sang-Lim Choi. 1983. Economic rationale of International Financial Centers. Ph.D Dissertation at University of Michigan. Ann Arbor, Michigan, pp. 32-34.

9. McCarthy (1979), p. 45.

10. Harvey A. Poinacheck. 1982. International financial markets. In Ingo Walter (ed.), *Handbook of international business*. New York: John Wiley & Sons, pp. 18, 67.

11. A. K. Bhattacharya. 1982. Costs and benefits. In Philip D. Grub, Tan Chwee Huat, Kwan Kuen-Chor, and George H. Rott (eds.) *East Asia: dimensions of international business*. Sydney: Prentice-Hall Internal, p. 86.

12. Y. S. Park. 1982. The economics of offshore financial centers. *Columbia Journal of World Business*. Winter:32-33.

13. Chown and Keller, op. cit., p. 149.

14. Tan Chwee Huat. 1982. Singapore as an International Finance Center. In Phillip D. Grub, Tan Chwee Huat, Kwan Kuen-Chor, and George H. Rott (eds.), *East Asia: Dimensions of international business*. Sydney: Prentice-Hall, Inc, p. 37.

15. For a more detailed discussion, see G. W. Shaw, *Financial Deepening in Economic Development*, Oxford University Press, 1973. Also R. W. Goldsmith, *Financial Structure and Development*, Yale University Press, 1969.

16. Hugh T. Patrick. 1966. Financial development and economic growth in underdeveloped countries. *Economic development, and cultural change*. January:182.

17. See R. Cameron, *Banking and Economic Development*, Oxford University Press, 1972.

18. Ian McCarthy, op. cit., p. 46.

19. D. Germidis and A. Michalet. 1984. *International banks and financial markets in developing countries*. Paris. 1 OECD.

20. Park, op. cit., p. 31.

21. Ministry of Finance, Taiwan. 1982. Study on the establishment of OBC in Taipei. Unpublished staff paper.

22. Ronald I. McKinnon. Offshore markets in foreign currencies. In Monetary Authority of Singapore, *Papers on Monetary Economics*, pp. 146-147.

23. MAS. 1973. *Annual report*.

24. A. K. Bhattacharya. 1977. *The Asian dollar market: international offshore financing*. New York: Praeger, pp. 69-70.

11. COST/BENEFIT ANALYSIS OF ESTABLISHING AN OFFSHORE BANKING CENTER: THE CASE OF ANCHORAGE

Musa Essayyad
University of Alaska, Anchorage

M. M. Haddad
Wayne State University

Omar Benkato
University of Detroit

INTRODUCTION

The unabated fluctuation of oil prices in the world markets and their drastic decline since 1985 has prompted the state of Alaska, and other states whose economies rely primarily on oil, to look more seriously into the possibilities of diversifying the sources of their income. One possibility is to consider the establishment of an international financial center (IFC) in Anchorage, the largest city in Alaska. The proposed center would function as an interbank market, comprised of foreign and local financial institutions, in which short-term, medium-term and long-term international lending and borrowing--for purposes of investment, financing, hedging, and speculation--denominated in Eurocurrencies are consummated. Lenders and borrowers would include multinational corporations, banks, and governments.

The willingness of Anchorage's financial community and the state of Alaska's government to host an IFC is tied up to the estimated magnitude of the positive net welfare gains that can be generated from this undertaking. Past experience indicates that the size of benefits and costs differ from one center to another. The type and magnitude of benefits and costs are also related to the nature of the offshore banking center, whether it is a booking, full-fledged center or merely an International Banking Facility (IBF).

The potential benefits and cost of establishing an IFC also vary with the ever-changing international financial markets, monetary systems, depth of advancement in technology and automation, and finally the degree of international markets' integration. Since the advent of the floating exchange system in 1973 and the prevalence of the managed float or "dirty float" in the 1980s, the potential gains of establishing an IFC are expected to outweigh those that would be derived under the pre-1973 fixed parity systems. Moreover, with more integrated and automated financial markets, we would be expecting lower transaction and administrative costs than in the case of segmented and less automated markets. Another development that created opportunities for more profits, and yet more risk, is the 1979 major change in the monetary policy of the U.S. Federal Reserve Board. In October 1979, the Board decided to target its money management operations on the monetary aggregates rather than on the level of interest rates. As a result of this change in policy, U.S. interest rates became much more volatile than they were previously. Since much of world financing and investing is tied directly or indirectly to U.S. dollar interest rates, this change has had a significant effect on the degree of bond coupon risk faced by international financial managers.

This paper is divided into two main sections. The first section discusses the IFC's potential benefits to Alaska banks and non-banks, the benefits of enhanced access to international capital markets, and direct and indirect benefits of the internationalization of the Alaska Permanent Fund Corporation. The second section discusses the potential cost and disadvantages of establishing an IFC in Anchorage. Finally, the paper concludes with a summary.

POTENTIAL SOURCES OF BENEFITS

In general, the main source of benefits derived from attracting offshore banks is their local operating expenditure and their direct effect on the welfare of the domestic economy. To have a general idea of the magnitude of IFC economic benefits, McCarthy (1979) points out that the estimated operating expenditures are as high as 8 percent of the host country's gross national product (GNP) in some centers. An economic impact analysis may be used to estimate the cash flows associated with the establishment of an IFC in Anchorage. With some adjustment, the economic multiplier can also be used in this regard to give a rough idea on how many times the local income will expand, given an increase in local investment. The economic multiplier is $1/[1-C(1-t)]$, where C denotes the marginal propensity to consume, and t is the effective income tax rate. Due to the special nature of the proposed center, the tax effect should be eliminated from the multiplier. Caution should also be employed in interpreting the results, since capital expenditure is not substantial in creating the IFC.

Benefit to Banks

Irrespective of the approach utilized in determining the net positive welfare gains, the following are the *banks'* potential benefits attached to setting up a full-fledged offshore banking center in Anchorage:

(1) Employment expansion. Despite the political and economic significance of employment, the financial literature on offshore banking centers provides only a few cursory estimates of the direct effects of employment on the host countries. In July 1987, experts in the field were assembled in Anchorage to discuss, among other things, the viability of setting an IFC in Anchorage. Unfortunately, none of those experts has provided specific estimates of the effects

of employment on Alaska. The impact of international banking activities on local employment varies from one country to another. For example, Lessard and Tschoegl (1985) find that the employment-generating ability in the Bahamas was about one thirty-second of that in Panama. In another study on the direct employment effects on Panama's international banking center, Lessard and Tschoegl (1986) used simple methods to calculate the total and marginal direct employment effects of Panama's international banking center. They have shown that the results, "which appears reasonable, suggest that international banking activities are not very labor-intensive and provide even fewer jobs than many observers infer from the relatively impressive asset amounts involved." In another paper, Tschoegl (1987) points out that although the absolute number of jobs which offshore banking creates is slight, this creation is a relative term.

(2) Generation of net cash inflows from short-term Eurocurrency trading. The magnitude of these benefits and others mentioned below is, however, related to volume and frequency of trading.

(3) Generation of net cash inflows from medium and long-term Eurosyndication in loans, Eurobonds, foreign bonds, cocktail bonds, commodity-indexed bonds, etc., and spreading risk among Eurobank participants.

(4) Production of net cash inflows from new financial innovations: currency futures, interest rate futures, currency swaps, currency coupon swaps, interest rate swaps, basis rate swaps, etc.

(5) Generation of net cash inflows from international fiduciary activities.

(6) Increased net cash inflows from export-import financing.

(7) Countertrade financing. It is hoped that Alaska's future export markets would be in the Asian developing countries, particularly China, whose currency is inconvertible. Countertrade arrangements are a possible solution to circumvent the shortcoming of currency inconvertibility. Countertrade arrangements are complex and risky. The establishment of an IFC in Anchorage will enhance access to international expertise in countertrade financing.

(8) Diversification of existing bank services. Prior to the 1985 collapse in world oil prices, the performance measures of most banks in Alaska have shown that those banks were

reaping the benefits of a strong and booming state economy that was attributed to increased and relatively stable oil prices, increased disposable personal income of Alaskans that accompanied the $8-billion Alaska Oil Pipeline project, and the unprecedented explosive growth of demand for real estate assets. The deep involvement of local financial institutions, particularly banks and savings and loans associations, in real estate loans, and the lack of rational and efficient long-term strategic diversification of their loan portfolios were the reasons that constrained those institutions' flexibility in weathering the shock of the decline in oil prices. 1986 statistics indicate that construction and land development loans as a percentage of domestic loans were extremely high for Alaska Mutual Bank (47.8 percent). United Bank Alaska (47.4 percent), United Bank of Alaska Southeastern in Juneau (39.6 percent), the First Interstate Bank of Alaska (24.5 percent). The deep involvement of banks in real estate loans have propelled the nonperforming loans ratio to total loans to escalate to 6.51 percent, thus exceeding the national average of 1.94 percent. More prudent and diversified banks, such as the National Bank of Alaska and the First National Bank of Anchorage, were able to survive the dramatic decline in oil prices.

Therefore, the establishment of an IFC in Anchorage would motivate local financial institutions to diversify their services, especially in international banking. As of the end of 1986, there are five banks in Anchorage rendering international banking services via money-center correspondent banks in the lower 48. Three of the five banks generate their business primarily from export-import financing and, to a lesser extent, from money transfer services that do not require an advanced level of sophistication. The potential gains of international diversification, whether in investing or financing, are well substantiated in the financial literature and reported by multinational financial institutions. See, for example, Essayyad and Wu (1988), Essayyad, Haddad, and Benkato (1988), Lessard (1974), and Kidwell, Marr, and Thompson (1985).

(9) Enhancing efficiencies (allocational, operating, and market) in the Anchorage banking market.

(10) Building of local human capital and expertise in international banking and finance.

Benefits to Non-Banks

The following potential benefits can be realized by non-bank businesses in Anchorage and Alaska:

(1) Alleviation of the present slump in the real estate sector. Establishment of an IFC in Anchorage would result in a

surge of demand for office space and commercial properties. This may improve the ailing financial position of savings and loan associations operating in Alaska.

(2) Improved income of the retail sector (hotels, restaurants, department stores, utilities, telecommunications, etc.)

(3) Building of the financial human capital in the fields of international finance, international legal counselling, international accounting, and general international business.

(4) Improved profits of insurance companies as a result of the possible increase in premium volume and business of co-insurance.

(5) Improved profits of local brokerage houses as a result of increased trading and commissions.

(6) Improved profits of local credit unions because of the generally improved personal savings.

(7) Improvement of local and state government revenues through license fees, expatriate taxes, etc.

(8) Joint ventures and venture capital opportunities. Of particular importance to Alaska reap the benefits associated with joint ventures and venture capital possibilities between non-residents and local businesses or state government agencies, such as the gas pipeline project, fisheries, timber, tourism, etc.

Some of the above advantages may not be relevant if the International Banking Facility (IBF) model is regarded as more appropriate than a full-fledged IFC model to adopt in setting up an international financial center in Anchorage. In fact, Moffett and Stonehill (1987) argue that the potential benefits derived from IBF operations are limited to the participating banks and states of residence, and employment and tax effect generations are minimal. Moreover, the authors conclude that although the profitability of operations in isolation is unknown, IBF operations officers followed a passive approach to marketing and management indicative of the secondary importance of the operations themselves.

Benefits of Enhanced Access to International Capital Markets

A firm's access to international money or capital markets is a function of its creditworthiness, which is measured by its business (default) and financial risks. These risks in turn are tied up to the state's economic stability as well as political stability. While Alaska is far more stable politically and economically than all the offshore banking units in Panama, Singapore, Hong Kong, and Bahrain, nevertheless, it is still more constrained in its access to capital markets than some other states in the lower 48 and some Western industrial nations, such as Greece, Spain, and Portugal. Regardless of IFC feasibility, Alaska's access to international capital markets would be definitely enhanced through the establishment of an IFC in Anchorage. Economies of scale and competition in the Euromarkets would provide substantial savings in borrowing costs. In fact, many U.S. corporations have reported substantial savings with Eurodollar bond sales between 25 and 100 basis points in the Eurodollar, as compared with the domestic market. Kidwell, Marr and Thompson (1985) and Kidwell, Marr and Trimble (1987) have empirically substantiated the savings associated with Euromarkets financing. Others who have also attested to these savings include Cooper (1985), Fisher (1979)d, Karp (1982), Li (1987), and Mabuchi (1987).

Role of the Permanent Fund: Direct and Indirect Benefits

The considerable assets size of the Alaska Permanent fund, the state saving account, not only generates substantial earnings but also tremendous leverage and networking in the international financial markets. The Fund was created in 1976 by the state of Alaska's legislature in order to achieve three objectives: to save a portion of the state's one-time oil wealth to benefit present and future generations of Alaska; to protect those savings from loss of value through inflation-proofing and avoidance of speculative strategies; and to invest those savings to produce income for uses provided by the state legislature. According to SEI Corporation, a San Francisco consulting firm which was hired by the Permanent Fund to evaluate the performance of the Fund's portfolio, the principal and the inflation-proofing among of the Fund was approximately $9 billion as of June 30, 1986. The conservative investment policy as formulated by the state legislators was behind the following breakdown of the Fund's 1986 portfolio: fixed income securities (76.6%); equities (18.6%), real estate (2.5%); Alaskan CDs (1.7%); and mortgages (0.6%). Equity managers for the period are: Bankers Trust (73.2%); Rosenberg Capital Management (9.5%); Lehman Capital Management (9.3%); and Eaton Vance (8.0%).

The potential cardinal role of the Fund in the future would be a determining factor in generating sizable benefits that would make the idea of establishing an IFC in Anchorage viable. With assets of $9 billion in June 1986 and estimated assets of $30 billion dollars by 1998, the Fund would be able to help create the center. Moreover, it has been predicted that in five years, the Fund will provide more income for the state than the oil industry. For comparison purposes, it is germane to mention that the total assets of banks in Singapore amounted to $17 billion in 1976 and those of Hong Kong were only $6.8. Prior to the Lebanese civil war in 1974 and the subsequent setback of Beirut as the most active and seasoned international banking center in the Middle East and West Asia, the total assets of Beirut's banks were only $4.5 billion compared to $9 billion of the Permanent Fund in 1986, let alone the total deposits of Anchorage banks. The estimated assets size of the Fund at $30 billion by the end of the next decade would produce a colossal leverage for the state of Alaska.

I would not exaggerate if I would say that the Alaskans' hope lies in the Permanent Fund, untouched.

Notwithstanding the Permanent Fund capability of assuming a nucleus role in the proposed IFC, the IFC's feasibility should be first convincingly established, and the state legislature should seriously consider the relaxation of the current laws so the Fund would be allowed to diversify internationally its assets. This relaxation would then help the Fund to function flexibly as the nucleus of the proposed IFC. So far, the Fund is not permitted to invest internationally, and bills have been submitted in the House and Senate to allow the Fund to invest in securities of foreign governments, foreign governmental agencies, and foreign corporations. In addition to the direct benefits--in terms of more favorable risk-return mix--of international portfolio diversification that it will reap, the fund will acquire considerable international leverage and unique networking that can be used to generate the following indirect benefits:

(a) Greater access to international capital markets. Currently, there are many untapped natural resources and different small business projects and ventures that are encountering local financing problems emanating partly from credit rationing by local financial institutions. Moreover, Alaska's international trade is seeking financing solutions. Solving the above problems would serve considerably the objective of diversifying Alaska's economy. The Permanent Fund's visible involvement in international investment would attract foreign financiers and bankers to consider financing local businesses and/or participating in international syndications to finance local projects.

(b) Mitigating the slump in the real estate market. The leverage of the Permanent Fund can also be used to help alleviate the problems facing the local real estate markets. Using its networking and leverage, the Fund can draw the attention of many foreign investors, who are desirous of investing for long-term appreciation purposes, to two important considerations: first, there are numerous undervalued commercial properties in Alaska that deserve investing in, and second, the drastic decline of the dollar vis-a-vis many foreign currencies would provide potential investors unique opportunities to acquire these properties at very low prices in terms of their own local currencies.

(c) Solving the "brain drain" problem. The Fund's involvement in international investment would help substantially build up Alaska's financial human capital. This would be achieved by using the leverage of the Fund. In addition to in-house internships, the Fund would capitalize on its clout to help the University of Alaska's business students to obtain internships at its equity and real estate managers mentioned above. Such internships would give Alaskans first-hand experience in managing portfolios and securities and thus would help solve the "brain drain" problem from which local financial institutions are currently suffering. Providing internships is a universally established marketing practice and investment managers thus recognize it and are receptive to it. In fact, they use it as a "sweetener" to attract funds from prospective institutional investors, such as the Permanent Fund. In the long run, Alaska might even have a financial cadre that is capable of managing locally all the huge estimated future assets of the Fund.

POTENTIAL COSTS AND DISADVANTAGES

The following are the potential costs and disadvantages of establishing an IFC in Anchorage:

(1) Cost of hiring non-Alaskans. If the feasibility of setting up an IFC in Anchorage were established, and given the limitation on local expertise in international banking and finance, there would be a need to recruit non-Alaskan employees with expertise in this area. To estimate the cost of hiring non-Alaskans in local banks, a survey was conducted. The following question was asked: Considering all relevant cost when initially hiring new employees (relocation, interviewing and advertising costs), what is the additional expense incurred when hiring non-Alaskans?.

Table 1 indicates that one bank incurred 10% in additional expenses, three banks incurred 30%, and four banks incurred more than 50% in additional expenses relative to local hire.

The second question addressed to local banks was: What is the *permanent* additional expense of hiring non-Alaskans (i.e., it may cost more to lure non-Alaskans into Alaska), if any? Table 1 shows that five of the eight banks responding to this question did not incur any *permanent* additional cost, while the remaining four banks incurred 5 percent, 10 percent, 15 percent and 30 percent respectively.

It can be inferred from the above results that non-Alaskan hire is not substantially more costly than local hire. We would attribute these unexpected results to many factors including: many new hired professionals accept lower-paying jobs because they are either unemployed, have some relatives in Alaska, or they used to live before in Alaska and would like to come back to stay. Some would come here because they were interested in wilderness, fishing and hunting. Some find additional business opportunities and less competition than is available in other states. Some may relocate to escape the pressure and tension they have in their jobs in the lower 48.

The relative cost of overseas hire was not, however, investigated in the survey. Given the great demand for and supply shortage of professionals in international business and its allied fields, it is felt, *a priori*, that the cost of hiring this type of professional, whether U.S. or foreign nationals, would be higher than the cost of hiring professionals in the field of domestic banking and finance. The main reason is that there are few universities and colleges in the U.S. and abroad which offer international business concentration in their undergraduate business program, and yet fewer institutions who afford to offer master and doctorate degrees. Currently, there is a fierce competition among multinational corporations, banks, governments and academic institutions in their pursuit of luring specialists in international finance, international banking, international accounting and international business law. Another factor for the very high cost of recruiting those experts is the sizable premium or allowance that they would require to induce them to relocate in Alaska. The reasons for requiring such a high premium are: first, the negative perception by non-Alaskans toward the quality of life in Alaska, and second, the relative high cost of living in Alaska.

The murky waters of politics of the "local hire" law should also be evaluated carefully by prospective multinational financial institutions making up the proposed IFC. If passed, "local hire" would apply to any contract in which the state is acting as a "market participant" and only to natural resources industries. Notwithstanding this interpretation of the law, and the vague recent declaration of its unconstitutionality by the Supreme Court, yet you would find some unpredictable politicians who would wish to please their ultra-conservative constituents by vowing to widen the application of this state law to encompass "market nonparticipant." Some observers try to draw an analogy of this law to the sovereign risk whose underestimation led to the current Third World debt crisis. Though unclear, the declared unconstitutionality of the law, however, renders this analogy as an overstatement.

(2) Cost of training and rehabilitating some local bank employees to make banks more competitive in international financial services.

(3) Sunk cost. The cost of commissioning a full-fledged feasibility study may range from $100,000 to $1,000,000. It would cover planning, economic, financial, banking, accounting, legal, and other technical analyses. The sunk cost would be borne by the state government, local financial institutions, or both. Though this cost is not substantial, getting the financial institutions involved would commit them to make the IFC's idea workable. A less costly pre-feasibility study may also be prepared to determine the general outlook of the concept.

TABLE 1*
Cost of Hiring Non-Alaskans

Cost of Hiring Non-Alaskans	Alaska Pacific Bank	Rainier Bank Alaska	National Bank of Alaska	United Bank Alaska	Ak. Natl. Bank of the North	Alaska Mutual Bank	1st Interstate Bk of Ak	Alaska State Bank	Alaska Conti-nental Bk
Initial hiring, additional expense									
10%				X					
20%									
30%	X							X	X
40%									
50%									
Greater than 50%			X		X	X	X		
Permanent additional expenses of non-Alaskans									
no additional expense	X		X	X	X		X		
5%						X			
10%									X
15%									
20%								X	
30%									
Greater than 30%									

* Alaska Pacific Bank has changed its name to Key Bank; United Bank and Mutual Bank merged in the newly established Alliance Bank; Bank of the North and 1st Interstate Bank merged with National Bank of Alaska.

(4) Costs of designing separate accounting systems, management information systems and international counselling. This is a negligible cost for well-established multinational banks already having branches in the existing IFCs. The cost would be substantial, however, for local Alaskan banks wishing to operate in the proposed IFC.

(5) Foreign competition of foreign and non-Alaskan banks with Alaska's domestic banks in case a full-fledged offshore banking center is developed along the lines of those located in Bahrain, Hong Kong, Singapore and Panama. If the IBF model were deemed more appropriate, the competition could come from other U.S. participating banks having IBFs and from Canadian International Banking Centers (IBCs) in Vancouver and Montreal. This competition could be destructive if non-Alaskan banks were allowed to deal with on-shore borrowing and lending. The experience of other financial centers in Singapore and Hong Kong indicate that regulations can be enforced to preclude offshore institutions from dealing with domestic businesses. With the cooperation of local banks, the state government may take measures to help banks avoid this kind of mischief.

(6) Cost of economic infrastructure. Despite an adequate international airport in Anchorage, the state government may consider improving other elements of economic infrastructure to make IFC a viable and attractive idea. Improvement of economic infrastructure is aimed at promoting trade and direct investment flows which would consequently contribute to the advancement of international banking services in the proposed center. The process would include connecting Alaskan towns with paved highways, railroads and communications. It is not a secret, however, that the weather and topographical nature of Alaska would make it a very difficult and costly undertaking.

(7) Monitoring cost. The direct and overhead cost of monitoring the activities of the proposed IFC would be borne by the state government. Effective control of the fast and intricate activities of an IFC is a cumbersome and costly task for the state government to do.

(8) Tax revenue loss. If the decision is made to establish an IFC in Anchorage, the state government will have to enact more lenient and attractive tax legislation which will exempt the profit of all foreign financial institutions operating as offshore entities. Loss of revenue attributed to this policy represent an implied cost.

(9) Immigration and social problems. Taking advantage of the unconstitutionality of the state "local hire" laws, the branches of foreign banks established in Anchorage's proposed IFC may prefer to recruit their own nationals, thus depriving Alaskan residents from reaping the potential benefits of employment in the IFC. To facilitate smoother communication and to maintain profitable business with their domestic headquarters, some multinational banks prefer to hire their own nationals because of their knowledge of language and culture. This may lead to local political and social problems in the host state. Although the Immigration and Naturalization Services (INS) of the Department of Justice has legal solutions for expatriates, such as issuing H-1 visas for such professionals, it is expected that the INS office in Anchorage would incur more expenses in rendering service to and monitoring activities of more people. Despite these shortcomings, it might be a blessing to some financial centers, such as Miami, to utilize bilingual or multilingual immigrants in international banking, let alone furnish a decent source of income for some "ethnic" banks.

(10) Local inflation cost. It is documented in the literature on IFCs that a possible rise in local inflation comes from the increased demand on local transportation, communication, hotel and entertainment services, etc. This situation may create economic as well as political problems for the state government. Adverse effects of inflation is more relevant to an IFC, particularly situated in a commodity-producing state such as the state of Alaska. Many experts believe in the traditional link between commodity inflation and wage inflation. Should the price of oil surge, inflation of wages would accelerate, according to those experts. Some economists, however, argue that the traditional relationship has weakened considerably in the last decade, as competitive pressures from overseas have inspired employers to resist wage demands, and as painful memories of staff cuts, layoffs, and plant closures have led workers to temper those demands. Notwithstanding the possible harm that a hike in oil prices would cause to local wage inflation, the benefits of price increase to Alaska would definitely outweigh the inflationary cost.

SUMMARY

This article discusses the potential benefits and costs associated with establishing an international financial center in Anchorage. The potential benefits for local banks are: employment expansion; generation of net cash inflows from Eurocurrency trading, loan Eurosyndication, trading in new financial innovations, and export-import financing; countertrade financing;

and diversification of local banking services. The potential benefits that can be derived by non-banks are: alleviation of the present slump in the local real estate sector; improved profitability of the retail industry, saving and loan associations, insurance companies, brokerage house, finance companies, and credit unions; increase of local and state government revenues through license fees and expatriate taxes; creation of joint license fees and expatriate taxes; creation of joint ventures and venture capital opportunities to finance Alaska projects; and enhanced access to international capital markets through the proposed IFC as well as the Permanent Fund which will be able to generate tremendous international leverage and networking for Alaska businesses. Furthermore, one of the important benefits of an IFC is that it would help solve the "brain drain" problem from which local financial institutions are currently suffering. The potential costs and inconveniences of setting up an IFC in Anchorage are: cost of hiring non-Alaskans; cost of training and rehabilitating local employees; sunk cost of commissioning a full-fledged feasibility study; cost of designing separate accounting and management information systems; local concern of destructive competition of foreign and non-Alaskan banks with domestic banks; cost of building local economic infrastructure; government monitoring cost; tax revenue loss; immigration and social problems; and cost of higher local inflation.

REFERENCES

Alaska Permanent Fund Corporation. *1986 Annual Report.*

Alaska Statute. Title 36: Public Contracts. Sections 36.10.005, 36.10.006, and 36.01.990 on employment preferences and local hire.

Cooper, W. 1985. Some thoughts about Eurobonds. *Institutional Investors*: 157-158.

Essayyad, Musa, M. Haddad, and O. Benkato. 1988. Intratemporal stability of international diversification gains. A paper accepted for presentation at the Financial Management Association Meeting, New Orleans, forthcoming.

Essayyad, Musa, and H. K. Wu. 1988. The performance of U.S. international mutual funds. *Quarterly Journal of Business and Economics*, Autumn, forthcoming.

______________________. 1988. International portfolio diversification and the mean-semivariance CAPM: The case of U.S.-based international mutual funds. *Advances in Quantitative Finance and Accounting*, 1:1.

Fisher, F. J., III. 1979. *The Eurodollar bond market.* London: Euromoney Publications Limited.

Karp, R. 1982. How U.S. companies are catching the Eurobond habit. *Institutional Investors*, August: 208-212.

Kidwell, D. S., M. W. Marr, and G. R. Thompson. 1985. Eurodollar bonds: Alternative financing for United States companies. *Financial Management*, Autumn: 18-27.

Kidwell, D. S., M. W. Marr, and J. L. Trimble. 1987. Domestic versus Euromarket bond sale: A persistent borrowing cost advantage. A paper presented at the Financial Management Association Meetings, Las Vegas, October.

Laws of Alaska: Chapter No. 69. 1986. An act relating to preferential hire of Alaskans, approved by the Governor: May 31, 1986.

Lessard, Donald R. 1974. World, country, and industry relationships in equity returns: Implications for risk reduction through international diversification. *Financial Analyst Journal*, 32:32-38.

Lessard, Donald R., and Adrian E. Tschoegl. 1984. The Panama's international banking center: The direct employment effect. A paper prepared in connection with a report of the USAID technical assistance project to the Panamanian Ministry of Planning and Economic Policy.

Lessard, Donald R., and Adrian E. Tschoegl. 1985. Panama's international banking center: Where does it stand and what can be done to insure its continued viability and increase its contributions to the Panamanian economy?. Discussion Paper 85-2, Miami: International Banking Institute, University of Miami.

Li, David. 1987. Tapping international capital markets for Alaska projects: A Hong Kong banker's perspective. A paper presented at the International Banking and Finance Conference, Alaska Center for International Business, Anchorage.

Mabuchi, Nortioshi. 1987. Tapping international capital markets to finance Alaska projects: An analysis of sources and methods. A paper presented at the International Banking and Finance Conference, Alaska Center for International Business, University of Alaska, Anchorage.

McCarthy, Ian. 1979. Hosting offshore banks: Benefits and costs. *Finance and Development*, December: 45-48.

Moffett, Michael, and Arthur Stonehill. 1987. International Banking Facilities revisited: An alternative for Alaska? A paper presented at the International Banking and Finance Conference, Alaska Center for International Business, University of Alaska, Anchorage.

SEI Funds Evaluation Services. 1986. *Alaska Permanent Fund Investment Performance Report*.

Tschoegl, Adrian E. 1987. The benefits and costs of hosting financial centers. A paper presented at the International Banking and Finance Conference, Alaska Center for International Business, University of Alaska, Anchorage.

12. THE BENEFITS AND COSTS OF HOSTING FINANCIAL CENTERS

Adrian E. Tschoegl
SBCI Securities (Asia) Ltd., Tokyo Branch

INTRODUCTION

Should the government establish an offshore banking center within its jurisdiction? This question is one which many governments have faced and answered in the affirmative. The number of countries which have established such offshore centers has perhaps given rise to a common perception not only that the benefits must outweigh the costs, but also that the benefits of hosting financial centers are quite substantial. I present a framework here for evaluating the benefits and costs, direct and indirect, of hosting a financial center. At the same time I review the existing evidence to assess the net position and thus the implications for the supply of financial centers. The result is an assessment that, although the benefits are slight, the costs of hosting a center in small countries are often slighter. Thus, we see the frequent creation of such centers in open, island economies.

Much of the growing literature on international financial centers and on offshore banking in particular has focused on the growth of the offshore currency market and the implications for monetary policy. Kindleberger (1974) in his seminal study remarked that *financial centers* had not attracted much serious academic attention in the years following World War II. Since Kindleberger's study, there has been limited progress with work by Johnson (1976), Reed (1980 and 1981), Park (1982), and Choi (1984). Grubel's (1982) work on the welfare effects of free economic zones is also relevant, though more general. The growing journal literature on the costs and benefits of hosting an offshore banking center remains sparse. A number of articles address the issue of costs and benefits, but the estimates of the relevant factors are typically imprecise (Bhattacharya 1980 & 1982; Francis 1985; Hodjera 1978; Johnson 1976; McCarthy 1979; Sicat 1984). I draw on this literature for the evidence it can provide.

The next section provides some definitions and terminology. The third section deals with the benefits to a country hosting a center. The fourth section then looks at the other side of the issue, the costs. The final section presents the conclusions.

I would like to thank Tom Murtha and the participants at the Conference on Anchorage as a Financial Center sponsored by the Alaska Center for International Business for helpful comments on an earlier draft, and Virginia Hayes for her helpful editorial assistance.

TYPES OF CENTERS

The term "international financial center" in its broadest sense usually means a locus where foreign and external intermediation takes place, and which serves a region extending beyond the national boundaries of the host country. As Choi (1984) points out, the term "international financial" center has at least five different, nonexclusive meanings. These five meanings are:

a) a source of global financial influence

b) the apex of a hierarchy in financial central places

c) a market with peculiar sets of regulations

d) a geographic area for financial activities, and

e) an external currency market.

In this chapter I will use the term to include the last three meanings, in particular the sense of a locus for an external or offshore currency market.

It is common to distinguish two types of financial centers: the booking center and the functional center. The booking center is a legal home of record for transactions conducted elsewhere. Such a center simply provides an attractive jurisdiction. We will discuss the nature of the attractions below when we discuss free economic zones or offshore banking centers.

The functional financial center is a central marketplace for financial services, which encompass lending and borrowing, money transmission, corporate finance, and foreign exchange and money market trading. The need for a center grows out of the characteristics of many financial services. Generally, one cannot store or transport services because production and consumption take place simultaneously; instead, one must produce the services in contact with the customer. A bank can serve some of its customers' requirements indirectly via a correspondent relationship with another, local bank, but the deliverable range is quite limited. Although electronic communication has somewhat extended the range of types of services which banks can provide at a distance, many services require negotiation and intensive communication between bank and client. For these services, the banks must be physically close to their customers in order to minimize the transportation costs of bringing customers and service providers together.

Banks have two major motivations to go abroad: to service trade and to follow their corporate customers (Grubel 1977). The cities, which host the centers in which banks actually work, provide a convenient location for such activities. They are often major distribution points, sites for many corporate headquarters, and the centers of communication networks. All that a bank requires to operate in such a location is a sufficient volume of business from its customers. However, the agglomeration of several institutions in one place can have two additional consequences.

The first consequence of agglomeration of institutions is that an interbank market may develop in foreign exchange and deposits. Banks with an expertise in trading may enter when trading provides a profitable activity in itself. Callier (1986) argues that the economics of trading is such that banks wishing to trade profitably must be capable of trading around the clock, which now requires a presence in at least the three major financial centers of Tokyo, London and New York.

The second consequence of agglomeration of institutions is that a new entry can have two opposite effects on the market which the pre-existing institutions face. An entering bank increases the number of competitors for the existing business. It also can cause an increase in the total size of the market. The enlargement follows from the reduction in buyers' search costs due to the wider choice of services now available in the center when the new entrants are sellers of similar but not necessarily identical services. The reduction in buyers' search costs results in an increase in the demand for the sellers' services as buyers can now profitably come from further afield or even for minor purchases.

Some functional centers offer a more limited menu of services. Park (1982) distinguishes funding and collection centers. A funding center is a center which primarily is a locus for arranging credits to customers in the regions. The banks and financial institutions in the funding center have a net demand for funds which they satisfy by borrowing in the worldwide interbank market. In a collection center, on the other hand, the banks and other financial institutions are net collectors of deposits which they then sell to the worldwide interbank market.

In addition to specifying whether a center is a booking center or a functional center, one should also specify whether or not the center is a free economic zone. Grubel (1982) defines the free economic zone as an institutional innovation which "involves the deregulation of, or the lowering of tariffs and taxes on, a range of economic activities that can be effectively separated from the regulated, taxed and protected industries of which they are a part." All booking centers and many functional centers are also free economic zones.

In banking, the free economic zones are more usually called offshore banking centers. Offshore banking centers are completely analogous to free trade zones for manufactured goods. In offshore banking centers, the host country's regulatory authorities apply more lenient regulations to activities involving nonresidents or currencies which are not the legal tender of the host jurisdiction than to those transactions involving home country residents or the national currency. Generally, the most important exemption in such offshore banking centers is the exemption of deposits from the implicit tax of required reserves. Frequently the authorities also exempt the banks' income from services to nonresidents from income taxation. The regulatory authorities take limited responsibility for the institutions in the offshore center with respect to prudential supervision. The authorities particularly take no responsibility for providing a lender of last resort facility to the offshore banks with respect to their offshore currency deposits.

BENEFITS

Direct Benefits

Employment. Despite the political saliency of employment effects, the existing literature on financial centers contains almost no estimates of the proportion of the jobs in those centers which one can attribute to offshore banking alone. One exception is a recent paper on Panama's international banking center (Lessard and Tschoegl 1987). Lessard and Tschoegl (1987) found that, in 1983, international banking activities provided employment for 1,430 Panamanians (and 213 expatriates), representing about 16.4 percent of the total Panamanian employment in banking. This contrasted with the fact that the international assets of U.S. $37.5 billion accounted for 87.6 percent of the total banking system assets in 1983. These 1,430 jobs earned an average U.S. $10,807 each, producing the payroll contribution of international activities of U.S. $15.5 million. Inclusion of expatriate salaries (averaging US$25,282 each) increased the total contribution to U.S. $20.6 million, or 1.1 percent of Panama's GDP. This compares favorably with the overall employment in international banking representing only about 0.3 percent of the total employment in Panama.

Francis and Tschoegl (1987) have made similar calculations for the contribution of offshore banking to employment in the Bahamas. The calculations suggest that international activity generates 426 jobs in the domestic commercial banks, 40 in the other local financial institutions, and 536 in the offshore banks. The total of 1,002 jobs represents 32.7 percent of the total employment of 3,060 persons in the financial sector in the Bahamas. By contrast, the total external assets of B$143.67 billion represent 99.2 percent of the country's banking system assets. Thus, the 0.8 percent of domestic assets was associated with 66.1 percent of the total employment in banking in the Bahamas. At the margin, a B$1,000 million change in international assets was associated with a change of about one job.

This marginal impact in the Bahamas is substantially smaller than the marginal impact Lessard and Tschoegl (1987) found in Panama. Lessard and Tschoegl (1987) found that a U.S. $1,000 million change in international deposits and a commensurate change in international assets was associated with a change of about 27 jobs for Panamanians, and 4 to 5 jobs for expatriates. The exchange rate between the U.S. and the Bahamian dollars is almost one for one. The employment generating ability of international banking in the Bahamas was therefore about one thirty-second of that in Panama. The difference in employment intensity may reflect the greater proportion of pure booking activities in the Bahamas.

Panama has always insisted that all foreign banks in Panama maintain a functional presence, not merely a legal one.

Gerakis and Roncesvalles (1983) estimated the employment creation of Offshore Banking Units (OBUs) in Bahrain in 1978 at 1,000 jobs. They arrived at 1,000 jobs by multiplying the fifty or so OBUs by 20, which they stated was a reasonable assumption of the average number of Bahrainis for each OBU, either on its staff or in ancillary services. The total Bahraini labor force at the time was on the order of 80,000 workers, and total assets of the offshore sector were US$23.4 billion.

Jones (1984) provides some figures for the Cayman Islands. In June of 1983, the foreign currency liabilities of U.S. bank branches in the Cayman Islands totaled US$46 billion. Four hundred and fifty banks made up the financial sector. The 38 principal banks or trust companies of this group had a total staff of 858 persons. Ninety-two percent of these people were employed in banks or trust companies with an A license. An A license permits the institution in question to operate as a full service bank and to carry on business both within and outside the islands. Thus some, perhaps substantial, part of this employment represents staffing for local retail banking.

These results support the general consensus in Bhattacharya (1980 & 1982), Francis (1985), McCarthy (1979), and Sicat (1984) that the absolute number of new jobs which offshore banking creates is slight. Often, much of the assets and deposits on the books of offshore banks represent assigning a legal jurisdiction for tax and administrative purposes to transactions arranged and processed elsewhere. The transactions generate employment, but not necessarily in the offshore center. However, "slight" employment creation is a relative term. As these authors have argued, countries with small populations and few alternative sources of employment may nevertheless be interested in creating and maintaining an offshore center.

Government Revenues. As with any other industry, banking and financial services add to government revenues through the corporate taxes the firms pay, and the income and consumption taxes the employees pay. Furthermore, the governments of some financial centers charge those banks resident in the centers an annual license fee. Just as in employment, the net revenue benefits of offshore centers are likely to be smaller than might appear at first glance. The reason is that governments compete away the revenues and may provide socially costly services free to the banks in an attempt to draw bank establishment. This is especially true for offshore banking centers. We will deal more with this point under the rubric of the costs of hosting offshore centers.

Bhattacharya (1982) reports that bank and trust company license fees generated 6 percent and 13 percent of local government revenues respectively in the Bahamas and Cayman Islands. In 1983, the total license and fee income of US$12 million generated by offshore activities in the

Cayman Islands represented some 21 percent of government revenues (Jones 1984). Francis (1985) reports that the Bahamian government's annual intake from license fees from the 363 institutions licensed to conduct business within or from within the Bahamas fluctuates between $3.2 to $4.6 million. The 26 OBUs in the Philippines paid a total of US$12.5 million in taxes over the period 1977 to June 1983. Total assets of OBUs in the Philippines in June of 1983 were US$4.47 billion (Sicat 1984).

One must offset an unknown but possibly sizable tax cost of the center against these amounts. Banks engaged in both onshore and offshore activities within a center can reduce their corporate tax obligation on domestic activities by allocating some of the costs they incur on offshore activities against the local onshore operations. By allocating joint costs such as, for example, those of the computer system or the salary of the general manager to its onshore activities, a bank operating in a center could shift profits from its taxed onshore activities to its untaxed offshore activities.

Expenditures. The operations of banks involve expenditures which have a multiplier effect throughout the economy, generating additional employment. Offshore activities do not, however, generate extensive expenditures. McCarthy (1979) suggested that a ratio of 0.05 percent of international assets would give a reasonable estimate of expenditures in the case of pure booking activities. Combining figures for the Bahamas from Francis (1985) on total expenditures, with an estimate of offshore liabilities in June of 1983 of US$137 billion, gives ratios of expenditures to total international assets of 0.085 percent (including government fees) and 0.082 percent (net of government fees).

A study for the Australian government on the establishment of an offshore banking center in Sydney used ratios ranging between 0.1 percent and 0.3 percent (Whitlam 1984). The Whitlam (1984) study used a multiplier of 1.75 to calculate the sum of the direct and indirect expenditures. Lessard and Tschoegl (1985) applied ratios of between 0.05 percent and 0.3 percent and a multiplier of 1.75 to international assets of banks in Panama of US$37.5 billion. The resulting estimate of annual direct and indirect expenditures ranged between US$33 million and US$197 million.

Human Capital Formation. The jobs an offshore banking center creates may contribute to human capital formation when employees receive training and learn skills on the job. This human capital formation may result in some positive externalities. For example, employees changing jobs can transfer skills learned in the banking sector to other firms.

None of the studies of which we are aware has attempted to quantify the net amount of human capital formation. The study by Lessard and Tschoegl (1985) comes closest. They estimate that average annual salaries for Panamanians in international banks were US$767 higher than those of Panamanians in domestic banking in private banks. This suggests that the contribution to Panama in 1983 of having 1,430 persons engaged in international activities rather than in domestic banking was about US$1.1 million. If we use a real (net of expected inflation) discount rate of 2 percent, the present value of a perpetual annuity of US$1.1 million is US$55 million. If one were to assume that the relevant opportunity cost was not what the employees could earn in domestic banking but rather what they could earn in some other, less skilled, clerical occupation, the amount would be higher. Even so, the amount of human capital formation would be of only limited interest to a developed economy with close to full employment.

Indirect Benefits

The presence of foreign banks in an international banking center can provide major indirect benefits to the host country. These benefits derive from the presence of foreign banks and hence flow from functional centers, but not from pure booking centers. One indirect benefit is the effect of the foreign bank presence on the center host country's access to capital. The second, and perhaps more important, benefit is the effect of the presence of the foreign banks on the efficiency of the domestic banking system. A number of authors have made the argument that the presence of a center in a country should aid the country's integration into the world capital market, resulting in increased availability and lower cost of capital to potential borrowers. Grubel (1980) suggests this capital access effect as a benefit which would follow from the establishment of a regional currency market in Nairobi.

The common argument for the positive effect of a banking center on host country access to world capital markets is that familiarity with a country, by reducing uncertainty, increases a bank's willingness to lend to that country, other things being equal. One argument in the debate on establishing an offshore financial center in India was that "the foreign banks linking in a Centre in India are bound to get closer and better perceptions of the strengths of the Indian economy and its political stability than from abroad" (Tandon 1984). Sicat (1984), discussing offshore banks in the Philippines, suggests that "The physical presence of some offshore banks may be good reason to provide larger credit lines for the country than would otherwise be the case." Thus there are arguments for both the price effect, i.e., a lower cost of borrowing, and the quantity effect, i.e., the larger amount borrowed. Whatever the logic of the argument, there is no empirical evidence on the price effect. The empirical evidence on the quantity effect is limited, though supportive of the argument of a positive effect of foreign bank presence.

Tschoegl (1987) used data on Panama, Turkey, and India to examine the evidence on the relationship between banks' presence in a country and their willingness to lend to that country or arrange borrowing for it. For all three countries, the results showed that among the top managers or providers of loans to Latin America, Turkey, and India, those banks with an organizational presence in the countries in question were more likely to be lenders to the country or to have arranged a greater volume of loans. In addition to their function as catalysts for country borrowing, foreign banks in a center could be catalysts for flows of private capital. In 1977 the Bank of Thailand explained its decision to permit the establishment of the European Asian Bank in Bangkok, the first approval in ten years (Tschoegl 1981). The Bank of Thailand said, "The establishment of a branch of a German commercial bank in Thailand might bring benefits to the Thai economy, and encouraged (sic) investors from the EEC to give increased interests (sic) to Thailand."

One can question how much foreign banks do in fact attract investment from their home countries to the host country. We do have some anecdotal evidence from an anonymous, unpublished and confidential internal document from a bank assessing the effect of foreign banks in Atlanta as of 1983. The author(s) of the report quote the Deputy State Banking Commissioner for the State of Georgia to the effect that after two or three years of foreign banks in Atlanta, he could cite no instances where foreign banks attracted investment in the area which would not have come otherwise. However, the Commissioner did feel that the foreign bank presence provided "one piece of the puzzle" which determined whether a company might invest in the Southeast United States. The presence of home country banks could prove decisive to firms choosing between otherwise identical foreign locations. By speeding up information flows, the presence could also speed up the rate of decision making.

For developed countries, the possibly more important indirect benefit of bank presence is the effect on the efficiency of the domestic banking system. The efficiency gains have two dimensions. First, there are the benefits of increased competition on the prices of existing services. The entry of foreign banks, for whom the local market is but a small part of their worldwide operations, increases the scope for competitive rivalry in the local market. The result will be a narrowing of spreads between lending and deposit rates either to the legal or to the competitive minimum, whichever is more binding. Similarly, prices for other services such as foreign exchange, letters of credit, and so forth will also come under competitive pressure.

We are not aware of any formal studies of the magnitude of this effect in any country. The author(s) of the just discussed anonymous, unpublished and internal report on the effect of foreign banks in Atlanta found that foreign banks had aimed primarily at the top corporate accounts where credit was not a problem and where the banks could hope to garner market share on the basis of price alone. Few of the foreign banks had aimed at the middle market, and the banks generally had avoided both secured and riskier credits. The middle market, in the author(s) opinion, had seen limited results from foreign bank presence.

The second efficiency gain derives from the introduction of new services. The foreign banks, in an attempt to carve out unique niches, may introduce service hitherto unavailable in the local market. Given demand, the foreign banks can readily make available those products and services that they offer elsewhere. As a result, customers will face lower search (including travel) costs for new bank services. The anonymous study of foreign banks in Atlanta, referred to earlier, reported that foreign banks did appear to have provided some assistance in foreign trade. Local companies may have had easier access to foreign markets because the foreign banks had a familiarity or presence in countries where the local banks could not be of service. The effect, though, was not measurable, and many of the services were available from United States banks from other states.

COSTS

A financial center can generate not only benefits for its host country, but also costs. The costs may be direct, such as the need to provide physical and legal infrastructure and the loss of revenue from the waiving of taxes, or indirect, such as the effect on the government's freedom of action.

Direct Costs

Banking centers require some physical infrastructure in the form of transportation and communication services, buildings, and hotel facilities for visiting customers. Grubel (1980) points out, with respect to Nairobi, that a sudden influx of banks would increase demand for housing and office space. This could add to upward pressure on prices and adversely affect the living standards of existing residents if wage increases did not keep pace with the increased cost of living. In the longer run, one could count on supply to respond to the change in demand. The legal and regulatory environment is another major aspect of a banking system infrastructure. Regulation involves expenditure because of the need to monitor, evaluate, and intervene when necessary in the banks' activities. The reputation of a center is a public good and a function of the oversight of the regulatory authorities, an oversight that is costly to create and maintain.

Part of the attraction of a center lies in the waiving of taxes on particular activities, as we have noted earlier. When a government waives taxes on the existing activities of existing firms in order to draw new activities and entrants, the net revenue effect may be negative. Singapore had to lower its taxes on earnings from offshore activities from 40 percent to 10 percent because of competition from Hong Kong where a 10 percent rate was in effect. Florida repealed the intangible tax (U.S. $1 per U.S. $1,000) relating to international banking transactions such as notes, loans, accounts receivable, bonds and stocks. It also eliminated the documentary tax (U.S. $0.15 per $100) for all documents and instruments whose primary purpose was payment or repayment of money (Roussakis 1981).

Indirect Costs

The major indirect costs of a banking center reside in the limitations on the government's freedom of action which accompany offering such a center. Not only is there a constraint on tax policy, but governments may find that the presence of foreign banks or the desire to draw the banks gives rise to other constraints. For instance, the coexistence of domestic and foreign banks limits the ability of the government to engage in cross-subsidization of selected sectors through the banking system (Tschoegl 1981).

The limitations on the government's freedom of action are more meaningful issues for national governments than for those of sub-national jurisdictions. In discussing the competition between San Francisco and Los Angeles, Choi (1984) pointed out that both centers were rule takers rather than rule makers as both fell under the regulatory supervision of the U.S. and California authorities. Any regulatory changes imposed by either level of government would apply to both centers, and thus there was little scope for differentiating the centers in terms of their regulatory environments. That is, there was little scope for either city government to engage in policies or to refrain from policies in order to influence bank location decisions.

The limitations on the government's freedom of action are more meaningful for socially activist governments than for laissez faire governments. It also matters whether the financial center would represent a large political interest in the country or not. A government committed to an activist role and intolerant of opposition would be less willing to permit the creation of an alternative important center of power than would a government committed simply to providing a favorable environment for commerce. Malta's government has not so far encouraged the development of the island as an offshore banking center despite the island's many otherwise favorable economic characteristics (Haney 1984). The government took over and completely owns the largest commercial bank in the country, and is a majority shareholder in the other two commercial banks. Tschoegl (1981) found that government ownership of major commercial banks, a proxy for a desire to control the economy, was negatively correlated with openness to foreign banks. He also found a correlation between government ownership of banks and countries' political and economic systems.

CONCLUSION

We have not dealt with the issue of the effects of financial centers on global welfare. Plender (1987) suggests that the competitive approach to deregulation in different financial centers is a zero-sum game. That is, attracting footloose international banking business by offering reduced regulation and lower taxes and transactions costs may simply shift business and jobs from one location to another with little net benefit to the world economy apart from a marginal increase in financial efficiency. Grubel (1983) argues that the desire to avoid taxes has led to the development of locational and currency diversion costs which are likely to be large and to be continuing to grow in the future.

The picture that emerges from our discussion of the costs and benefits to a government of hosting a center suggests that the benefits of an offshore center are slight, but the costs are often slighter. For many governments, particularly those of small, open economies, the direct costs of regulatory infrastructure and the indirect costs of constraints on policy freedom are minimal. The governments minimize the costs by limiting their oversight and by insulating the banking center in a free economic zone. The slight direct benefits in terms of employment creation, human capital formation and fee income, and the similarly slight indirect benefits of efficiency and capital attraction effects are still of interest to those governments whose economies provide few alternative sources of employment and income.

Functional centers are both more costly and provide more benefits. However, a government policy initiative in the form of the regulatory and tax environment which they create are a necessary but not sufficient condition for the development of a functional center. A government can make a center possible. Whether or not a functional center develops is a question of bank demand for a center in the location in question.

REFERENCES

Bhattacharya, A. K. 1980. Offshore banking in the Caribbean by U.S. commercial banks. *Journal of International Business Studies*, 11(1):37-46.

Bhattacharya, A. K. 1982. Offshore banking costs and benefits. In Phillip D. Grub, Tan Chwee Huat, Kwan Kuen-Chor, and George H. Rott, eds., *East Asia: Dimensions of international business*. Sydney: Prentice-Hall of Australia.

Callier, Phillipe. 1986. Professional trading. Exchange rate risk and the growth of international banking: A note. *Banca Nazionale del Lavoro Quarterly Review*, 159:423-428.

Choi, Sang-Rim. 1984. *Economic rationale and consequences of international banking and financial centers*. Unpublished PhD dissertation, University of Michigan.

Choi, Sang-Rim, Adrian E. Tschoegl, & Chwo-Ming Yu. 1986. Banks and the world's major financial centers, 1970-1980. *Weltwirtschaftliches Archiv*, 122(1):48-64.

Francis, Carlene Y. 1985. The offshore banking sector in the Bahamas. *Social and Economic Studies*, 34(4):91-110.

Francis, Carlene Y., and Adrian E. Tschoegl. 1987. Offshore banking in the Bahamas: The direct employment effects. Paper in progress, University of Michigan.

Gerakis, Andreas S. and O. Roncesvalles. 1983. Bahrain's offshore banking center. *Economic Development and Cultural Change*, 31(2):271-293.

Grubel, Herbert G. 1977. A theory of multinational banking. *Banca Nazionale del Lavoro Quarterly Review*, 123:349-364.

______________. 1980. About the establishment of an Afro-currency market in Nairobi. In John S. Chapman and Charles P. Kindleberger, eds., *Flexible Exchange Rates and the Balance of Payments*. Amsterdam: North Holland.

____________. 1982. Towards a theory of free economic zones. *Weltwirtschaftliches Archiv*, 118(1):39-62.

____________. 1983. The new international banking. *Banca Nazionale del Lavoro Quarterly Review*, 146:263-284.

Haney, Siobhan. 1984. Malta sticks to domestic banking. *The Banker*, August:43-44.

Hodjera, Z. 1978. The Asian currency market: Singapore as a regional finance center. *International Monetary Fund Staff Papers*, 25(2):221-253.

Johnson, Harry G. 1976. Panama as a regional financial center: A preliminary analysis of development contribution. *Economic Development and Cultural Change*, 24:261-286.

Jones, David. 1984. US shadow over the Caymans. *The Banker*, May:43-51.

Kaufman, George C. 1970. Bank employment: A cross-section analysis of the world's largest banks. *Journal of Money, Credit and Banking*, 2(1):101-111.

Kindleberger, Charles P. 1974. *The formation of financial centers: A study in comparative economic history*. Princeton: Princeton Studies in International Finance, Princeton University.

Lessard, Donald R. and Adrian E. Tschoegl. 1987. Panama's international banking center: The direct employment effects. *Journal of Banking and Finance*, 11(4) forthcoming.

Lessard, Donald R. and Adrian E. Tschoegl. 1985. *Panama's international banking center: Where does it stand and what can be done to insure its continued viability and increase its contributions to the Panamanian economy?* Discussion Paper 85-2, International Business and Banking Institute, University of Miami.

McCarthy, Ian. 1979. Hosting offshore banks: Benefits and costs. *Finance and Development*.

Park, Yoon S. 1982. The economics of offshore financial centers. *Columbia Journal of World Business*, 17(4):31-35.

Plender, John. 1987. London's big bank in international context. *International Affairs*: 39-48.

Reed, Howard Curtis. 1980. The ascent of Tokyo as an international financial center. *Journal of International Business Studies*, 11(3):19-35.

Reed, Howard Curtis. 1981. *The preeminence of international financial centers*. New York: Praeger.

Roussakis, Emmanuel N. 1981. The edges come to Miami. *The Bankers Magazine*, 164(3):82-91.

Sicat, Gerardo P. 1984. Offshore banking and the Philippine economy. *Journal of Philippine Development*, 11(2):203-229.

Tandon, Prakash. 1984. Transnational banking. *State Bank of India Monthly Review*, May 23 (5):203-220.

Tschoegl, Adrian E. *The regulation of foreign banks: Policy formation in countries outside the United States*. Monograph 1981-2, Monograph Series in Finance and Economics, Salomon Brothers Center for the Study of Financial Institutions.

Tschoegl, Adrian E. 1987. Foreign bank presence and developing country access to world capital markets. Unpublished paper, University of Michigan.

Whitlam, Nicholas, Chairman. 1984. Report of the committee established by the premier of New South Wales to report on the steps necessary to establish offshore banking activity in Australia, with particular reference to Sydney. Unpublished report.

PART III

NEW APPRAISAL OF INTERNATIONAL BANKING FACILITIES

13. THE DEVELOPMENT OF INTERNATIONAL BANKING FACILITIES

Sydney J. Key and Henry S. Terrell
Division of International Finance
Board of Governors of the Federal Reserve System

INTRODUCTION

The Federal Reserve Board permitted banking offices located in the United States to establish International Banking Facilities (IBFs) beginning in December 1981. The purpose was to allow these banking offices to conduct a deposit and loan business with foreign residents, including foreign banks, without being subject to reserve requirements or to the interest rate ceilings then in effect.[1] IBFs are also exempt from the insurance coverage and assessments imposed by the Federal Deposit Insurance Corporation. In addition, a number of states have encouraged banking institutions to establish IBFs by granting favorable tax treatment under state or local law for IBF operations. As a result, banking offices located in the United States can, through their IBFs, conduct transactions with foreign residents in a regulatory environment broadly similar to that of the Eurocurrency market without having to use an offshore facility.

As of December 1987, more than 540 banking institutions--including U.S.-chartered banks, U.S. agencies and branches of foreign banks, and U.S. offices of Edge corporations--had established IBFs. (See Table 1.) Although IBFs have been established by banking offices in 24 states and the District of Columbia, more than three-quarters of total IBF assets are accounted for by institutions located in New York. As is also common in other international banking centers, a large portion of IBF activity consists of interbank transactions, that is, transactions with other IBFs and with banks in foreign countries. U.S. agencies and branches of foreign banks (especially Japanese banks) play a major role in IBF activity, accounting for more than two-thirds of IBF assets.

With total external assets of more than $275 billion, IBFs accounted for nearly 7 percent of worldwide external banking activity as of December

---

The authors wish to thank their colleagues at the Federal Reserve Board for their comments and suggestions. The views expressed in this paper are those of the authors and should not be interpreted as representing the view of the Board of Governors of the Federal Reserve System or anyone else on its staff.

TABLE 1

Number of IBFs, by State and Type of Establishing Entity, December 31, 1987

State	U.S.-chartered banks	Agencies and branches	Offices of Edge corporations	Total
New York	47	190	17	254
California	20	69	11	100
Florida	26	29	24	79
Illinois	7	19	2	28
Texas	10	0	4	14
District of Columbia	7	3	1	11
Pennsylvania	5	2	1	8
Washington	3	4	0	7
Georgia	4	2	0	6
Ohio	6	0	0	6
Massachusetts	3	1	2	6
New Jersey	5	0	0	5
Others[1]	17	0	2	19
TOTAL	160	319	64	543

[1] Arkansas, Colorado, Connecticut, Delaware, Hawaii, Kentucky, Louisiana, Michigan, North Carolina, Rhode Island, South Carolina, Virginia, and Wisconsin.

Source: Federal Reserve Board.

1987; another 5-1/2 percent of this activity is recorded on the domestic (non-IBF) books of institutions located in the United States.[2] In comparison, London accounts for 21 percent of total external banking activity, and the Japanese offshore market, which is similar to IBFs and was introduced in December 1986, accounts for about 4 1/2 percent. Although IBFs have continued to grow since their introduction in 1981, this growth does not appear to be associated with any major shift of business away from London. For U.S.-chartered banks, the main effect seems to have been a shift of business that would otherwise have been booked at their Caribbean branches to their IBFs.

The history of the IBF proposal is reviewed in the second section of this chapter. Federal Reserve Board regulations for IBFs are summarized in the third section, and the fourth section discusses state tax treatment of IBFs. IBF activities and the use of IBFs in comparison with domestic offices and with foreign branches are analyzed in the fifth section. The sixth section evaluates the growth of IBFs in relation to activities in other international banking centers. The final section presents the conclusions.

HISTORY OF THE IBF PROPOSAL

During the 1960s, the Eurocurrency market grew rapidly, as did participation in that market by foreign branches of U.S.-chartered banks. The development of the Eurocurrency market resulted in part from U.S. regulatory requirements such as interest rate ceilings, maturity limitations, and reserve requirements on deposits at banks in the United States. In addition, at least initially, some large depositors had a preference for holding dollar-denominated deposits at banking offices beyond the jurisdiction of U.S. law.[3] U.S. measures to reduce net capital outflows from the United States that were in effect from the mid-1960s until January 1974 also contributed to the growth of the offshore banking market.[4]

Although dollar-denominated assets and liabilities predominate, Euromarket activity now includes transactions in all major currencies and is conducted in international financial centers around the world. However, the "Eurocurrency" market is a rather narrow concept in that it includes only deposits and loans booked outside the country in whose currency they are denominated; transactions conducted with foreign residents that are denominated in domestic currencies, an important part of international banking, are not included. Thus, strictly speaking, IBF transactions with foreign residents denominated in U.S. dollars are not part of the Eurocurrency market because IBFs are located in the United States. However, the traditional concept of the Eurocurrency market has been supplanted by a broader concept of "international" banking transactions that is now widely used.[5] This concept includes *all* "external" transactions (that is, transactions with foreign residents denominated in domestic or foreign currencies) as well as transactions with domestic residents in foreign currencies.

Proposals for banking facilities similar to IBFs were first put forward in the early 1970s to allow U.S. banks more flexibility under the Voluntary Foreign Credit Restraint (VFCR) program, which set ceilings on claims on foreigners held by U.S. banking offices. The proposals would have enabled domestic banking offices to lend funds raised abroad to foreign residents without being subject to these ceilings. After the removal of the VFCR and other U.S. capital controls in January 1974, IBF-type proposals reemerged as a possible method of reducing the burden of domestic reserve requirements and interest rate limitations. Proposals for a "foreign window" or a "free-trade banking zone" were studied within the government as a way of granting regulatory relief. The Federal Reserve Board was, however, concerned about the effect that the adoption of such proposals might have on the conduct of monetary policy and on competition among groups of U.S. banks.

The proposal that culminated in the final IBF regulations was submitted to the Board by the New York Clearing House Association in July 1978. The month before, the New York state legislature had enacted a statute granting favorable tax treatment to IBFs under New York state and city law, subject to the condition that the Federal Reserve Board take action to exempt IBF activities from reserve requirements and interest rate limitations.

The Board considered the IBF proposal in December 1978, and decided to request comment on a number of its features and to analyze further the issues involved. After passage of the Monetary Control Act of 1980, which broadened the Federal Reserve Board's authority to impose reserve requirements and explicitly confirmed the Board's authority to exempt IBFs from such requirements, the Board again considered IBFs. In June 1981 the Board adopted final regulations, which became effective December 3, 1981.

FEDERAL RESERVE BOARD REGULATIONS

Although IBFs are often regarded as engaging in loan and deposit transactions, in reality an IBF is not an institution but rather a set of asset and liability accounts segregated on the books of its establishing entity. Under Federal Reserve Board regulations, IBFs may be established by a U.S.-chartered depository institution, a U.S. branch or agency of a foreign bank, or a U.S. office of an Edge or Agreement corporation.[6] No formal application is required to establish an IBF. However, before doing so, the establishing entity must notify its Federal Reserve Bank and agree to comply with the Federal Reserve Board's regulations, including recordkeeping, accounting, and reporting requirements.

Transactions that may be booked at an IBF are specified in the Federal Reserve Board's Regulation D (Reserve Requirements of Depository Institutions). In exempting IBFs from reserve requirements and from the interest rate ceilings then in effect, the Board intended to facilitate the provision of international banking services to foreign customers at banking offices in the United States. However, to avoid complicating the conduct of domestic monetary policy, the Board wanted to insulate U.S. economic activity from IBF transactions. Among the Board's principal concerns was the possibility that IBF accounts might be substituted for transaction accounts included in the monetary aggregates or be used to circumvent reserve requirements or interest rate ceilings. Consequently, the Board's regulations impose a number of limitations on IBF activities that do not apply to foreign branches of U.S.-chartered banks.

First, IBF loan and deposit customers are restricted to foreign residents (including banks), other IBFs, and the entity establishing the IBF. Lending to or accepting deposits from any other U.S. resident is prohibited. Net funds obtained by a U.S. banking office from its own IBF are subject to Eurocurrency reserve requirements in the same manner as net funds obtained from its foreign offices because such funds are used to finance the bank's domestic activities in the United States.

Second, limitations are placed on the maturity of "IBF time deposits," which may be in the form of deposits, borrowings, placements, or similar instruments. An IBF may offer such deposits with an overnight maturity to banks in foreign countries, to other IBFs, and to domestic and foreign offices of its establishing entity. However, in order to ensure that they are not close substitutes for reservable transaction accounts at domestic banking offices, IBF time deposits of nonbank foreign residents are required to have a minimum maturity of two days.[7]

Third, transactions of nonbank customers at IBFs are subject to a minimum amount of $100,000; a withdrawal of less than this amount is permitted only to close out an account or to withdraw accumulated interest. The Board believed that this limit would be sufficient to preserve the wholesale nature of IBF business but would not be so high as to prevent smaller banking institutions that engage in international transactions from making use of an IBF. Deposits and withdrawals of banks at IBFs are not subject to any minimum amount.

Fourth, IBFs are prohibited from issuing negotiable instruments because such instruments might be purchased from the original holders in secondary market transactions by U.S. residents who are not eligible deposit customers of IBFs.

Fifth, an IBF may extend credit to a foreign nonbank customer only if the proceeds are used to finance operations of the borrower (or its affiliates) outside the United States. Similarly, under the Board's regulations, an IBF may accept a deposit from a foreign nonbank customer only if the funds are used to support operations of the depositor (or its affiliates) outside the United States.[8]

Sixth, IBFs may engage in secondary market transactions only to the extent that such transactions are consistent with the Board's overall restrictions on IBF activities. IBFs may purchase (or sell) assets such as loans, loan participations, securities, certificates of deposit, and bankers acceptances from (or to) any domestic or foreign customer (except domestic affiliates of the establishing entity), provided that the assets are IBF-eligible and that the transactions are at arm's length and without recourse.[9] A negotiable instrument issued by a third party and acquired by an IBF on the secondary market may be sold by the IBF only if the instrument is not guaranteed by the establishing entity or its affiliates. The purpose of this limitation is to prohibit transactions that would be functionally equivalent to the issuance of negotiable instruments by an IBF.

The Federal Reserve Board's limitations on IBF activities are more restrictive than those it imposes on the activities of foreign branches of U.S.-chartered banks.[10] In contrast to IBFs, such branches are not prohibited from accepting deposits from and making loans to U.S. residents. There are no limitations on the maturities of deposits at such branches provided that they are payable only outside the United States. In addition, unlike IBFs, foreign branches of U.S. banks may issue negotiable instruments, such as certificates of deposits and bankers acceptances, and they may purchase or sell assets in secondary market transactions without restriction.

For purposes of U.S. reserve requirements, foreign branches and IBFs are treated in a similar manner. Deposits at foreign branches of U.S. banks that are payable only outside the United States are not subject to U.S. reserve requirements. Net advances by a foreign branch to its U.S. parent bank, purchases of assets from its parent bank, and branch loans to U.S. residents are included in the calculation of the parent bank's required Eurocurrency reserves because such transactions provide sources of funding for the bank's domestic activities.

TAX LAWS AND REGULATIONS

Favorable tax treatment under state and local statutes has been an important factor for banks in assessing the attractiveness of establishing an IBF. Where favorable state or local tax treatment for IBFs has been granted, there are usually tax advantages in booking loans at an IBF rather than at a domestic office. For some U.S.-chartered banks, particularly under New York state and city law prior to 1985 and also under an optional method of taxation under present New York law, there have also been tax advantages to booking loans at an IBF rather than at a shell branch. The reason is that, in some instances, the tax authorities have attempted to apply state and local tax laws so that certain income from shell branches would, in effect, be treated as income of the domestic office and thus subject to state and local taxation. In such a situation, a bank might prefer to use an IBF instead of a shell branch in order to rely on specific statutory provisions granting tax relief to IBFs.

At least ten states, including New York, have enacted special tax legislation for IBFs.[11] The provisions for tax relief differ among the states, reflecting differences in both the underlying state tax structures and the amount of tax relief provided for IBF operations. There have been no modifications to federal tax statutes for IBFs; as a result, income arising from IBF activities is subject to U.S. federal income taxation in the same manner as other income of the establishing entity.

Because the bulk of IBF activity is located there, the tax treatment of IBFs under New York law will be summarized briefly. Although New York was the first state to grant favorable tax treatment to IBFs, it initially limited that relief in a number of ways. The 1978 New York statute established a complex formula for determining the amount of IBF income that could be deducted from New York taxable income in computing New York state and city income taxes. This procedure reflected the provisions of New York tax law then in effect for determining the portion of a bank's overall income subject to New York taxation.[12]

In 1985, in order to tax banks in a manner similar to other corporations, to treat banks and thrifts similarly, and to make tax calculations more predictable and less likely to require adjustment upon audit, New York changed its overall approach to taxation of banks with the introduction of a three-factor apportionment formula, and the treatment of IBFs also changed.[13] Under the 1985 statute, the portion of a bank's adjusted federal taxable income that is subject to New York taxation is determined by an apportionment formula that takes into account the ratio of New York to total receipts, deposits, and payroll. In accordance with this approach, banks now have the option of treating IBF receipts, deposits, and payroll as if they were located outside New York for purposes of the formula, that is, treating IBFs in the same manner as branches located outside New York state.

Under the new law, the state also allowed banks the option of continuing to use the pre-1985 separate accounting approach for IBFs. Under this option, adjusted federal taxable income may be reduced by the amount of the IBF's "adjusted eligible net income," which, as noted above, is computed according to a rather complex formula.[14] Most of the major domestic banks have chosen to continue to use the separate accounting option for their IBFs. By contrast, the vast majority of U.S. agencies and branches of foreign banks use the formula apportionment option.

IBF ACTIVITIES

IBFs have continued to grow since their inception in December 1981. Their activities consist primarily of transactions with banks, a pattern similar to that in other Euromarket centers. As of December 1987, claims on unrelated parties (that is, total assets excluding claims on the establishing entity and its foreign offices) at large IBFs amounted to about $180 billion.[15] (See Table 2.)

Claims on unrelated banks, including both foreign banks and other IBFs, were the largest component of IBF assets, accounting for nearly 60 percent of the claims of large IBFs on unrelated parties. However, this overall figure masks differences between U.S. banks and agencies and branches of foreign banks in their use of IBFs. In the aggregate, claims on banks accounted for more than two-thirds of claims on unrelated parties at large IBFs of agencies and branches; the comparable figure for large IBFs of U.S. banks was less than one-third.

This difference in the importance of interbank activity is accounted for by the more extensive use of the inter-IBF market by the agencies and branches of foreign banks. The less extensive use of the inter-IBF market by U.S. banks reflects the fact that domestic banks are relatively more active in the federal funds market and other U.S. money markets than are the agencies and branches. In comparison with the agencies and branches, claims at large IBFs of U.S. banks are more heavily concentrated in commercial and industrial lending and loans to foreign governments and official institutions.

On the liability side, IBF business also consists primarily of interbank and intrabank transactions. The agencies and branches are the major borrowers in the inter-IBF market, where they accounted for about 90 percent of liabilities due to other IBFs as of December 1987. Large IBFs of both U.S. banks and agencies and branches were, in the aggregate, net borrowers from related foreign offices; such borrowings serve as one

TABLE 2

**Assets and Liabilities of
Large International Banking Facilities
December 31, 1987[1]
(billions of dollars)**

Balance sheet item	U.S.-chartered banks	Agencies and Branches	Total all entities
A S S E T S			
1. **Claims on unrelated parties[2]**	**56.11**	**24.51**	**80.6**
2. **Loans and balances due from other IBFs**	2.84	1.64	4.5
Balances due from:			
3. Banks in foreign countries	4.32	6.33	10.7
4. Foreign governments and official institutions	1.	1.1	1.2
5. **Securities of foreign residents**	.24	.74	.9
Loans to foreign residents:			
6. Commercial and industrial loans	15.1	10.1	25.2
7. Banks in foreign countries	11.0	19.0	30.0
8. Foreign governments and official institutions	17.3	7.2	24.5
9. Other loans	.6	.1	.7
10. **Other assets in IBF accounts**	1.5	2.8	4.2
11. **Gross claims on foreign offices of establishing entity[2]**	22.7	54.1	76.7
12. **Total assets other than claims on U.S. offices of establishing entity (item 1 plus item 11)[2]**	78.7	178.6	257.3

(continued)

Table 2, Continued

L I A B I L I T I E S			
13. **Liabilities due to unrelated parties**[2]	30.9	130.2	161.1
14. **Liabilities due to other IBFs**	5.6	40.4	46.0
15. Overnight maturity or notice	.82	.02	.8
16. **Liabilities due to banks in foreign countries**	10.0	62.2	72.2
17. Overnight maturity or notice	2.4	3.8	6.2
18. 2-6 days maturity or notice	1.5	2.5	4.0
19. 7 days or over maturity or notice	6.1	55.9	62.0
20. **Liabilities due to foreign governments and official institutions**	5.6	6.3	12.0
21. Overnight maturity or notice	2.0	3.0	4.9
22. 2-6 days maturity or notice	.7	.6	1.2
23. 7 days or over maturity or notice	3.0	2.8	5.8
24. **Liabilities due to other foreign residents**	5.2	2.7	7.9
25. 2-6 days maturity or notice	.4	.2	.6
26. 7 days or over maturity or notice	4.8	2.5	7.3
27. **Other liabilities in IBF accounts**	2.0	2.3	4.2
28. **Gross liabilities due to foreign offices of establishing entity**[2]	47.1	67.8	115.0
29. **Total liabilities other than those due to U.S. offices of establishing entity (item 13 plus item 28)**[2]	78.1	198.0	276.1
R E S I D U A L			
30. Net due from or net due to (-) U.S. offices of establishing entity (item 29 minus item 28)[2]	-.7	19.4	18.8
MEMO: Net due from or net due to (-) foreign offices of establishing entity (item 11 minus item 28)[2]	-24.5	-13.7	-38.2
Number of reporters	13	38	51

[1] Includes data only for entities whose IBFs had assets or liabilities of at least $2 billion on December 31, 1987 or any previous report date during the preceding year. (Details may not add to totals because of rounding.)

[2] Includes amounts denominated in both U.S. dollars and foreign currencies; unless noted, figures on all other lines include only amounts denominated in U.S. dollars. As a result, the figures shown for claims on (liabilities due to) unrelated parties exceed the sum of their components (for which foreign-currency denominated items are not reported) by the amount of claims (or liabilities) denominated in foreign currencies.

Source: Federal Reserve Statistical Release G-14.

source of funding for the U.S. current account deficit. However, in comparison with IBFs of agencies and branches, IBFs of U.S. banks relied much more heavily on these borrowings to fund IBF activities. As of December 1987, large IBFs of U.S. banks were funding almost 45 percent of their claims on unrelated parties with net advances from related foreign offices; the comparable figure for large IBFs of U.S. agencies and branches of foreign banks was 11 percent.

The bulk of deposits at IBFs of both agencies and branches and U.S. banks have maturities of seven days or more. Deposits of private nonbank customers remain relatively small, totaling only about $8 billion, and although deposits with maturities as short as two days are available to these customers, more than 90 percent of their deposits have maturities of seven days or more. Thus, there is no evidence that private nonbank customers have tried to use IBF deposits as a substitute for transaction accounts at U.S. banking offices, which was one of the Board's initial concerns. By contrast, IBF deposits with an overnight maturity are permitted for foreign governments and official institutions and account for about 40 percent of the deposits of these customers at large IBFs. The rates paid on IBF deposits have been virtually the same as rates on Eurodollar deposits of comparable size and maturity.

IBF deposits and loans may be denominated in either U.S. dollars or foreign currencies. Although U.S. banks had sought this ability, to date the volume of their IBF business denominated in foreign currencies has been moderate. As of December 1987, business denominated in foreign currencies accounted for about 5 percent of total assets and total liabilities at large IBFs of U.S. banks. These figures compare with a share of business denominated in nondollar currencies of about 5 percent of total assets and total liabilities at Caribbean branches of U.S. banks and more than 35 percent at London branches of U.S. banks. Business denominated in foreign currencies accounts for nearly 20 percent of total assets and total liabilities at large IBFs of agencies and branches, although almost all of this business is concentrated at IBFs of Japanese agencies and branches.

With regard to IBF activities in general, the consensus in the banking community is that IBFs have not created a substantial amount of new business. Rather, the business now on the IBF books was either shifted there from establishing entities or their foreign offices or would, in the absence of IBFs, have been booked at the establishing entities or their foreign offices.[16]

In the case of large U.S.-chartered banks, most of the assets and liabilities shifted to IBFs were originally on the books of their foreign branches, primarily those in the Caribbean; without IBFs, most of the other assets and liabilities now at IBFs of U.S. banks would probably also be on the books of the Caribbean branches. Because many of the transactions booked at Caribbean branches of U.S. banks were actually conducted in New York or other financial centers in the United States, IBFs simply permitted a more rational and operationally efficient pattern of booking for such transactions. As a result, there do not appear to have been substantial income or employment gains in the United States associated with the introduction of IBFs.

With regard to state and local taxes, some U.S.-chartered banks may find it advantageous (in particular, under the optional separate accounting method of IBF taxation in New York) to book loans at an IBF rather than at a shell branch in the Caribbean. (See the section on TAX LAWS AND REGULATIONS). By contrast, in general there is no incentive under federal tax law to book transactions at an IBF rather than a foreign branch. The reason is that for purposes of federal income taxation, U.S. banks are taxed on their worldwide income, which includes income of both their IBFs and their foreign offices.

In contrast to the pattern at U.S. banks, most of the assets and liabilities shifted to IBFs by U.S. agencies and branches of foreign banks were originally on the books of the U.S. offices. Had IBFs not been introduced, it is not clear whether these assets and liabilities would have remained on the U.S. books or would have been shifted to offshore locations in order to receive more favorable treatment with respect to reserve requirements or taxes.

Prior to the implementation of the International Banking Act of 1978 (IBA), agencies and branches were not subject to federal reserve requirements.[17] When IBFs were introduced in 1981, federal reserve requirements for U.S. agencies and branches of foreign banks were still in the process of being phased in under the IBA and the Monetary Control Act of 1980. As a result, foreign banks had not fully adjusted their U.S. activities to the costs imposed by such requirements. If IBFs had not been introduced, it is not clear how the activities of the agencies and branches would have changed after federal reserve requirements had been fully phased in. It seems likely, however, that at least some portion of the business that would otherwise have been booked at the U.S. agencies and branches would have been moved offshore.

Taxes are also an important consideration for the agencies and branches. It is difficult, however, to generalize about tax incentives that apply to the operations of U.S. agencies and branches of foreign banks because such incentives depend on a variety of factors such as home- and host-country tax laws and provisions of bilateral tax treaties, as well as on the circumstances of each individual bank. Income arising from the activities of an IBF at a U.S. agency or branch of a foreign bank is, like that of an IBF of a U.S. bank, subject to U.S. federal income taxation in the same manner as income arising from the activities of the agency or branch itself. By contrast, income associated with activities at non-U.S. offices of foreign banks is not subject to U.S. federal taxation, provided that the income is not "effectively connected" with the activities of a U.S. agency or branch.

As a result, a foreign bank would, in general, increase its U.S. federal income tax liability by shifting assets from a foreign office to an IBF. However, such an increase in U.S. federal tax liability would not necessarily increase the worldwide taxes paid by the foreign bank. The outcome would depend on the tax laws of the bank's home country and provisions of tax treaties between the home country and the United States and between the home country and third countries.

Use of IBFs as Opposed to U.S. Books

Despite the introduction of IBFs, a number of banking institutions still have some claims on foreign residents and liabilities due to foreign residents on their U.S. books. These include loans to foreign banks and foreign governments, business loans to foreign residents, and time deposits and borrowings from unrelated foreign banks and foreign governments.[18] At least on the surface there would appear to be tax advantages under state or local law to booking the loans at an IBF, reserve requirement advantages to booking the deposits and borrowings at an IBF, and, for the deposits, FDIC insurance-assessment benefits as well. However, as discussed below, other considerations may explain the observed pattern of booking.

One explanation is that the foreign assets and liabilities still on the U.S. books are not eligible for transfer to IBFs under the limitations imposed by the Federal Reserve Board on IBF activities. With regard to assets, it is possible that some portion of business loans to foreign residents, especially those to foreign affiliates of U.S. corporations, may not meet the IBF use-of-proceeds requirement. Loans to foreign banks are not required to meet this test. However, a considerable portion of the amounts reported as loans to unaffiliated foreign banks on the U.S. books may result from overnight overdrafts that arise in the normal process of clearing and funds transfer activities.

With regard to liabilities, it seems likely that most of the time deposits of foreign residents still on the U.S. books are negotiable certificates of deposit, which are not eligible for booking at an IBF. By contrast, borrowings from foreign banks and foreign governments (which are also subject to a three percent reserve requirement) could be shifted from U.S. books to IBFs. However, if a banking institution in the United States is already a net borrower of funds from its foreign offices and its IBF and wants to use the funds borrowed from unaffiliated foreign banks at its domestic office, there would be no reserve requirement advantage to booking the borrowings at an IBF because funds advanced to the domestic office from an IBF are subject to Eurocurrency reserve requirements.

It is also possible that the character and extent of the tax relief granted to IBFs may be affecting the incentive for banks to shift IBF loans and deposits that are IBF-eligible from their U.S. books to the IBFs. In New York, but only under the separate accounting option for IBF taxation, two aspects of the tax treatment of IBFs may contribute to the booking of IBF-eligible loans on the domestic books.

First, there is no New York state or city tax advantage resulting from the shifting of additional assets to IBF books if such assets are funded by advances from the U.S. office, which would constitute "ineligible funding" for purposes of calculating an IBF's adjusted eligible net income. (See note 14.) A bank could try to arrange for the funding to be "eligible" by routing it through a foreign branch. However, in the case of a shell branch, some or all of such funds might be treated by the state and local tax authorities as "ineligible funding."

Second, but also only under the separate accounting option of New York state and city law, tax benefits associated with an IBF would not be fully realized if a loan on the IBF books were written off. Because the resulting increase in the amount of the bad-debt deduction would be attributable to the IBF, it would have to be subtracted from the IBF's eligible gross income. Moreover, if the amount of such loans were sufficiently large, a bank could actually increase its state and city tax liability by having shifted the loan to its IBF.[19] It is possible that some U.S. banks that use the separate accounting option for their IBFs may be keeping certain foreign loans on their domestic books for this reason.

By contrast, under the New York option of treating an IBF as if it were outside New York for purposes of the apportionment formula, it is advantageous to be able to allocate receipts, deposits, and payroll to the IBF as opposed to the domestic office. Under this option, whether an increase in the amount of the bad-debt deduction resulted from the charge-off of a loan recorded on the books of the domestic office or the IBF generally would not have a substantial effect on the portion of adjusted federal taxable income that is subject to New York taxation.

Use of IBFs Compared With Foreign Branches

It is impossible to determine conclusively what changes in activities at foreign branches of U.S.-chartered banks would have occurred in the absence of IBFs. Both the structure and growth of international banking since 1980 have been affected by a variety of factors such as the international debt problem, the financing requirements associated with the large U.S. current account deficits, market innovations that have resulted in securitization of international assets for nonbank investors, and pressure by U.S. and other regulatory authorities for banks to increase their capital ratios. However, certain changes in the structure of activities at foreign branches of U.S.-chartered banks do appear to be related to the introduction of IBFs. In particular, U.S. banks appear to have shifted loan and deposit transactions with foreign customers from their Caribbean branches to their IBFs in the United States.

From December 1980 to December 1987, the share of claims on unrelated parties attributable to foreign residents at Caribbean branches of U.S.-chartered banks declined from 90 percent to 62 percent. Over the same period the share of liabilities to unrelated parties attributable to foreign residents declined from 56 percent to 28 percent. (See Table 3.) Discussions with bankers support the view that this decline in business with foreign customers at Caribbean branches of U.S. banks is related to the introduction of IBFs. Because the management and record keeping activities associated with accounts at Caribbean branches had been conducted primarily in the United States, the transfer of this business to IBFs was relatively easy to implement.

However, as of December 1987 nearly $50 billion in claims on unrelated foreign residents and about $25 billion in liabilities due to unrelated foreign residents remained on the books of Caribbean branches of U.S. banks. Four reasons have been suggested for the existence of this business; three are relevant only for nonbank customers, which account for about one-sixth of the claims and one-half of the liabilities. First, the activities of some nonbank customers might not meet the use-of-proceeds or use-of-funds tests for IBF transactions, particularly if the customers are foreign affiliates of U.S. corporations. Second, some nonbank customers may want to keep their accounts outside the United States for reasons of secrecy because they view such accounts as subject to less scrutiny by U.S. and other authorities than an account at an IBF. Third, some nonbank depositors may not want to be subject to the two-day minimum maturity requirements of an IBF.[20] Fourth, some banks may adhere to an internal "matched funding" rule under which, if funds are raised through an offshore branch, the associated loan must be booked there as well. The last reason does not, however, seem sufficient to explain why about $34 billion in claims on unrelated foreign banks and about $11 billion in liabilities due to unrelated foreign banks remain on the books of Caribbean branches of U.S. banks.

The introduction of IBFs did not affect transactions with U.S. residents at Caribbean branches of U.S. banks because, as noted above,

IBFs are not permitted to lend to or accept deposits from U.S. residents other than the establishing entity or another IBF. Thus, U.S. residents wishing to hold deposits at a bank's domestic office have continued to bear the burden of part or all of the bank's costs of reserve requirements and FDIC insurance assessments. As a result, interest rates on domestic office deposits have been relatively unattractive to large corporate customers who are typically willing to accept the small country risk of having a deposit account domiciled at a Caribbean branch of a U.S. bank.

In order to attract funds from these corporate customers, various types of accounts have been developed for U.S. residents at Caribbean branches of U.S. banks. Because these accounts are managed by the U.S. office of the bank, customers have the advantage of being able to communicate with the bank's U.S. office rather than with its Caribbean branch. One of the most widely used types of accounts being offered to U.S. residents is a "sweep account," in which collected funds in various domestic office accounts are automatically deposited at Caribbean branches at Eurodollar rates at a certain time in the business day.The funds in a sweep account can be transferred back to a deposit in a U.S. office for use on the next business day. The availability of sweep and other accounts led to a near doubling of deposits of nonbank U.S. residents at Caribbean branches of U.S. banks between 1980 and 1983.

London branches of U.S. banks experienced slow growth in activity from 1980 to 1987. This experience reflects the generally slow growth of international activities of U.S. banks both in absolute terms and in relation to banks from other countries, particularly Japanese banks. In general, the activities of the London branches of U.S. banks have remained oriented towards non-U.S. customers who wish to have loan and deposit accounts in London. This focus does not appear to have been affected by the introduction of IBFs. However, specific comparisons of the structure of the activities of the London branches over time are difficult because of the importance of negotiable certificates of deposit, which were not reported as a separate category until 1985.[21]

The growth of negotiable certificates of deposit issued by London branches of U.S. banks reflects in large part the issuance of Eurodollar certificates of deposit to money market mutual funds, particularly those domiciled in the United States, and to other large investors. Because IBFs are prohibited from issuing negotiable certificates of deposit, there is no possibility of this business being transferred to IBFs. In addition, London is a desirable location for banks to issue their negotiable certificates of deposit because the infrastructure for sales, custody, and transfers is very well-developed.

TABLE 3

Selected Assets and Liabilities of Caribbean and London Branches of U.S. Banks, 1980-87[1] (billions of dollars)

	Caribbean branches			London branches		
	December 1980	December 1983	December 1987	December 1980	December 1983	December 1987
Total assets/liabilities	123.8	151.5	160.3	144.7	158.7	159.2
Claims on unrelated parties	97.9	86.4	79.0	104.7	93.1	91.9
U.S. residents	5.1	27.0	25.3	2.2	5.3	5.2
Banks	}5.1	}27.0	14.3	}2.2	}5.3	1.3
Nonbanks	}	}	11.0	}	}	3.9
Foreign residents	88.6	55.4	48.9	96.4	82.8	75.8
Banks	54.9	36.8	33.8	58.7	43.4	36.7
Public/official	12.6	6.1	7.4	6.7	5.9	4.8
Nonbanks	21.1	12.6	7.7	31.0	33.5	34.3
Other assets	4.2	3.9	4.8	6.1	5.0	11.0
Liabilities to unrelated parties	78.6	87.9	87.8	125.1	125.7	112.9
U.S. residents	31.5	60.6	60.6	17.6	41.8	10.2
Banks	7.4	15.7	17.2	5.7	11.3	1.7
Nonbanks	24.1	44.9	43.4	11.8	30.5	8.5
Foreign residents	44.2	25.0	24.6	102.1	76.8	65.6
Banks	29.9	11.9	10.8	56.3	41.6	34.3
Public/official	4.4	1.9	1.5	21.4	10.2	11.0
Nonbanks	9.9	11.2	12.4	24.4	25.0	20.3
Negotiable CDs	-	-	.9	-	-	27.0
Other liabilities	3.0	2.3	1.7	5.5	7.1	10.0
Memorandum: Net claims on parent banks and its other foreign offices	-19.2	1.5	8.8	20.4	32.6	20.9

[1] Includes all foreign branches with total assets of at least $150 million on the end of month report date or on any previous report date in the same calendar year. Prior to June 1984, shell branches with total assets between $50 million and $150 million are also included. The assets and liability categories shown in the table include amounts denominated in both U.S. dollars and foreign currencies. (Details may not add to totals because of rounding.)

Source: Board of Governors of the Federal Reserve System. **Annual Statistical Digest.**

IBFs AND OTHER INTERNATIONAL BANKING CENTERS

In providing special treatment for IBF operations, federal and state authorities hoped that the introduction of IBFs might enhance the competitiveness of the United States as a location for conducting international banking transactions. As Table 4 shows, external assets on the books of banks in the United States more than doubled between December 1980 and December 1983.[22] By contrast, external assets in other banking centers grew much more slowly. As a result, the share of external banking activity conducted in the United States increased substantially during this period. (See Table 5.)

The data in Table 4 indicate that almost all of the increase in the volume of external banking activity conducted in the United States from 1980 to 1983 is statistically associated with activity at IBFs. However, this statistical association overstates the likely impact of IBFs because some of the assets booked at IBFs, particularly at IBFs of U.S. agencies and branches of foreign banks, may represent assets that were, prior to the introduction of IBFs, booked at U.S. offices. A previous study estimated that during the year following the introduction of IBFs, about two-thirds of the external assets of IBFs were associated with a net increase in international banking business conducted in the United States while the remaining one-third represented assets shifted from domestic office books.[23]

Thus, even after taking into account assets shifted from domestic office books to IBFs, it still appears that, at least initially, IBFs enhanced the relative importance of the United States as an international banking center. It seems likely the net effect of IBFs has continued to be positive in subsequent years. However, because most of the actual shifting of assets and liabilities from domestic offices to IBFs occurred before the middle of 1982, IBF activity in subsequent years would need to be adjusted to take into account assets that would, in the absence of IBFs, have been booked at U.S. offices, a figure which, as discussed in the above section on TAX LAWS AND REGULATIONS, is impossible to determine.

The preeminence of London as an international banking center does not appear to have been significantly affected by IBFs. As Table 5 shows, the share of external banking in the United Kingdom increased between December 1980 and 1983, although it is, of course, possible that the increase would have been greater in the absence of IBFs. The reported share of external banking conducted in the offshore centers remained about constant during this period, although coverage is limited in that the reported figures include only U.S.-chartered banks. The major observed loss of share between 1981 and 1983 appears to have occurred in Luxembourg, France, and other European centers. Although external banking activity was stagnant between 1980 and 1983 in these locations, there is no reason to

TABLE 4

External Assets of Banks in Selected Centers. 1980-87[1]
(billions of dollars)

	United Kingdom	United States			Japan			France	Luxembourg	Offshore Centers[2]	Grand Total[3]
		Total	IBFs	Other	Total	JOM	Other				
December 1980	336.3	176.8	--	176.8	65.7	--	65.7	143.2	88.6	141.0	1,321.9
December 1981	401.2	256.3	63.4	192.9	84.6	--	84.6	143.0	88.4	172.0	1,549.5
December 1982	431.4	361.4	143.6	217.8	90.9	--	90.9	148.1	90.5	172.9	1,686.7
December 1983(1)	485.2	398.3	174.2	224.1	109.1	--	109.1	141.3	85.4	179.8	1,754.5
December 1983(2)	488.9	398.3	174.2	224.1	109.1	--	109.1	139.7	85.4	498.8	2,093.0
December 1984	489.7	411.4	189.7	221.7	126.9	--	126.9	141.5	85.6	518.9	2,163.6
December 1985	587.2	417.8	202.8	215.0	194.6	--	194.6	163.5	108.6	555.2	2,568.7
December 1986	714.5	468.7	234.3	234.4	345.3	88.7	256.6	188.0	141.1	677.3	3,221.1
December 1987	875.6	508.9	277.3	231.6	576.9	191.9	385.0	266.4	182.3	878.5	4,157.2

1 "External" assets include claims on foreign residents denominated in both domestic and foreign currencies. Foreign currency claims on domestic residents are not included because data for such claims were not published for individual centers prior to 1983. In the aggregate, as of December 1987, foreign currency claims on domestic residents amounted to about $980 billion.

2 Prior to December 1983, data for offshore centers include only branches of U.S. banks. Beginning in December 1983, coverage was expanded to include all banks operating in the Bahamas, Bahrain, the Cayman Islands, Hong Kong, the Netherlands Antilles, and Singapore, as well as branches of U.S. banks in Panama. (At the same time, minor reporting changes were introduced that affected the figures for some of the other centers.) The table shows data for December 1983 on both the old and new basis.

3 Includes data for Canada and for European countries that are not shown separately.

Source: Bank for International Settlements, **International Banking and Financial Market Developments.**

TABLE 5

Shares of Selected Centers in Total External Bank Assets, 1980-87[1]
(percent of total)

	United Kingdom	United States			Japan			France	Luxembourg	Offshore Centers
		Total	IBFs	Other	Total	JOM	Other			
December 1980	25.4	13.4	-	-	5.0	-	-	10.8	6.7	10.7
December 1981	25.9	16.5	4.1	12.4	5.5	-	-	9.2	5.7	11.1
December 1982	25.6	21.4	8.5	12.9	5.4	-	-	8.8	5.4	10.3
December 1983(1)	27.7	22.7	9.9	12.8	6.2	-	-	8.1	4.9	10.2
December 1983(2)	23.4	19.0	8.3	10.7	5.2	-	-	6.7	4.1	23.8
December 1984	22.6	19.0	8.8	10.2	5.9	-	-	6.5	4.0	24.0
December 1985	22.9	16.3	7.9	8.4	7.6	-	-	6.4	4.2	21.6
December 1986	22.2	14.6	7.3	7.3	10.7	2.8	8.0	5.8	4.4	21.0
December 1987	21.1	12.2	6.7	5.6	13.9	4.6	9.3	6.4	4.4	21.1

1 The figures in this table are derived from the figures for external assets shown in table 4. (Details may not add to totals because of rounding.)

believe that this change was directly related to the introduction of IBFs in the United States.

In contrast to the 1980-83 period, the growth of external assets at banking offices in the United States was relatively slow from December 1983 to December 1987. The share of external banking activity conducted at offices located in the United States (both at IBFs and on the banks' domestic books) declined sharply. By contrast, the volume of external banking activity conducted in the United Kingdom and in the offshore centers increased rapidly during this period; nevertheless the share of total external banking activity conducted in these locations declined slightly. The reason was an extraordinarily rapid increase in the volume of external assets at banking offices located in Japan. As a result, the share of external banking conducted in Japan rose rapidly, increasing from about 5 percentat the end of 1983 to nearly 14 percent at the end of 1987. In terms of total external assets, Japan eclipsed the United States as an international banking center.

The rapid rise in the share of external banking activity conducted in Japan reflects a variety of factors. First, the appreciation of the Japanese yen since 1985 has increased the dollar value of yen assets. Second, the liberalization of Japanese financial markets, including the development of the yen certificate of deposit and the yen bankers acceptance market, has been an important factor in enhancing Japan's role as a banking and financial center. Third, the introduction of the Japan Offshore Market (JOM) in December 1986, which is similar to IBFs in the United States, has also contributed to the growth of Japan as an international banking center. Finally, the excess of domestic saving over investment in Japan, as reflected in the large cumulative current account surplus of Japan, has been associated with the acquisition of external assets by both domestic and foreign banking institutions located in Japan and also with the rapid growth of worldwide total assets of Japanese banks in relation to large banks headquartered in other countries.[24]

An important component of this rapid growth of worldwide total assets of Japanese banks has been the increase in business conducted at offices of Japanese banks in centers outside Japan. In London, for example, where activity at branches of U.S. banks has been relatively stagnant (as shown in Table 3), Japanese banks have played an important role in the growth of international banking activity. The London branches of Japanese banks accounted for about one-half of the growth of total international assets at all banking offices in the United Kingdom from December 1984 through December 1987.[25]

CONCLUSION

IBFs have not turned out to be the dramatic innovation that some had predicted, and London remains the major center of Euromarket activity. Moreover, the view that depositors would perceive clear advantages in the sovereign risk associated with deposits subject to U.S. law does not seem justified. Sophisticated international depositors do not appear to perceive a significant difference in sovereign risk between deposits at branches of a U.S. bank located in other major international financial centers and deposits at that bank's IBF in the United States; in both cases the deposits are backed by the U.S. bank, which is supervised on a worldwide consolidated basis by U.S. bank regulatory authorities.

IBFs appear to be used for a large proportion of transactions with foreign residents that were, or would otherwise have been, booked at Caribbean branches of U.S. banks. As a result, the introduction of IBFs appears to have resulted in a substantial decline in the volume of business with foreign residents conducted at these branches. However, the same management and communication considerations that facilitated the transfer of transactions with foreign customers from Caribbean branches to IBFs have also facilitated the reverse shifting of some business with U.S. customers from domestic offices to Caribbean branches. Paradoxically, U.S. banking regulations are now structured so that non-U.S. residents have certain incentives to conduct banking transactions in the United States while U.S. residents are offered incentives to conduct banking transactions at branches of U.S. banks in the Caribbean.

IBFs appear to have had a negligible impact on the structure of activities at London branches of U.S. banks. In particular, the prohibition against issuance of negotiable certificates of deposits by IBFs has prevented them from sharing in the growth of activity in such instruments that has occurred at London branches of U.S. banks.

The creation of IBFs does appear to have enhanced the overall competitive environment for international banking in the United States from the time of their inception in December 1981 through December 1983. Since 1984, however, the share of total external banking activity conducted in the United States has declined sharply, in large part because of an increase in the share of external banking activity conducted in Japan. Throughout the entire period, however, London has remained the world's largest international banking center.

In sum, IBFs simply provide another center for booking transactions with foreign residents in a regulatory environment broadly similar to that of the Euromarket. To date, the operation of IBFs has not presented a problem either for the conduct of domestic monetary policy or for bank supervision. As noted above, since the early 1980s, international banking activity, including that conducted at IBFs, has been affected by a variety of factors such as the international debt problem, the financing requirements associated with the large U.S. current account deficits, market innovations that have resulted in securitization of international assets for nonbank investors, and pressure by U.S. and other regulatory authorities for banks to increase their capital ratios. Activities at IBFs have also been affected by the specific constraints on IBF operations, by the type of state tax relief offered to IBFs, and by the fact that establishment of IBFs has occurred in an environment of deregulation and structural change in the U.S. banking system as a whole.

NOTES

1. Except for the prohibition against payment of interest on demand deposits, interest rate ceilings on deposits at banking offices in the United States were eliminated by the Monetary Control Act of 1980 with a phase-out period that ended in 1986.

2. "External" assets comprise claims on nonresidents (including related foreign offices) denominated in both domestic and foreign currencies. Figures for IBF external assets, which are reported on the Treasury International Capital Reports, are used in the section IBFS AND OTHER INTERNATIONAL BANKING CENTERS for purposes of international comparisons. However, the analysis of the structure of IBF activities in the section IBF ACTIVITIES uses data from reports submitted to the Federal Reserve for "large" IBFs only; these reports differ in content and coverage from the Treasury reports.

3. One of the first depositors in the Eurodollar market was the Russian government, which wanted to hold its dollar-denominated deposits outside the United States because of fear that the deposits might be confiscated. The term Eurodollars is said to have been derived from the telex code (Eurobank) of a Russian-controlled bank in Paris, Banque Commerciale pour l'Europe du Nord.

4. These measures included the Interest Equalization Tax, which was enacted in 1963, and the Voluntary Foreign Credit Restraint Program, which began in 1965. A third measure was the Foreign Direct Investment Program, which was introduced on a voluntary basis in 1965 and became mandatory in 1968.

5. See, for example, Ralph C. Bryant, *International Financial Intermediation* (The Brookings Institution, 1987), pp. 23-30; Bank for International Settlements, *International Banking and Financial Market Developments*,

Fourth quarter 1987, p. 2; and Morgan Guaranty Trust Company, *World Financial Markets*, July 1988, p. 15.

6. Edge corporations are chartered by the Federal Reserve Board to engage in international banking and financial operations and may be established in locations outside the state in which their owner operates. Agreement corporations are state-chartered corporations that have entered into an agreement with the Federal Reserve Board to limit their activities to those of an Edge corporation.

7. IBF transactions with foreign governments and official institutions are treated in the same manner as IBF transactions with foreign banks. Deposits of foreign governments and official institutions, like those of foreign banks, are not included in the U.S. monetary aggregates.

8. This policy must be communicated in writing to IBF nonbank customers when a credit or deposit relationship is first established; foreign affiliates of U.S. entities must supply a written acknowledgement that such notice has been received.

9. In order for an asset to be eligible to be held by an IBF, the obligor (or in the case of bankers acceptances, both the customer and any endorser) must be IBF-eligible.

10. Foreign branches of U.S.-chartered banks are, of course, also subject to regulations imposed by the host-country authorities.

11. Others include California, Connecticut, Delaware, Florida, Georgia, Illinois, Maryland, North Carolina, and Washington; the District of Columbia has also enacted IBF tax legislation.

12. Prior to the 1985 taxable year, almost all New York banks computed taxable income on a separate accounting basis under which each item of income and expense was identified as attributable to business conducted either inside or outside New York.

13. See Marilyn M. Kaltenborn, "Is New York's Bank Tax Ready for the 1990s?," *Journal of State Taxation*, Vol. 4 (Fall 1985) pp. 225-34, regarding taxation of banks under the 1985 New York statute.

14. In order to compute an IBF's "adjusted eligible net income," certain expenses are deducted from "eligible gross income" (as defined in the statute), and the "ineligible funding amount" is also deducted. The latter adjustment reflects a decision to give an IBF a tax benefit only to the extent that the IBF is funded by foreign persons, including other IBFs. (An additional adjustment for the "floor amount" was designed to avoid an

abrupt decrease in tax revenues by reducing the tax benefit granted to an IBF in proportion to any decline in foreign lending activity on the domestic books of its establishing entity. However, because the base period for the calculation is 1975-77 and the floor amount is phased out over a ten-year period, in general the practical effect of this adjustment is now negligible.)

If the separate accounting option is chosen, the IBF must be excluded from the allocation formula, that is, the IBF must be excluded not only from New York receipts, deposits, and payroll (the numerators of the apportionment factors) but also from total receipts, deposits, and payroll (the denominators of the apportionment factors).

15. Large IBFs are defined as those with total assets or total liabilities of at least $2 billion. As of December 1987, 13 U.S. banks and 38 U.S. agencies and branches of foreign banks operated large IBFs.

16. See Sydney J. Key, "International Banking Facilities," *Federal Reserve Bulletin*, vol. 68 (October 1982), pp. 572-575, for an account of initial shifting of assets and liabilities to IBFs.

17. See Sydney J. Key and Gary M. Welsh, "Foreign Banks in the United States," in William H. Baughn and others, eds., *The Bankers' Handbook* (Dow-Jones Irwin, 1988), Chap. 5, pp. 58-71, regarding the activities and regulation of U.S. offices of foreign banks.

18. The data used in the section on IBFS AND OTHER INTERNATIONAL FINANCIAL CENTERS for external banking activity conducted in the United States but not booked at IBFs do not give an indication of these amounts. The reason is that the data in this section include gross claims on related foreign offices as well as external assets of nondepository institutions that are not eligible to establish IBFs.

19. Under the separate accounting option, if an IBF's adjusted eligible net income is negative, the amount of the loss must be added to the bank's New York taxable income in computing state and city income taxes.

20. The prohibition on issuance of negotiable certificates of deposit by IBFs does not explain the liabilities due to unrelated foreign residents still on the Caribbean branch books because U.S. banks typically issue Eurodollar certificates of deposit through branches in London rather than through branches in the Caribbean.

21. Prior to 1985, negotiable certificates of deposit issued by foreign branches of U.S. banks were classified for reporting purposes according to the holder of record, which was normally the custodial bank holding the certificate and not the ultimate beneficial owner.

22. As discussed in the section on THE HISTORY OF THE IBF PROPOSAL, "external" banking activity includes transactions with foreign residents (including related foreign offices) in both domestic and foreign currencies. "International" banking activity includes external banking activity and also transactions with domestic residents in foreign currencies. The figures in Tables 4 and 5 include only external activity because data for foreign currency claims on domestic residents were not published for individual centers prior to 1983.

As of December 1983, the coverage of the data series used in Tables 4 and 5 was expanded to include additional banking offices in offshore centers. The tables therefore contain two sets of numbers (on both the old and new basis) for December 1983 in order to permit comparison of consistent data for two separate periods, 1980-83 and 1983-87.

23. See Henry S. Terrell and Rodney H. Mills, *International Banking Facilities and the Eurodollar Market*, Staff Studies, no. 124 (Board of Governors of the Federal Reserve System, 1983) regarding this estimate.

24. See Robert S. Dohner and Henry S. Terrell, *The Determinants of the Growth of Multinational Banking Organizations: 1972-86*, International Finance Discussion Papers, no. 326 (Board of Governors of the Federal Reserve System, 1988) for an empirical analysis of the factors associated with growth of total assets at the world's largest banks.

25. In the United States, by contrast, the growth of activities of agencies and branches of Japanese banks during this period has been relatively more concentrated in domestic rather than foreign activity. This growth in domestic U.S. activities of the Japanese agencies and branches is not reflected in the figures for external assets at offices in the United States shown in Table 4.

REFERENCES

Bank for International Settlements. 1987. *International banking and financial market developments*. Basle. Fourth Quarter 1987 and previous issues.

Bellanger, Serge. 1981. Prospects for the International Banking Facilities from the European banker's viewpoint. *United States Banker*. July: 32-36.

Board of Governors of the Federal Reserve System. *Annual Statistical Digest*. Washington: Board of Governors.

Bryant, Ralph C. 1987. *International financial intermediation*. Washington: The Brookings Institution.

Dohner, Robert S. and Henry S. Terrell. 1988. *The determinants of the growth of multinational banking organizations. 1972-86*. International Finance Discussion Papers, no. 326. Washington: Board of Governors of the Federal Reserve System.

Hanabuchi, Satoshi. 1987. Tokyo Offshore Market. *The Japan Economic Journal*. November 14:14-16.

Horst, Thomas H. 1981. Taxation of international income of commercial banks. In Gary C. Hufbauer, ed., *The international framework for money and banking in the 1980s*. Washington: The International Law Institute, Georgetown University Law Center.

Kaltenborn, Marilyn M. 1985. Is New York's bank tax ready for the 1990s?. *Journal of State Taxation*. Fall:225-234.

Kawano, Michiaki. 1986. The Tokyo offshore market. *Tokyo Financial Review*. Bank of Tokyo. December:1-5.

Key, Sydney J. 1982. International Banking Facilities. *Federal Reserve Bulletin*. October:565-577.

Key, Sydney J. and Gary M. Welsh. 1988. Foreign Banks in the United States. In William H. Baughn, and others, eds., *The bankers' handbook*. Homewood, Illinois: Dow Jones-Irwin.

Kindleberger, Charles P. 1974. *The formation of financial centers: A study in comparative economic history*. Princeton Studies in International Finance, no. 36. Princeton: Princeton University Press.

Little, Jane Sneddon. 1975. *Euro-Dollars: The money-market Gypsies*. New York: Harper & Row.

McKinnon, Ronald I. 1977. *The Eurocurrency market*. Essays in International Finance, no. 125. Princeton: Princeton University Press.

Morgan Guaranty Trust Company. 1988. *World Financial Markets*. July.

Tamari, Shingo. 1986. Inauguration of Tokyo offshore market. *The Japan Economic Journal*. November 29:41-43.

14. INTERNATIONAL BANKING FACILITIES REVISITED

Michael H. Moffett
Arthur I. Stonehill
Oregon State University

INTRODUCTION

The Federal Reserve Board amended its regulations regarding reserve requirements (Regulation D) and payment of interest on deposits (Regulation Q), effective December 3, 1981, to allow the establishment of International Banking Facilities by commercial banks in the United States. An "International Banking Facility" or IBF means a set of asset and liability accounts segregated on the books and records of a depository institution, United States branch or agency of a foreign bank, or an Edge or Agreement Corporation that includes only international banking facility extensions of credit.[1] In addition, Federal legislation exempted IBFs from F.D.I.C. coverage and assessments. Finally, nine states have granted special tax status on the operating profits of IBFs or have altered restrictions in order to encourage their existence within state borders.

The IBF represents an attempt by U.S. government regulators to "internalize" the Euromarkets into the U.S. banking system. The purpose of the IBF was to eliminate or at least minimize the size and growth of the offshore shell branches of U.S. banks, while providing the domestic banking system with new profit opportunities in international banking within U.S. legal jurisdictional boundaries. The move was seen by the public and private sectors as long overdue and was anticipated with great expectations.

The IBF, however, was very narrowly defined. An IBF could offer:

(1) To foreign nonbank residents time deposits of two-day minimum maturities (or notice of withdrawal) of $100,000 minimum size and withdrawals

(2) To foreign offices of U.S. banks, foreign banks, other IBFs, or their U.S. parent institutions time deposits of minimum one-day or overnight maturity. An IBF could extend credit to foreign residents, including banks and other IBFs and the parent institution of the IBF, denominated in either U.S. dollars or in any other foreign currencies free of reserve requirements and interest rate restrictions.[2] In essence, this

---

The authors would like to gratefully acknowledge the research assistance of Jan Ciranny.

deregulation has allowed domestic onshore offices of U.S. banks to accept foreign currency denominated deposits and to make loans on terms competitive with the Euromarkets. The major constraint was the continued division of these international operations from the domestic banking operations of U.S. banks.

THE EXPECTED COSTS AND BENEFITS OF IBFS

The purported benefits of IBFs which were successfully used in the passage of initial enabling legislation were:

(1) Tax considerations. IBFs could potentially increase Federal tax revenue if their creation shifted assets from foreign branches paying taxes to foreign governments. Account owners of this type were seen as claiming tax payments to other governments as credits against U.S. Federal income tax. If, however, the creation of IBFs shifted accounts from Caribbean shell branches to the United States, there would be no Federal income tax gain, given that income from those branches which pay no income taxes in their country of residence are already taxed by the U.S. government. Tax benefit considerations on the Federal level are then dependent on the geographic shift of deposits resulting from the formation of IBFs.

Tax considerations on the state level depend on the degree of new banking business generated by the creation of an IBF and the degree of switching from offshore to onshore accounts. Nine states have passed laws reducing or altogether eliminating state taxes on IBF operations in order to provide additional incentives for successful operations.

(2) Reduced bank operating costs. Banks could potentially reduce operating costs if the creation of IBFs eliminated the need for, and caused the closure of, offshore shell branches. Savings would include the elimination of the licensing fee and annual operating expenses of the branches. However, even at the initial stages of IBF enabling legislation, it was not considered likely that U.S. banks would choose to close offshore shell branches due to the continued need for offering offshore banking services to U.S. residents excluded from IBFs.

The access of U.S. banks to the Euromarkets could reduce costs for funds for operations to be conducted in international lending. It was proposed that interest rates paid for funds would be lower in U.S. IBFs relative to the shell branches due to the reduced country risk.

(3) Employment effects. Banks supporting IBF passage in the late 1970s emphasized the increase in jobs which would

> result in net increases in domestic bank employment, as well as secondary employment arising from the income generation effects of increased bank business. It was estimated that even among the major IBF formation bank group, the agencies and branches of foreign banks, the average IBF would increase employment per bank by six employees. The employment effects in terms of operating expenses would be somewhat offset by employee reductions in the offshore shell branch banks.

Additional concerns regarding IBF deposit impacts on U.S. monetary policy, credit availability, exchange rates, and the soundness of bank portfolios were considered and dismissed, given the absolute separation of IBF operations and domestic banking operations. Equity concerns, such as the fact that foreign corporations could enjoy U.S. country risk levels combined with Eurocurrency interest rates while American corporations could not, were considered inconsequential or unavoidable.

PERFORMANCE OF THE IBF TO DATE

IBF growth was rapid in the first two years of operation, 1981-1983, while slowing considerably in the period since then. Total IBF assets by the end of year 1981, less than one month after initiation, were $56.6 billion. By the end of 1982, total assets had increased to approximately $153 billion. After this initial startup period, however, the growth rate of IBF assets has slowed, though remaining steady throughout the last four-year period, totaling $317 billion by May 1987.

Table 1 provides a comparison of several international banking aggregates in order to put IBF growth in perspective. Total U.S. bank claims on foreign countries, the widest measure of international banking, has actually stagnated in the 1980s. The purpose of the creation of IBFs to a large degree was to draw the offshore shell branch assets onshore. Without implying causation, the assets of offshore banking centers have shown essentially no growth between 1981, the year of IBF operation commencement, and 1986.

The total international assets of banks by the nationality of banks in Table 2 provides further evidence of the role of IBFs in U.S. international banking growth (or their lack of). There are two notable characteristics of bank assets by nationality: first, the rapid growth demonstrated by Japanese banks in the 1984 to 1986 period, and secondly, the rapid loss of world market share of U.S. banks during this same period. Some of this disparity is probably due to expressing all values in U.S. dollars at a time when the dollar was rapidly depreciating.

PROFILE OF IBF OPERATIONS

The location of IBFs in the United States has followed traditional financial center standards by being dominated by New York banks, both U.S.-owned banks and the agencies and branches of foreign banks. Table 3 provides a detailed breakdown of the number of IBF operations by state, and also provides descriptive statistics on assets controlled by banks in New York. Although one would expect a traditional banking center such as New York to dominate in the early stages of growth of a new international financial instrument, the increasing domination of IBF assets by New York is surprising. By the end of 1986, New York contained 250 of the 549 reporting IBFs, and controlled over 78 percent of their total assets.

TABLE 1
United States International Banking Aggregates
(billions of U.S. dollars)

Year	U.S. Bank Claims on Foreign Countries[1]	U.S. Offshore Banking Center Assets[2]	Total IBF Assets
1980:	352.0	46.6	-----
1981:	415.2	63.5	56.6
1982:	436.1	67.5	152.7
1983:	433.9	70.5	191.6
1984:	405.7	65.6	227.6
1985:	391.6	65.4	260.5
1986:	395.5	65.6	298.2

Notes: 1. U.S. offices and foreign branches of U.S.-owned banks and of U.S. subsidiaries of foreign-owned banks. Offices not included are U.S. agencies and branches of foreign banks and foreign subsidiaries of U.S. banks. Source: **Federal Reserve Bulletin**, various dates.

2. Offshore Banking Centers include those located in the Bahamas, Bermuda, Cayman Islands and other British West Indies, Netherlands Antilles, Panama, Lebanon, Hong Kong, and Singapore. Source: **Federal Reserve Bulletin**, various dates.

TABLE 2
International Bank Assets by Nationality of Banks
(billions of U.S. dollars)

Country	December 1984 Assets	%	December 1985 Assets	%	December 1986 Assets	%
France	200.7	8.9	233.7	8.7	276.1	8.1
Germany	143.2	6.4	191.2	7.1	270.0	7.9
Italy	90.6	4.0	113.2	4.2	145.1	4.3
Japan	517.9	23.0	706.7	26.4	1117.7	32.8
Switzerland	82.9	3.7	109.2	4.1	152.0	4.5
United Kingdom	168.9	7.5	192.2	7.2	211.7	6.2
United States	594.5	26.4	589.5	22.0	598.3	17.6
Other	450.7	20.1	544.8	20.3	635.4	18.6
Total	2,249.4	100%	2,680.5	100%	3,406.3	100%

Source: Bank for International Settlements, **Fifty-Seventh Annual Report,** June 1987, Basle, page 104.

The performance of IBFs has also varied according to ownership. The growth of IBF assets has been steady and substantial for those IBFs established by U.S. agencies and branches of foreign banks ("foreign banks") compared to the lack of growth by IBFs established by U.S.-based banks ("domestic banks"). Figure 1 illustrates the relative performances of these two groups since the beginning of operations, while providing details on the numberof IBFs by establishing entity. IBF assets held by domestic bankshave shown essentially no growth since the end of 1983, while IBFs owned by foreign banks have continued to grow steadily. Foreign bank IBFs have maintained a two-thirds share of the IBF market since 1983, with all indications that the gap will continue to widen.

Much of the growth of IBFs is dependent on their ability to draw in funds from foreign residents, bank and nonbank, in order to,in turn, place the fund with nonresidents. Disaggregating the liability structures of IBFs by establishing entity gives some indication as to possible causes of the rather anemic performance of domestic bank IBFs. Table 4 provides a comparison of asset and liability structures by establishing entity. Each is separated into claims on and liabilities to three major subgroups:

(1) Foreign affiliated offices (either parent or foreign branches)

(2) Other IBFs in the United States

(3) Unaffiliated foreign residents (bank and nonbank nonresidents).

Two points appear most obvious regarding the comparison: first, foreign IBFs utilize the interbank IBF market much more heavily than do domestic bank IBFs; and second, domestic bank IBFs are much more heavily dependent on their foreign affiliated offices (in their case their foreign branches) to provide funding for IBF operations.

Foreign affiliated office liabilities consistently provide 50 percent of the funds for domestic bank IBF operations, while similar foreign bank liabilities are distributed much more evenly among the three major funding sources (affiliated offices 28 percent, other IBFs 24 percent, unaffiliated foreign residents 40 percent). Between 1983 and 1987, domestic bank IBFs increased their liabilities derived from unaffiliated foreign residents from $27 to $34 billion, while similar foreign bank IBF liabilities nearly tripled from $34 to $95 billion in the same period.

Closer examination of IBF unaffiliated foreign funding sources indicates that foreign bank IBFs dominate the foreign interbank market. In May 1987, of the total liabilities to unaffiliated foreign banks, foreign bank IBFs held $74.5 billion of the total $88.0 billion, nearly 85 percent. This inability or unwillingness of domestic bank IBFs to penetrate the foreign interbank markets, essentially the traditional Eurocurrency market, is indicative of the general limitations that IBFs possess due to their exclusive non-resident operations.

Much of the initial growth of IBFs did result from the shifting of assets from foreign branches. The majority of this asset shift was conducted by U.S.-owned banks, since they experienced no adverse tax effect. On the other hand, foreign banks would experience significant increases in their U.S. tax liabilities if they shifted a large amount of foreign branch/parent assets to the United States. For this reason, the balance sheets of domestic bank IBFs and foreign bank IBFs reflect the dissimilar tax incentives. Domestic bank IBF operations increased at the expense of assets shifted from foreign branches, whereas foreign bank IBF assets increased at the expense of their other operations in the United States.

Another indication of the inability of domestic bank IBFs to access the traditional Eurocurrency markets lies in the near total dominance of the U.S. dollar as IBF currency of denomination. One of the truly revolutionary aspects of IBFs for the American banking system was the creation of operations which could accept foreign currency-denominated deposits like that of the Euromarkets. As of May 1987, $286 billion of the total $317 billion in IBF assets were denominated in U.S. dollars, 90 percent of the total. This figure is in contrast to the relatively stable 70 percent dollar

TABLE 3
Profile of IBFs by Location
December 31, 1986

State	Banks & S&Ls	Agencies & Branches	Edge Act Corporations	Total
Arkansas	0	0	1	1
California	20	67	11	98
Colorado	1	0	0	1
Connecticut	2	0	0	2
Delaware	2	0	0	2
District of Col.	7	3	1	11
Florida	29	31	25	85
Georgia	4	2	0	6
Hawaii	2	0	0	2
Illinois	7	19	4	30
Kentucky	2	0	0	2
Louisiana	1	0	0	1
Massachusetts	4	1	2	7
Michigan	2	0	0	2
New Jersey	4	0	0	4
New York	44	187	19	250
North Carolina	2	0	0	2
Ohio	6	0	0	6
Pennsylvania	5	2	1	8
Rhode Island	1	0	0	1
South Carolina	1	0	0	1
Texas	13	0	4	17
Virginia	2	0	0	2
Washington	3	4	0	7
Wisconsin	0	0	1	1
Total	164	316	69	549

Source: **Federal Reserve Statistical Release G.14(518)**, December 1986.

New York State Dominance of IBF Assets
(billions of U.S. dollars)

Year	New York Assets	Percent	Total IBF Assets
1981	-----	-----	56.6
1982	-----	-----	152.7
1983	143.4	74.8	191.6
1984	172.3	75.7	227.6
1985	200.6	77.0	260.5
1986	233.7	78.4	298.2
1987[1]	253.9	80.0	317.2

Note: 1. 1987 values are annualized levels as of May 1987.
Source: Compiled by authors from **Federal Reserve Statistical Release G.14 (518)**, various issues.

TABLE 4
Asset and Liability Comparison of IBFs
By Establishing Entity
(billions of U.S. dollars)

Domestic Bank IBFs

- Claims on -

	Affiliated Offices	Other IBFs	Unaffiliated Residents	Total Assets
1982:	6.5	4.2	61.0	71.7
1983:	12.2	6.6	71.8	90.5
1984:	15.0	8.4	72.2	95.6
1985:	20.2	9.3	71.1	100.5
1986:	16.2	7.1	65.8	89.1
1987:[1]	18.4	7.7	63.8	90.0

- Liabilities to -

	Affiliated Offices	Other IBFs	Unaffiliated Residents	Total Assets
1982:	25.9	3.3	26.8	66.8
1983:	47.3	5.7	32.7	86.6
1984:	43.4	8.3	33.9	87.8
1985:	46.9	6.3	36.0	91.0
1986:	43.2	8.0	31.5	84.7
1987:[1]	43.3	6.1	33.9	85.6

Foreign Bank IBFs

- Claims on -

	Affiliated Offices	Other IBFs	Unaffiliated Residents	Total Assets
1982:	13.6	12.4	55.0	81.0
1983:	16.7	12.7	62.7	101.1
1984:	23.7	32.5	75.7	131.9
1985:	33.0	38.1	88.9	160.0
1986:	59.8	50.3	99.0	209.1
1987:[1]	63.6	52.4	111.2	227.2

- Liabilities to -

	Affiliated Offices	Other IBFs	Unaffiliated Residents	Total Assets
1982:	28.4	14.1	34.3	69.6
1983:	24.8	24.9	49.2	99.9
1984:	29.4	35.0	65.2	132.0
1985:	40.6	44.0	69.3	159.3
1986:	67.9	49.5	89.4	216.5
1987:[1]	66.6	55.4	94.6	234.2

Note: 1. Values for 1987 are as of May 27, 1987.
Source: Compiled by authors from **Federal Reserve Statistical Release G.14(518)**, various dates.

role in the Euromarkets over the last decade. Domestic bank IBFs, already heavily dependent on their own foreign branches and affiliates for funding, are seemingly not drawing upon the foreign currency deposits of the Euromarkets to any significant degree.

COMPETITION AND POTENTIAL MARKET NICHE

Much of the initial growth of the IBF was at the expense of U.S. bank foreign branches, as many U.S. banks quickly relocated the funds which met IBF specifications (primarily time deposits of foreign residents in U.S. foreign and shell branches). Table 5 provides an analysis of the impact that IBFs have had on the balance sheets of U.S. bank foreign branches. Most notably, the total claims on foreigners have declined in the 1980s on the books of foreign branches in roughly the same magnitude as the gains of the IBFs. It is important to note that by the end of 1986 the total assets of IBFs (all currency denominated claims on nonresidents) essentially equaled the total foreign assets held by all foreign branches of U.S. banks worldwide, approximately $300 billion.

Some similarities between IBFs and foreign branches of U.S.-owned banks exist.[3] Foreign branches and IBFs have the same interest rate and reserve requirement restrictions, and net advances by IBFs and offshore branches to parent institutions (or vice versa) are included in the calculation of the parents' required Eurocurrency reserves in identical fashion.

There are also some significant difference between IBFs and foreign branches.

1. Branches are not prohibited from accepting deposits from and making loans to U.S. residents, whereas IBFs are prohibited.

2. There are no limitations on maturities of deposits at foreign branches (payable outside the United States.). Maturities at IBFs to nonbanks are limited to a minimum of two days. Banks are limited to one day.

3. Foreign branches may issue negotiable instruments such as certificates of deposit and bankers acceptances. IBFs may not do so.
4. Foreign branches may purchase or sell assets in secondary markets without restrictions, whereas IBFs may not.

These distinctions will continue to have a significant dampening effect on the growth of IBFs in the near future. It is clear that U.S.

residents will continue to do their international banking in the offshore markets. They have no choice with respect to the IBF. On the other hand, foreign residents will continue to utilize IBFs.

NEW COMPETITORS TO THE IBF

The onshore Japanese offshore market commenced operations in December of 1986. By the end of 1986, the Japanese Offshore Market (JOM) had booked total external claims of $88.7 billion, nearly 26 percent of all Japanese bank external claims.[4] This figure had increased to over $116 billion by May 1987, approximately one-third of that of the U.S. IBF market in less than six months of operation.

The JOM is quite similar to the IBF in that deposits are subject to few regulations, although tax benefits are limited in the JOM to the elimination of withholding taxes on interest payments to nonresidents. Unlike the dominant role of foreign bank IBFs in the United States, the JOM has to date nearly exclusively consisted of Japanese banks. Given the small role which foreign banks have in the Japanese banking system, this is not surprising.

The primary threat which the JOM offers to the U.S. equivalent IBF is the level of operations the JOM is pursuing with foreign branches of Japanese banks and affiliates. This is purported to be particularly strong in the interbank operations of the JOM and Japanese bank branches in Hong Kong and Singapore, the dominant financial centers of the Asian Pacific.[5] Major foreign participation in the IBF market since its beginning has been dominated by the Japanese and Italian banks, both of which previously were not allowed operations akin to shell branch quantities of funds to the JOM could substantially slow future IBF growth. It should be noted that one of the primary purposes of the JOM, according to Japanese authorities, was to promote the role of the yen in international finance, as well as aiding in the more rapid development of Tokyo as an international financial center.

Recently, Canada announced plans to pursue the development of two international banking centers of their own. The two proposed offshore banking centers would be located in Montreal and Vancouver, although many in the Canadian government continue to support the inclusion of a number of other major cities. Both cities represent centers of some experience in international trade and banking, contributing to the potential success of their operations. The banking centers would provide tax breaks on international loans and deposits, and possibly the elimination of withholding taxes on interest payments to nonresidents. The impacts of an additional competitor are of course unknown at this banking like that of the Caribbean. The potential loss of large time, although the role of Canadian

TABLE 5
The Impact of IBF Operations on the Balance Sheets of U.S. Bank Foreign Branches
(billions of U.S. dollars)

	Claims on Foreigners[1]		Total IBF Assets[2]	
Year	all currencies	dollars	all currencies	dollars
1981:	379.0	277.0	56.6	55.2
1982:	358.5	259.9	152.7	148.8
1983:	342.7	247.4	191.6	187.7
1984:	320.2	228.6	227.6	221.1
1985:	315.7	209.9	260.5	247.9
1986:	314.3	196.4	298.2	275.6

Notes: 1. Source: Table 3.14, **Federal Reserve Bulletin.**
2. Source: **Federal Reserve Statistical Release G.14(518),** various dates.

banks in world banking--though growing over the last decade--is still relatively small.[6]

IBF MARKETING AND MANAGEMENT

In order to get a better feel for the operational aspects of IBFs, the authors contacted by telephone and mail 15 IBF officers and two members of the Federal Reserve International Banking Division staff. They were asked a series of questions regarding the performance, marketing, and management of their IBF operations since establishment. Although the sample has no statistical significance, the major points made by survey responders include the following qualitative comments:

(1) Successful IBF operation appears to hinge on the aggressiveness of marketing; marketing contacts through an established foreign branch network are the most

common. Once the deposits or loans are booked in foreign branches, they are often transferred to the domestic IBF books.

(2) Pricing is dominated by LIBOR, though some banks do use the U.S. prime rate. There is no indication that pricing differentiation occurs to any great degree for competitive reasons. Several respondents believe that a few depositors may be willing to accept lower IBF rates because of the legal comfort offered by deposits placed within the U.S. banking jurisdiction, although these deposits themselves are not guaranteed by the Federal Deposit Insurance Corporation.

(3) Major banks have maintained their existing branch and shell branch networks even after successful IBF operations due to the prohibition on dealing with U.S. domestic residents. Offshore shell branches already in operation have not reduced staff as a result of IBF operations.

(4) The employment effects of IBF operations appear to be negligible. The typical response was that IBF operations resulted in the addition of one employee--two at the maximum, with many IBFs sharing staff with general international banking operations.

(5) There is a clear attitude among respondents, particularly the domestic bank IBFs, that the IBF is "a set of books", and does not necessarily constitute a clearly separate operation from other international banking operations.

(6) Respondents indicated that on the whole the operation of IBFs in a U.S. legal jurisdiction did not constitute a major advantage, although it was seen as a positive feature. Respondents indicated that no more than 10 to 20 percent of IBF customers were attracted by U.S. legal jurisdiction.

(7) Respondents indicated that operation in a U.S. time zone constituted no significant advantage for U.S. IBFs.

(8) IBF operations have not resulted in the attraction of any significant new customer base.

SUMMARY

The benefits of IBFs are limited to very small increased profits from large volumes of transactions at interest rate spreads competitive with the Euromarkets. The narrowness of the IBF operation, however, precludes it from benefiting domestic residents in any appreciable fashion. Employment impacts of IBF operations have been negligible. Costs of operation are minimal mainly as a result of sharing staff and facilities with other international banking operations and the fact that the IBF is in essence just a set of books.

Public policy impacts of IBF operations have also been less than expected in that IBFs have not eliminated the need for offshore shell branches in the Caribbean, although they have significantly stifled growth in these financial centers. The entrance of the Japanese Offshore Market in December 1986 could well have serious long term negative impacts on the growth potential of U.S. IBFs.

NOTES

1. Federal Reserve Press Release, June 18, 1981. p.9.

2. Advances by an IBF to its parent institution will be subject to the reserve requirement on Eurocurrency liabilities of the U.S. office in the same manner as advances from a foreign office to its U.S. office.

3. A "branch" is here used to represent an extension of the establishing entity which provides full banking services in the location of its residence. A "shell branch" is simply a booking office, normally located in countries which do not tax income generated through the office and which do not provide banking services to the country of residence. Given this distinction, the IBF is seen as having the basic characteristics of a shell branch, hence the classification of an "onshore offshore banking market".

4. *Bank for International Settlements Annual Report*. June 1987, pp. 102-103.

5. The BIS estimates the increased Japanese interbank activity at $80 billion, $44 billion of it occurring between the JOM and Hong Kong and Singapore (*Bank for International Settlements Annual Report*, June 1987, p. 103).

6. In recent years, the number of countries considering opening international banking centers has grown rapidly, including Australia, Taiwan, and Macao, in addition to Canada and Japan.

REFERENCES

Bank for International Settlements. 1987. *Fifty-Seventh Annual Report*, Basle. June.

Chrystal, K. Alec. 1984. International Banking Facilities. *Federal Reserve Bank of St. Louis Bulletin*, April: 5-11.

Cumming, Christine M. 1985. Federal deposit insurance and deposits at foreign branches of U.S. banks. *Federal Reserve Bank of New York Quarterly Review*, Autumn: 30-38.

Key, Sydney J. 1982. International Banking Facilities. *Federal Reserve Bulletin*, Board of Governors of the Federal Reserve System, October: 565-577.

Morgan Guaranty Trust Company of New York. 1981. International Banking Facilities. *World Financial Markets*, November: 6-11.

Teeters, Nancy H. and Henry S. Terrell. 1983. The role of banks in the international financial system. *Federal Reserve Bulletin*, Board of Governors of the Federal Reserve System, September: 663-671.

Terrell, Henry S. and Rodney H. Mills. 1983. International Banking Facilities and the Eurodollar market. *Staff Study of the Board of Governors of the Federal Reserve System*, August.

The New York Clearing House Association. 1978. International Banking Facilities in the United States: An analysis of the economic policy issues, July 14.

Wise, David W. 1982. International Banking Facilities and the future of offshore banking. *The Fletcher Forum*, Summer: 299-329.

PART IV

GLOBAL PERSPECTIVE ON INTERNATIONAL FINANCIAL CENTERS

15. RECENT FUNCTIONAL CHANGES IN INTERNATIONAL FINANCE AND THEIR IMPLICATIONS FOR INTERNATIONAL FINANCIAL CENTERS

Yoon S. Park
George Washington University

INTRODUCTION

It is well known that the State of Alaska has experienced severe economic difficulties in recent years. The adverse economic impact on the people of Alaska is exacerbated by the fact that the state used to enjoy bountiful economic growth in the 1970s riding on the crest of the Alaskan oil boom.

The current economic difficulty poses a new challenge for Alaska. In this context, one can easily recognize the importance of international partnership for the future of Alaska's economic development, given the state's abundantly endowed natural resources and geographic and locational advantages. The relatively small population base of the state also requires the economies of scale made possible through external economic linkages. Therefore, international business should be a key part of the state's overall economic strategy, as Alaska needs foreign markets and international capital. Fortunately for Alaska, the state is strategically located within easy reach of the dynamic economies of the Asia-Pacific region.

Alaska can greatly benefit from diversification of its economic base, turning away from overdependence on a single resource industry. International business linkages will promote the process of economic diversification through foreign trade, foreign direct investments and the influx of entrepreneurial stimulus from the dynamic Asia-Pacific region. Foreign trade will not only provide the markets for Alaska's abundant natural resources such as fishery, timber, mining and energy, but also make it possible for Alaska's manufacturing industry to construct and operate optimum-size facilities, taking advantage of the economies of scale.

Alaska's geographic proximity to the Asia-Pacific region allows it a strategic advantage in accessing the region's countries, which can become attractive markets for Alaska's abundant natural resource products. Especially, the fast-growing countries such as Japan and the Asian NICs (the so-called "little Japans") lack the natural resources that are richly endowed in Alaska. Thus, Alaska and these Asia-Pacific countries are ideal partners in foreign trade and economic development.

Of course, development of Alaska's natural resources requires both capital and management. In addition to foreign trade, therefore, Alaska should also encourage foreign direct investments in the state. In recent years, the world debt crisis has led to increasing reluctance of both the international banking community and multinational corporations to make further financial commitments in most developing countries, which are suffering from heavy foreign debt burden. Since the world debt crisis emerged to the surface in 1982, the debt problems of developing countries have become worse rather than getting better. The total foreign debt of developing countries has increased from about $600 billion in 1982 to over $1 trillion in 1987. And there is still no prospect in sight for an early resolution of this world debt crisis.

Consequently, both international banks and multinational corporations will become extremely reluctant to transfer their capital resources to many developing countries, and instead they are likely to channel both capital and other business resources increasingly to politically stable, Western developed countries in search of investment opportunities. Alaska can greatly benefit in the coming years from the redirected flow of capital away from Third World countries. By developing a coherent strategy to attract this flow of capital, Alaska can become an important recipient of foreign direct investments, especially for many natural resource sectors.

RECENT DEVELOPMENTS IN INTERNATIONAL BANKING AND FINANCE

International trade and foreign direct investments go hand in hand with international finance. An international financial center in Alaska can attract and mobilize the needed international capital for the state's economic development. It can also boost foreign trade through both abundant trade financing opportunities and collection of worldwide commercial and economic intelligence. A successful international financial center expands employment in financial and ancillary services such as legal and accounting professions and also promotes development of such infrastructure as office buildings, hotels, restaurants, and other businesses.

During the past decade and a half, the international banking and financial markets have experienced phenomenal growth. The size of the Eurocurrency market grew from $110 billion in 1970 to over $4,000 billion by 1987, while the total international assets of all banking institutions rose from $130 billion to $4,800 billion during the same period. The development of international financial centers has also accompanied the rapid expansion of international banking and Eurocurrency activities. Some of the better known offshore financial centers are playing a major role in international financial markets, as demonstrated by the size of their international banking assets: Bahamas ($144 billion), Hong Kong ($130 billion), Bahrain ($46 billion), and Panama ($32 billion).

Not only has the scale of international banking and finance grown tremendously over the years, but also the market environment and financial institutions have undergone a marked change in recent years. This change can be characterized by: deregulation, internationalization, securitization, and financial innovations.[1] Major factors for deregulation were the substantial increases in inflation and interest rates in the 1970s and early 1980s. For the seven major industrial countries, inflation reached a peak in 1980, when the increase in the GNP deflator for these seven countries was 9.2 percent from the previous year, and the increase in consumer prices was 12.1 percent. Short-term interest rates in these seven countries reached a peak of 13.2 percent in 1981. Interest rate controls were in existence in several of the industrial countries as inflation and interest rates began spiraling upward in the 1970s. The United States was one of these countries. As interest rates rose, the institutions--most notably, banks--that were subject to interest rate controls in these countries came under competitive pressure from institutions that were not. The situation became particularly acute in the United States, where money market funds enjoyed exponential growth in the late 1970s at the expense of commercial bank deposits. The response of the U.S. government was to provide for the gradual phasing out of interest rate controls. This was done in the Depository Institutions Deregulation and Monetary Control Act of 1980, and the phase-out was completed in March of 1986.

The relaxation of interest rate controls was probably the major but certainly not the only aspect of deregulation. Functional distinction between different types of institutions has been breaking down, in part in response to the increasingly volatile economic environment. As financial institutions sought to expand the range of their products and services, they ran up against hostile laws, regulations, supervisory attitudes, and competitors. Although not always successful, those financial institutions seeking to overcome these impediments did so with sufficient frequency to cause a number of changes in the roles and relative importance of the different types of players in the financial arena.

Depository institutions are not the only financial institutions that have been caught up in deregulation. The securities industries in a number of countries, most notably the United States and the United Kingdom, have had to contend with changes in the rules of the game. In the United States, deregulatory measures in the 1970s increased competition by, among other things, ending the fixed rate structure for securities trades and lessening the power of the Big Board, the New York Stock Exchange. In the United Kingdom, the securities industry is undergoing more far-reaching alterations. Not only are rates and fees being deregulated; restrictions are also being dropped on divisions of functions between different types of securities firms and on the ownership of securities firms by banking organizations.

The global integration of financial markets is also a trend that has been underway for some time. The rise of the Eurocurrency and Eurobond markets in the 1960s was an important milestone in the development of this trend. International linkages increased in the 1970s and have accelerated in the 1980s. Internationalization is a commonly used term for the global integration of financial markets that is occurring. Neatness is not a characteristic of internationalization. The hodgepodge of institutions, financial instruments, flow of funds channels, and supervisory entities that make up domestic financial systems is reflected, and amplified, in the emerging international financial system.

Securitization is another feature of the current financial environment. Securitization is not a term that has achieved a generally accepted precise definition. Rather, it refers to what appears to be a move away from traditional bank lending and deposit-taking activities toward financial intermediation involving various kinds of negotiable financial instruments. The manifestations of securitization are numerous and varied. In the U.S. domestic market, loan-backed securities have achieved a significant presence. These are securities whose underlying assets are loans. Mortgage loans are the most common collateralization. In 1985, approximately one-fourth, or $366 billion, of one- to four-family residential mortgage loans ended up in mortgage-backed securities. In 1980, the dollar amount had been $114 billion, or only 13 percent of all one- to four-family residential mortgage loans.

Although mortgages are the predominant type of loans finding their way into loan-backed securities, a number of other types of assets have also been used. Among these are car loans, credit card receivables, computer leases, and Small Business Administration loans. The securitization of assets is limited only by the ingenuity of the packagers. The easiest assets to securitize, however, are those that are homogeneous, that is, that have similar terms and credit characteristics. To date, securitizing non-homogeneous assets, such as commercial and industrial loans, has not met with much success.

Both the richness and complexity of international funding sources and investment outlets bear a testimony to the robust spirit of financial innovations that has pervaded the international financial markets in recent years. Some of the innovations turned out to be faddish, but others have gained wide acceptance and made valuable contributions to the growth of international financial markets known as the Euromarkets. Both the development of markets for new financial instruments and the expansion

TABLE 1
Borrowings In The International Capital Markets
(U.S. dollars, in billions)

	1983	1984	1985	1987
Floating-rate bond issues	19.5	38.2	58.4	10.7
Other bond offerings	57.6	73.3	109.3	184.8
Syndicated loans	67.2	57.0	42.0	88.8
NIFs and other back-up facilities	9.5	28.8	46.8	29.9
Non-underwritten facilities and Euro-commercial paper programs	-	-	18.3	69.6
Total	153.8	197.3	274.8	383.8

Source: Organization for Economic Co-operation and Development, *Financial Market Trends*, June 1986 and May 1988, p. 5.

and deepening of markets for the pre-existing instruments are the results of the innovative spirit in the Euromarkets. Viewed in this way, the emergence of various Euromarket instruments since the early 1960s has been the result of financial innovation designed to meet the special needs of long-term international borrowers and investors.

The recent rapid expansion of Euromarkets has been promoted by further institutional innovations. The private use of both the European Currency Unit (ECU) and the Special Drawing Right (SDR) was first practiced for Eurobonds well before their use in bank deposits and Eurocredits. New clearing house mechanisms for international bonds and Euro CDs have greatly facilitated secondary market trading of these instruments. Gray market trading was pioneered in the Eurobond market and it still remains a unique feature of a Eurobond issue. Development of floating-rate notes (FRNs) in the 1970s is another example of Euromarket innovation.

Financial innovation involves more than development and diversification of new borrowing sources. It affects the entire range of financial intermediation, both domestic and international. In fact, the variety of services offered by financial intermediaries has been equally impressive on the liability side of their balance sheets. Liability management of modern financial institutions has become an important part of their integrated approach to financial intermediation. Innovations on the liability side have significant policy implications for monetary authorities.

CAUSES OF FINANCIAL MARKET CHANGES

The rapid pace of financial market changes in recent years is due to several factors. The first of these is the high level of interest rates worldwide since 1965 and especially since the late 1960s. High interest rates have reflected the serious inflation that the world economy has experienced over the years since the late 1960s. Rising inflation has led to anticipation of high future inflation, and lenders have sought higher interest rates as compensation for the depreciating purchasing power of their savings. Not only the high level of interest rates but also the greater fluctuation of interest rates increased significantly the risk exposure of most market participants. Savers and investment managers have been exposed to larger capital losses, as well as capital gains, on their financial portfolios due to widely fluctuating interest rates, since the market price of debt instruments moves inversely with interest rates. Also, banking institutions that have traditionally engaged in maturity transformation by funding medium to long-term loans with short-term liabilities are subject to greater uncertainty over their funding costs due to widely fluctuating money market rates.

Financial institutions have devised various counter measures to cope with this increased risk. On the one hand, the interest rates on medium to long-term loans have shifted increasingly from fixed rates to floating ones tied to certain short-term base rates such as three- or six-month LIBOR or the prime rate. Floating-rate loans significantly reduce the funding cost risk for financial intermediaries. Floating rates have been adopted not just for bank loans in the form of Eurocredits but also for long-term debt securities such as floating-rate notes, floating rate CDs and medium-term notes. On the other side of their balance sheet, financial institutions have also diversified their liabilities and lengthened their maturities. The trend toward liability diversification in terms of both instruments and maturities has intensified recently concomitant with the general deregulatory movement in the financial sector. In addition to traditional domestic CDs, banks now offer Eurodollar CDs as well as longer-term floating-rate CDs in various Euromarket centers. Medium- to long-term FRNs have been an important source of funds for banking institutions since the mid-1970s. Repurchase agreements (RPs) and Negotiable Order of Withdrawal (NOW) accounts have been extensively used by both thrift institutions and commercial banks in the United States. Interest rate swaps and currency swaps have been utilized by banks to tap longer-term funds at substantially reduced interest costs, while being hedged against foreign exchange risks.

High interest rates increase the opportunity cost of holding noninterest-bearing assets and encourage the economizing of such assets. Thus, high interest rates provide incentives for savers to shift out of demand deposits and into high-yield alternatives provided by new types of money market instruments. In order to slow down the disintermediation process, banks have had to devise new types of bank liabilities. Banks, forced to pay increasingly market-related rates in order to attract deposits, started to use actively a variety of new instruments for raising interest-sensitive funds, and they have also contributed to the creation of new secondary markets in which these assets are traded actively.

Variable-rate financing such as FRNs and floating-rate CDs enabled banks to raise medium- and long-term funds at a time when fluctuating interest rates continued to act as a major disincentive for savers to purchasing and holding long-term investment assets. The fast-growing interest rate futures market also serves as an example of continuing efforts to reduce risk exposure created by high and volatile interest rates. The Eurobond market has created new types of bonds designed to deal with the high and volatile interest rates. In addition to interest rate swaps and the FRNs, they include index-linked bonds, rolling rate notes (RRNs), extendable-maturity notes, medium-term notes (MTNs), zero coupon bonds, deep discount bonds, etc.

The floating exchange rate regime, that has been in force since early 1973 with the breakdown of the Bretton Woods system, greatly increased the volatility of exchange rate movements, increasing the level of financial risk exposure for market participants similar to widely fluctuating interest rates. Before 1973, many economists expected exchange rates to be fairly stable under the flexible exchange rate system. Because most market-determined prices are not volatile, it was believed that the market-determined price of foreign exchange would not be volatile either.[2] Instead of being stable, however, exchange rates have been highly volatile under the floating exchange rate regime. According to a study, the absolute percentage changes in the U.S.-German spot exchange rate between 1973 and early 1984 were 29.8 percent on a monthly basis and 107.4 percent on a daily basis.[3]

When spot exchange rates are volatile, the differences between forward exchange rates and future spot rates tend to be amplified,[4] thus lessening the degree of accuracy of the forward exchange rate as a predictor of the actual spot rate on a particular future date. Widening divergences between forward exchange rates and the subsequently observed spot rates for corresponding dates increase the degree of risk present in the financial market. Innovations such as currency swaps, currency options and currency futures contracts reflect the attempt by market participants to mitigate or even circumvent the heightened exchange risk perceived during the past decade and a half of floating exchange rates. A number of innovations in the Eurobond market have been designed specifically to lessen the foreign exchange risk exposure for international investors. They include currency option bonds, commodity-linked bonds, and bonds denominated in SDRs and European Currency Units (ECUs).

As the volume of outstanding loans to developing and Eastern European countries increased rapidly in the 1970s, international credit risk became a critical issue for financial intermediaries in the Euromarket. The recent world debt crisis accentuated the need for devising new ways to deal with the mounting international credit risk in general. In an attempt to supplement or even substitute the traditional Eurocredit mechanism (which was in itself a major financial innovation in the early 1970s), the Euromarket has experimented with a variety of new financing techniques such as bought deals, club loans, loan swaps, participation certificates, FRNs, and Euronotes with a revolving underwriting facility (RUF), note issuance facility (NIF), primary underwriting facility (PUF), etc. These new instruments are intended for certain specific needs perceived in this era of heightened international credit risk. Both NIFs and RUFs are designed to encourage continuing participation by U.S. and other banks in international banking activities despite the general decline of the traditional Eurocredit lending mechanism. To the contrary, club loans do away with the traditional loan syndicate structure with open invitations to banks for participation, and instead package the loans among a small number of pre-selected banks participating on an equal basis. Both loan swaps and participation certificates are designed to diversify the credit exposure of banking institutions among as many borrowing countries as desirable.

Another reason for rapid financial changes was the rise of computer and communications technology, which has provided financial institutions with the capacity to process massive amounts of data and to make financial transfers rapidly and economically. The introduction of new technology contributes to greater transactional efficiency and a higher degree of integration of world financial markets. The impact of new information processing techniques has been most visible in such new financial services as automated teller machines (ATMs), home banking systems and point-of-sale (POS) terminals. Corporate and individual depositors are now able to carry out significant portfolio shifts in order to economize on cash balances and low-yielding transactions accounts by quickly investing their liquid resources in various money market instruments.

Cash flow management has been enhanced significantly by such electronic fund transfer systems as the U.S. Federal Reserve System's Fed

Wire and the New York's Clearing House Interbank Payments System (CHIPS), which have made it possible to clear millions of transactions both efficiently and rapidly. London's new Clearing House Automated Payments System (CHAPS) plays a similar role, significantly reducing transactions costs. Automated international message transfer services such as the Society for Worldwide Interbank Financial Telecommunications (SWIFT) contributes to integration of world financial markets through efficient and almost instantaneous sharing of messages and information worldwide on a secure base. In many instances, sophisticated new equipment has resulted in sizable amounts of excess capacity, thereby creating incentives for expanding existing financial services and offering new kinds of services. New electronic banking technology has also produced significant structural changes in the organization of financial markets. For example, automated payment systems have facilitated the entry of non-banking institutions into the retail deposit business since ATMs have made it possible to avoid the heavy expense of building extensive branch networks.

Also, the regulatory environment for international financial transactions has been conducive to the kind of competitive and creative spirit needed in financial innovations. Regulatory authorities have traditionally allowed a greater operational leeway for "Euro" or foreign currency banking. In fact, this regulatory asymmetry was originally responsible for the creation of the Euromarket itself in the first place. For example, the absence of reserve requirements and interest rate ceilings encouraged the development of the Eurodollar market by providing the competitive advantage to banking institutions in Eurodollar funding operations. The Eurobond market was promoted in the absence of such strict securities regulations in domestic markets as registration requirements and disclosure rules.

Consequently, the Euromarket has provided a relatively fertile field for new financial experimentation free of stifling regulatory constraints. Even in the domestic financial markets of most Western industrial countries the process of financial deregulation has been at work during the past decade or so. In general, deregulation tended to follow rather than precede the introduction of new financial products and services which first would transform the financial market environment substantially enough to force the change in the traditional regulatory outlook. Deregulation would then accelerate further financial innovations, triggering more deregulation and so on in a self-reinforcing manner.

Between the Great Depression in the early 1930s and the expansion of Eurobanking in the 1960s, bank regulatory philosophy in major Western industrialized countries was dominated by a preoccupation with the soundness of individual institutions, mindful of the great financial crash in the late 1920s and early 1930s. Competition in banking was viewed as a double-edged sword, incorporating notable deficiencies as well as some generally recognized advantages in improving the quality of banking services to the public. However, recent regulatory changes were designed to promote competition not only among banks but also between commercial banks and other financial institutions, encouraging a rapid pace of financial innovations in the Euromarkets.

REQUIREMENTS FOR AN INTERNATIONAL FINANCIAL CENTER

Development of international financial centers has been a natural response by banking institutions to benefit from economies of scale in their international operations. Modern international financial centers require sophisticated and costly infrastructure, such as telecommunications, air transportation, and accounting and legal services. It would be cost inefficient to establish an elaborate infrastructure in each country to service just one national market. By locating most international banking and financial infrastructure in one central place, banks can spread their overhead costs in servicing clients in various countries.

Additionally, a sufficient number of banking and financial institutions must be located in one financial center to provide the critical mass needed to service international clientele effectively and efficiently. International banking requires both sophisticated financial expertise and up-to-date market information. Such knowledge cannot be generated in a vacuum; it needs constant innovation and cross-fertilization of ideas among bankers and other finance professionals. An accurate and up-to-date sense of financial markets can be obtained only through active market participation in the financial center.

Further, modern international banking frequently requires teamwork among many banks in loan syndication and other credit transactions. The amount of money involved is often huge and no one bank can prudently handle such transactions alone. International banking syndication necessitates close coordination and smooth working relationships among banks. Familiarity with each other's strengths facilitates such coordination and teamwork. A financial center provides the environment for frequent interaction among bankers and other finance professionals.

Apart from syndication and risk sharing, a cluster of international banking institutions in one place is helpful for funding and investment operations. The existence of active interbank money markets leads to efficient channeling of financial resources. Banks invest surplus funds in the interbank market from which other banks obtain funding to finance their international operations. Such a market is possible only where a large number of banking institutions are clustered together in one place. Attractive international financial centers serve not only as locations for international financial communities serving clients in various countries but also as havens for international savings and pools of liquidity seeking profitable investments free from monetary and exchange control restrictions. Efficient interbank markets provide the opportunity to invest these surplus funds easily and with minimal risk.

Location economics is important for international banking. Financial centers should be easily accessible in terms of geography and time zone to both investors and borrowers. Contact with potential borrowers is essential to bankers for marketing purposes and for packaging and negotiating customer loans. Location economics in international banking implies that a financial center should be in or near countries whose economies are dynamic and industrializing quickly, and thus requiring extensive borrowing. The development stage of these economies should also be high enough to assure reasonable credit risk for banks.

The availability of good air transportation to neighboring countries as well as telephone and telex communication links is essential for a financial center. It also needs liberal government regulation of banking and foreign exchange transactions, taxation, securities dealings, and work permits for expatriate staffs functioning in an environment of political and economic stability. Locally available internationally-oriented personnel in the legal, accounting, and clerical professions is also useful.

Anchorage possesses many advantages as a potential international financial center, such as political stability, convenient air transportation links with major cities in North America, Europe and the Asia-Pacific region, well-developed telecommunication facilities, and competent legal and accounting personnel. Another important advantage of Anchorage is its time zone, being conveniently linked during business hours to New York and Chicago on the one hand, and when these markets close, then to Tokyo, Hong Kong and Singapore on the other. As international financial markets are developed into one global market place with 24-hour trading, the Anchorage financial center could play a crucial trade linkage role by taking over the trading positions of New York and Chicago at the close of their business hours and off-loading them unto Tokyo, Hong Kong and Singapore as these markets open up.

Thus, the Anchorage financial center could provide valuable services in international trading of foreign currencies, domestic and international bonds and stock, Eurocurrency deposits, financial futures and options, currency swaps and interest swaps, etc. As Anchorage develops its international financial expertise and reputation, it will also attract offshore Eurocurrency deposits, insurance and reinsurance business for the Asia-Pacific region, investment and financial counselling, commodity broking, precious metals trading, and other related business.

CONCLUSION

Some might be skeptical at this point over the possibility of ever developing an international financial center in Anchorage, but the recent history of international financial centers gives us encouragement in this regard. About ten years ago in 1975, a tiny Middle East country, called Bahrain, boldly proclaimed to the international banking community its intention to become an international financial center. At that time, the odds seemed to run heavily against Bahrain, which is located in the middle of almost nowhere literally on the sea of desert sand, with no oil, no name recognition, no industry, no international financial experience or expertise, no trained personnel, no infrastructure, and, above all, no money. It only had a dream, a hope. Ten years later today, Bahrain is an important international financial center, with close to 200 financial institutions located there and almost $50 billion deposits, and lively financial trading activities in all sorts of financial instruments for Middle Eastern, European, and Asian customers.

Of course, it is erroneous to say that it will be easy to develop an international financial center in Alaska. But it is equally erroneous to conclude that it will be impossible for Alaska to do so. With both judicious planning and the cooperation between government officials and the private sector in the state, a viable international financial center can be established in Anchorage.

NOTES

1. The following discussion benefits heavily from an excellent treatment of the topic by David Holland. 1988. *Off-Balance Sheet Activities of Commercial Banks*, Ph.D. dissertation, George Washington University, Washington, D.C., 1988.

2. For example, see Harry G. Johnson, 1969. The Case of Flexible Exchange Rates. *Federal Reserve Bank of St. Louis Review*, June.

3. Craig S. Hakkio. 1984. Exchange Rate Volatility and Federal Reserve Policy. Federal Reserve Bank of Kansas City *Economic Review*, July-August.

4. See, for example, International Monetary Fund, *Annual Report 1982*, Washington, D.C. 1982, pp. 42-45.

16. FINANCIAL CENTER HEGEMONY, INTEREST RATES, AND THE GLOBAL POLITICAL ECONOMY

Howard Curtis Reed
Managing Director and CEO
Curt Reed & Co., Little Rock, Arkansas

INTRODUCTION

In recent years, concern about the continued vitality of the world economy has led some observers to conclude that international financial institutions and markets, as they are presently structured, may not be fully capable of performing the traditional functions of providing:

(1) Large amounts of capital at relatively cheap rates for borrowers, and

(2) Safety and liquidity for savers and investors.

Since 1973, the developing countries have amassed a staggering amount of debt. At year end 1986, the total debt of developing countries was $967 billion; approximately 70 percent of this amount is owed to the large internationally active commercial banks.

Brazil, the country with the largest amount of debt ($109 billion), announced in March 1987 that it was suspending payments on $68 billion of its foreign debt, and freezing $5 billion of short-term deposits owned by foreign banks. Brazil's objective is to have these loans restructured by lengthening the maturity and lowering the interest rate. Other developing countries with large external debt positions are eagerly waiting to see the terms of Brazil's restructuring agreement. The most interested countries are Mexico with $107 billion of outstanding foreign debt; Argentina, $52 billion; Venezuela, $35 billion; Philippines, $28 billion; and Peru, $22 billion. Bankers, government officials, and politicians generally agree that the stagnant level of world trade and economic growth has virtually eliminated any possibility that most of these loans will ever be repaid.

The question then arises as to how the banks and the regulating authorities should handle the accounting for these problem loans. Should these loans be written off entirely, partially, or carried on the books as if no problem existed? Additional questions that must also be answered are: Can a sovereign country go bankrupt? Is it reasonable to expect that the central banks will (and can) act as lenders-of-last-resort in the event of a major default? What powers should creditors have to collect their debt? What changes should be made in the international financial system? Who should manage the international financial system? And, how should the international system be managed?

These problems can clearly be traced to the 1973-74 quadrupling of world oil prices. In 1979-80 another major oil price increase exacerbated the situation that had developed in 1973-74. Oil prices, in 1979-80, increased to $32.50 per barrel from $14. As a result of these price increases, the OPEC countries accumulated enormous current account surpluses, while the non-OPEC developing countries and the industrialized nation were experiencing sizable current account deficits. The industrialized nations in varying degrees were able to offset their deficits. The deficits of the industrialized nations were, in a large part, offset by direct and portfolio investments from the OPEC countries.

The non-OPEC developing countries, on the other hand, did not attract OPEC capital. In addition, the non-OPEC developing countries generally discouraged direct investments from the multinational corporations apparently in the belief that these large organizations fostered dependency. Direct loans from banks, etc. were deemed, by the developing countries to be more acceptable than capital inflows coming from the multinational corporations because bank loans carried no direct financial control of an indigenous asset. The OPEC surpluses and the non-OPEC deficits for selected years is given in Table 1.

TABLE 1
Current Account Balances
(Billions of U.S. Dollars)

	1974	1980	1986
OPEC Surplus (Deficits)	$ 64	$105	$(33)
NON-OPEC Developing Country Surplus (Deficit)	(20)	(69)	(9)
NON-OPEC Bank Loans	44	195	524

Source: **World Financial Markets**, Morgan Guaranty Trust Co., various issues.

This trend, and to some extent the magnitude, of these flows was clearly seen and predicted as early as 1974. I am therefore perplexed at the behavior of interest rates since 1973. A question that remains unanswered is why interest rates did not fall precipitously (perhaps as much as 300 to 400 basis points) in the weeks and months following the oil price increase of 1973-74. At the time of the oil price increases, the international financial system was still adjusting to the consequences of the demise of the fixed exchange rate system that had been in existence since the conclusion of the Bretton Woods conference following World War II. Worry over rising unemployment land inflation and the economic health of LDCs was also being voiced.

In early 1974, the magnitude of the shift in wealth from the industrialized Western nations to the oil exporting countries was becoming quite clear. OPEC oil revenues in 1973 were $22 billion. Early estimates of 1974 OPEC oil revenues ranged from $100 to $115 billion (the actual revenues were slightly less than $90 billion). Armed with this information, it seems reasonable to have expected that London, the principal beneficiary of OPEC funds, would have bid down substantially the price it was willing to pay for new deposits. New York, the only other center capable of handling such a large influx of funds, was not receiving, directly, any of these new deposits from OPEC--for obvious political reasons.

It was clear at the time that these new liabilities, accruing to London, would be converted into assets by primarily increasing the loans made to developing countries, which were already having difficulty meeting their financial obligations. It should have been clear that rising interest rates have a destabilizing effect on the world's equity markets which make it difficult for corporations to maintain the appropriate debt/equity mix in their capital structure, which is vitally important to investor confidence. London, and the American banks which dominate the Eurocurrency market, should have realized that rising interest rates increase the general level of uncertainty, which has a tendency to slow capital investment activity in favor of shorter-term cash management actions. This puts additional upward pressure on inflation and unemployment.

This paper attempts to shed some light on interest rate behavior since 1973 by showing what happened and by arguing that the behavior has been misguided. The misguided behavior results from a theoretical framework that analyzes interest rate behavior by emphasizing financial institutions and financial markets, instead of "financial centers." In other words, interest rate behavior is a product of financial center determinants, not just the activity of the large internationally active commercial banks or the activity of the internationally active financial markets.

FINANCIAL CENTERS

Financial centers can be classified into three distinct groups:[1]

(1) *Host centers*. These centers enhance their own financial infrastructures and capabilities by attracting relatively large numbers of foreign financial institutions from a large number of countries.

(2) *International Centers*. These centers are headquarters for large internationally active banks which influence events that pertain to global asset and liability management.

(3) *Supranational Centers*. These centers are managers of large amounts of foreign financial assets and liabilities; net suppliers of foreign direct investment capital to the rest of the world; located close to a large number of large (measured by assets) industrial corporations; active users of global communication facilities (i.e., airplanes, telephone, telex, etc.); and management meccas that attract and generate ideas and information in ways that eventually establish the organizational and operating norms that govern internationally active organizations (private and governmental).

Financial centers are not only organized in a hierarchical structure for finance but they are also organized hierarchically for communications and management. As a result, the "supranational" centers are preeminent in finance, communications, and management. Finance centers facilitate the flow of goods, services, and capital within its own national economy and between its national economy and the other national economies of the world. Communication centers are places where interaction occurs, ideas are exchanged, and information is gathered, analyzed, and disseminated. Management centers are locations that require and subsequently attract skilled persons to organize the sourcing, reformulation, and marketing of resources in a clearly defined manner, a manner that lends itself to standardization and eventually the adoption of these practices on a wide scale.

The supranational centers, it is argued, provide the environment, the mechanism, and the competence for evaluating, on a continual basis, the policies and activities of the institutional components of the global political economy. These centers are important for:

(1) Financial sourcing and allocation

(2) Evaluating the policies, strategies, and activities of nations[2]

(3) Industrial project evaluation and pricing

(4) Monitoring the activities of the institutional components of the political economy, and

(5) Providing money and capital management services. The level of efficiency with which a center can perform these functions is dependent on its astuteness in gathering, evaluating, and utilizing information from around the world. Additionally, a center's astuteness is largely dependent upon the number (and size) of its locally headquartered banks, the management acumen of these institutions, the collective connections (to other centers) of these institutions, and the industrial power (and reach) of the nation's corporations.

The 1981 study (by Reed, Note 1) provided considerable insight into what is required to build financial center infrastructure over time (i.e., institutions, connections, markets, etc.), and into the organization, distribution, and influence of these centers. That study, however, left unexplored a whole range of factors that have emerged in the past ten to fifteen years that may have a significant influence on the building of financial center infrastructure, organization, and influence. The 1981 study uses a nine-variable analysis. The analysis in this study uses sixteen variables (six variables from the 1981 study plus ten new variables).[3]

In this sixteen-variable study, the organizational structure was determined by (in the order of their statistical significance) the amount of international currency clearings, the size of the Eurocurrency market, foreign financial assets, and headquarters for the large internationally active commercial banks (Figure 1).

As a result of the analysis, supranational centers can be characterized as centers whose principal operating currency(ies) is (are) widely used for settling international trade and capital transactions and whose financial infrastructures (primarily the large commercial banks) are developed to the extent that they are entrusted with the management of the world's foreign financial liabilities and assets. The large internationally active commercial banks have the primary responsibility for facilitating international clearings which in 1985 amounted to a U.S. equivalent of $324 billion a day. U.S. dollars accounted for approximately $225 billion of the total, and New York was clearing approximately 90 percent of these dollar transactions. In addition to the currency transactions, the clearing infrastructure is also used for coupon, dividend and interest payments on securities; and it is used to facilitate the transfers and registration of securities.

INTEREST RATE THEORY AND FINANCIAL CENTER INFRASTRUCTURE

The theories of interest rate determination and structure are based in large part on market expectations about the future. Traditional interest rate theory determines the rate of interest by intersecting the supply and demand curves for all financial assets.[4] The assumption is made that economic units:

(1) Are risk averse, and

(2) Base their utility preferences on the expected return and risk associated with a particular financial asset. It is further assumed that the principal objective of an economic unit is to maximize its total utility by selecting a diversified portfolio of financial assets that is optimal with respect to expected value of return and risk.

Theories that attempt to explain the yield-maturity relationship of financial assets argue that the behavior of interest rates is a function of the level of expected future short-term rates. The unbiased expectation theory argues that long-term interest rates are an unbiased average of current and future short-term rates. Therefore, an upward sloping yield curve implies that interest rates are expected to rise, and a downward sloping yield curve says that interest rates are expected to decline. Another theory, the expectations and liquidity preference theory, argues that investors generally prefer to lend short unless they receive a liquidity premium large enough to offset the risks associated with lending long-term. Liquidity premiums are thought to be a function of risk, where risk is a function of time (i.e., maturity schedule). The bias in this theory is toward upward sloping yield curves.

In the classic economic environment, it is perfectly legitimate to conclude that interest rates are determined by market supply and demand. For the large internationally active banks, the objective is largely traditional, i.e., maximizing total utility and optimizing income and wealth. For the supranational center (hereafter, financial center) the objective is quite different. The financial center's objective is, at the very least, to maximize the welfare of the political economy by optimally distributing financial resources throughout the world. The financial center is a synthesized infrastructure of institutions and markets whose function is to evaluate the operating efficiencies of the financial, industrial, commercial, and political organizations that utilize the center's capital, information and management resources.

The large internationally active commercial banks in addition to performing the traditional intermediary function of accepting deposits and making loans are also instrumental in gathering, analyzing, and disseminating information. These banks provide the principal direct links by which the financial centers access and disseminate information. Through the global branch networks, the internationally active banks transmit information between centers presumably at greater speeds, and at higher levels of quality and accuracy than information transmitted between center through relatively public networks. The strategic role of these banks naturally leads to the question: In international finance, is it the banks or is it the centers that are preeminent? The question is perhaps best answered by examining some aspects of the relationship between banks and centers.

In Japan, for example, the large internationally active banks headquartered in Osaka (Sumitomo, Sanwa, and Diawa), Kobe (Taiyo), Nagoya (Tokai) have their "top" international people in Tokyo and have recently split their top domestic people between their home office and Tokyo. Similar activities have taken place in California (USA). Bank of America has officially split its headquarters into a northern division in San Francisco (the original headquarters), headed by the president (chief executive officer) and a southern division in Los Angeles, headed by the chairman of the board (chief operation officer). The other large San Francisco bank, Wells Fargo, now has its chief executive officer spend 40 to 50 percent of his time in Southern California. This reflects the growth of Los Angeles as a significant financial center.

The importance of New York as a financial center is underscored by pointing out the impact of its international clearing facilities on the status and influence of international banking activity. Foreign banks have made it quite clear that having access to New York's Clearing House Interbank Payment System (CHIPS) is an important consideration when deciding on whether to open an office (or enlarge an existing office) in New York. Apparently the large U.S. banks headquartered outside of New York also feel that way. In the early years of this decade, a group of large U.S. banks headquartered outside of New York, led by Bank of America and Continental Illinois, attempted to delay and perhaps prevent New York from receiving final approval from the Federal Reserve to establish International Banking Facilities (IBFs). The support of this group was contingent upon their being given direct access to the CHIPs computer from their home offices outside of New York. It was argued that with IBFs and CHIPS at their disposal, the 12 settling banks headquartered ind New York will be able to obtain deposits at lower costs and make loans more profitably, thus giving the New York banks an unfair competitive advantage. (The ploy did not work. New York's IBFs began operating on December 1, 1981 and the non-New York banks do not get direct computer access to CHIPS).

Another action which appears to clearly favor the importance of the center over the banks is the behavior of the Arab Organization of Petroleum Exporting Countries (AOPEC) in 1973-74. When AOPEC quadrupled oil prices in 1973 and 1974, its members initially chose to employ their cash reserves (billions of new dollars) in London, even though comparable deposit rates in New York were 50 to 75 basis points higher. The London branch and subsidiary offices of the New York banks were the principal recipients (receiving more than 70 percent of the total) of the funds going to London.

If the banks were preeminent, then why not take advantage of the higher yields being offered in New York, since the London affiliates of the New York banks were the principal depositories for these AOPEC funds? This example points to the significance of politics and confidence, in addition to the more quantifiable variables, as important determinants of financial centers structure, particularly the perceived willingness of a center to use economic means to achieve a political objective. As important as the banks are, the evidence appears to clearly show that the large internationally active banks are not more important than the centers. The evidence also appears to clearly show that the reach, scope, and influence of the center is far greater than the total, reach, scope, and influence of its various institutions when measured independently.

Financial markets are comprised of a wide range of intermediary institutions, including the large internationally active banks. Financial markets are the formal mechanism by which savings are efficiently allocated. The efficiencies of these markets are reflected in the economies generated in the coordination of a wide range of financial transactions, such as providing the mechanism for:

(1) Clearing checks, stock certificates, etc.

(2) Larger and cheaper security issues for those that need capital, and

(3) Greater liquidity for lenders of capital. These rationing and coordinating activities are governed largely by the cost/price relationship of the supply and demand for these activities.

The foreign exchange markets are much more representative of the financial center than are the banks and securities markets. The foreign exchange market reflects immediately that center's evaluation of a nation's political economy. In the intermediate and very near term, it is reflected in the spot rate. In the future, or long term, it is the forward rate. The exchange rate is (at least, it should be) a synthesized evaluation of a nation's overall status--its policies, strategies, and activities. Nations, including their economic organizations, are active users of the products and services of financial centers.

A shift in a nation-state's policy, strategy, or predicted activity could substantially alter the portfolio quality of the center, and, in turn, of its investors. Accurate evaluation is also essential to evaluating and pricing industrial projects that are targeted for investment in foreign countries or projects that are dependent upon cash flow emanating from that country. Industrial project evaluation is also important for the initial pricing of the borrowed capital. Monitoring the progress of the projects is necessary so that the current value of the outstanding principal can be assessed. The quality of the money and capital management services offered by the center is largely a function of how well these other functions are managed.

INTEREST RATE BEHAVIOR: A FINANCIAL CENTER PERSPECTIVE

The expectation theory looks at future interest rates from the financial market's point of view. The theory concedes (albeit implicitly) that financial markets themselves have no significant influence over the future level of interest rates. Long-term interest rates are merely the market's expectation about the level of future interest rates. A financial center view of the future level of interest rates is more explicit about what influences future rate levels. The financial markets cannot determine or significantly influence the future level of interest rates, because these markets are only the mechanism by which the center makes the results of its evaluation known. The center's evaluation then results in a future level of interest rates being established.

The large internationally active banks and other financial institutions do not independently evaluate projects, price capital, and allocate resources. They do not independently set interest rate levels. The evaluation, pricing, and allocation is the result of all of the center's institutional components acting and reacting to the environment in a predictable manner. Succinctly stated, the financial center at any given period of time has the power and the responsibility to significantly influence the future level of interest rates by determining the direction of future interest rate trends. Interest rates should not necessarily be determined or significantly influenced by the supply and demand for financial assets.

The financial center does have a set of expectations about future interest rate levels. The expectations are based on the center's forecast of inflation, savings, consumption, industrial activity, trade, money supply, source(s) of funds, and so forth. Based on these predictions, the future trend (direction) of interest rate movement is initiated. Therefore, the center's expectation about future interest rate levels at any given time is a function of the accuracy of the center's forecast and its ability to speed up, slow down, or leave unchanged the forecasted trends (and levels) of inflation, savings, consumption, industrial activity, and so on. The direction of movement in the level of rates, as initiated by the center, is designed to speed up, slow down, or leave unaffected (or at least minimally so) the various environmental components (i.e., inflation, savings, etc.)

The expectations and liquidity preference argument holds that investors (lenders) require a liquidity premium sufficient to offset the risk associated with longer-term investments (loans). From the financial center's point of view, the expected future level of interest rates is a function of the accuracy of its forecasts and the extent to which it can carry out its desired purpose with respect to the environmental components. All investments that are not free of default require a liquidity (risk) premium for the investor. The center, however, has the option of determining whether the risk is initially absorbed by the saver (depositor) through lowering the interest rate paid to the saver or the borrower by increasing the interest rate charged. The center's earnings (and risk premiums) are generated from the spread between what it pays for funds and what it charges.

When focusing on earnings, the center must first take steps to ensure the success of its clientele. This means that the center is concerned foremost with the earnings and overall value of the portfolio of its clients and less concerned with its own earnings and investment portfolio. The reason for this is twofold. First, the center operates as an intermediary providing capital, information, and management products and services. And second, the center's total portfolio of clients represents the center's investment. The financial center is unlike the corporation, in that the lower the expected risk, the greater the expected return for the center. The center's primary concern at all times will be to reduce the expected risk of return on its portfolio of activities. For example, in cost of capital considerations, and where interest rates are an important determinant, the center's behavior will be to bid down the amount it pays for funds so as to minimize what it must charge for funds. The higher the capital servicing requirements for the borrowing firms, the greater the probability of problems occurring with the center's portfolio.

Figure 2 shows the financial center's risk-earnings possibility curve. The center's earnings are derived principally from fees and the spreads received between bid and ask on a wide range of intermediary activities. The negative slope of the curve suggests that, along with the benefits derived from an increase in the volume of activity, the center could widen the spread between bid and ask and increase the base rate of its fee schedules without significantly increasing risk or reducing volume of activity. By increasing the spreads and adjusting upwardly the base rate for its fees, the center adds to its reserves and capital accounts. The risk premiums required by the center varies inversely with the level of interest rates. The center wants to enhance the quality of its asset portfolio by providing capital to users at a cost that minimizes the risk of capital depreciation (e.g. being unable to service debt obligations; omitting or reducing dividend payments; etc.) and capital destruction (e.g. being unable to repay the principal from debt obligations; having the value of stockholder's equity reduced; etc.)

The large internationally active commercial banks, in most instances, respond quite differently to events. The behavioral differences between banks and the centers are primarily the results of their operating within inherently different market structures. The number of large internationally active banks competing on a global scale in a large number of product markets is considerably more than one hundred; and when regional competitors are included, the number of competitors exceeds two hundred. The number of financial centers with global capability is limited to New York and London. There are five centers with "near" global capability--Tokyo, Frankfurt, Paris, Zurich and Amsterdam. The market structure in which banks operate is considerably more competitive than the market structure in which the centers operate.

An example of the significance of the market structure constraints on banks can be seen when capital adequacy is examined. There are no absolute capital requirements for banks operating outside of their home countries, but investors, depositors and regulators impose their own standard as to what constitutes a sufficient amount of capital. A bank may also recognize that the quality of its portfolio, and the level of its earnings, will be enhanced if interest rates were lower. But when the bank lowers the interest rate it pays for deposits, it will lose future deposits as well as maturing deposits to competitor banks paying a higher interest rate. In other words, it is very unlikely that a bank will unilaterally lower the rate it pays for deposits prior to its reaching its minimal capital/deposit ratio. Even at this minimum, an interest rate reduction will not be necessary because the depositors will shift future additional funds to competitor banks (i.e., those banks with a more favorable capital/deposit ratio). Any bank moving unilaterally and precipitously to lower the interest rate it pays for deposits, exposes itself (in the short run) to the risk of having to fund its asset portfolio.

The comprehensive nature of the financial center (i.e., institutional infrastructure, investment instruments, and sophisticated clients) precludes the banks from having to move unilaterally to lower interest rates and reduce risk. The process of lowering the center's cost of capital to its clients will begin, for example, when one of the large internationally active banks reaches (or approaches) its minimum capital/deposit ratio. The depositors will direct future flows to other, better capitalized, banks. The undercapitalized bank will continue to lose deposits until the capital adequacy (in this particular situation it's the capital/deposit ratio) of all competitor banks has been minimized. Once the minimal capital/deposit ratio has been reached, the competitor banks will then lower their interest rates.

As a result of all banks now paying lower interest rates, future flows of funds to banks will be reduced. In addition, maturing deposits (in the short-run) will seek alternative investments. This will result in a net outflow of funds from the banking industry, which will result in a capital/deposit ratio that is optimal (particularly from the depositor's perspective) instead of minimal. The beneficiary of the outflow of funds from the banks will be the center's other money and capital market instruments (i.e., commercial paper, bonds, common stock, etc.). These actions will lower the overall cost of capital to all capital seekers using (and operating within) the center.

The interest rate behavior of both the large internationally active banks and the supranational financial center is illustrated in Figure 3a and 3b respectively. The interest rate paid is measured on the vertical axis and the quantity of funds supplied is measured on the horizontal axis. Figure 3a shows the behavior of the large internationally active banks operating within the center. The vertical lines labeled C_1, C_2, and C_n denotes the amount of capital in bank 1, bank 2, and bank n. The supply curve is labeled S. If the banks operating in a financial center believe that their capital resources are not being fully utilized, they take steps to increase deposits (liabilities) and, in turn, assets.

Assuming a competitive environment, price elasticity, and industry leadership, the most influential bank (perhaps C_n, if it is also the largest) will increase the rate of interest it pays for deposits. In due course, the rest of the center's banks also increase their interest rates. At interest rate I_1, the bank represented by the capital constraint line C_1 has reached its minimal capital/deposit ratio. At this point, X, bank C_1 will no longer compete with the rest of the industry for deposits on the basis of price. It will not be compelled to follow the industry in increasing its interest rates paid for future deposits because future deposits will flow to banks C_2 and C_n. At point Y, bank C_2 reaches its minimal capital/deposit ratio. Depositors will now direct all future deposits to bank C_n. At point Z, the center's banking industry will be fully utilizing its operating capital. The broken lines of the supply curve, S, represents the quantity of funds that will seek employment in the other money and capital market instruments available in the center.

There are two types of funds available to the center's banking industry:

(1) Unique Funds - capital that is made available to a financial center on the basis of that center's operating character (e.g. AOPEC funds in London during 1973-74, or clearing deposits maintained in New York).

(2) Volatile Funds - capital that continuously moves between all financial centers, usually seeking a higher return.

The cost of "unique" funds to the banking industry will not begin to decline until the capital/deposit ratio of all banks operating in that financial center falls below some minimum level. The cost of "volatile" funds to the banking industry will not begin to decline until the capital/deposit ratio of all banks, in all financial centers, falls below some minimum level. Therefore, each financial center's capital resources are classified as "unique" and "volatile". The center's influence over the future trends of interest rates is confined to its "unique" funds' portfolio. A center's "unique" funds' portfolio becomes vulnerable only when its capital/deposit ratio becomes unfavorable, when compared to other competitor centers.

Figure 3b shows the interest rate behavior of the financial center. The vertical line labeled C_* is the amount of capital supporting the center's activities. The TFS curve represents the total amount of funds available in the center (TFS = unique funds + volatile funds). The UFS curve represents the amount of unique funds available in the center. At the interest rate level I_*, the financial center is operating at its minimal capital/deposit ratio. At point A, the center will lose its volatile funds to other centers with more favorable capital positions. The supply curve for the center now shifts to UFS. The center's supply of unique funds will continue to 'increase beyond A', because of the "special" relationship between these funds and the center. After a while, the center recognizes its monopoly position with these funds, and at this time (point B) the center begins to lower the interest rate it pays for these funds. With lower interest rates being paid on deposits, the spread between interest paid for liabilities and interest earned on assets can be widened. The increased earnings permit the center to add to its reserves and increases its capital base.

The general supply curves facing the financial center is shown in Figure 4. The center has two supply curves (1) the relatively inelastic "unique" funds curve, s_u; and (2) the relatively elastic "volatile" funds curve, s_v. The center's relative influence over its "unique" funds fall somewhere in between monopoly and oligopoly. And the market structure for volatile funds is between monopolistically competitive and perfectly competitive markets.

MISGUIDED BEHAVIOR?

Developing a theoretical framework to explain behavior is not only important because it may explain the events that have already taken place, or because it may explain future events, but in this instance, a theory is also important because it is useful in identifying those factors that may be impeding the more "logical" and the more "rational" behavior of financial centers. Since the early 1970s, financial center behavior has been at odds with the theoretical framework argued for in this paper. A case in point: since the initial quadrupling of oil prices in 1973-74, the global economy has generated virtually no real growth, unemployment has more than doubled, inflation has increased threefold, corporate bankruptcies have more than doubled, and the international financial system is precariously plodding along without a clear plan for solving the problems associated with the prohibitively high costs.

Many (perhaps most, or even all) of these problems could have been avoided if London had reduced the interest rates it paid for Eurodollar deposits after the two major oil price increases: in 1973-74 and again in 1979-80. Table 2 gives the average annual Eurodollar and U.S. dollar rates (overnight and three month) for the years 1973 through 1981; and it also gives the oil price levels for the same time period.

Perhaps the theoretical framework presented in this paper will in some small way illuminate the importance and the significance of the supranational financial centers. London's view (in 1973-74 and again in 1979-80) of its supply curve with respect to AOPEC funds was, in my opinion, misguided. Apparently, London believed the AOPEC funds were unique and relatively inelastic, depicted in Figure 5b[5]. If London had lowered the price it was paying for capital, AOPEC funds would have been forced to: accept the lower rate, place substantial amounts in other European and Asian centers, accept the risk and utilize New York, or pursue a direct investment strategy.

Lower rates would have reduced OPEC's incentive to increase oil rates further, restrained inflation and enhanced the level of confidence in the global economies, and indirectly forced OPEC to absorb some of the costs associated with recycling their surplus.

In addition, the problems that the large internationally active banks are now encountering (i.e., the danger that a substantial percentage of their asset asset portfolios will become non-performing) would have been avoided.

TABLE 2

Eurodollar and U.S. Dollar Deposit Rates
(Yearly Average)

	Overnight		Three Month		Oil Prices Index
Year	Euro	U.S.	Euro	U.S.	(1974 = 100)
1973	8.80	8.73	9.35	8.49	
1974	10.40	10.49	11.23	10.28	100
1975	5.77	5.82	6.90	6.33	98
1976	5.07	5.05	5.55	5.20	106
1977	5.70	5.54	6.11	5.73	114
1978	8.09	7.90	8.97	8.41	117
1979	11.29	11.15	11.94	11.31	178
1980	13.40	13.41	14.35	13.32	306
1981	16.11	16.35	16.47	15.31	327

Surely, London realized that the developing countries would be requiring substantial amounts of capital, over and above the large amounts that they already owed, just to finance their oil imports. London must also have realized that the growth in non-oil world trade would certainly slow down, and more likely would shrink. It therefore seems reasonable to conclude that London recognized that the demand for its funds was relatively inelastic (Figure 6).

From the perspective of the theoretical framework presented in this analysis, London's behavior was clearly "misguided". But the explanations given by private (and central) bankers, multinational corporate executives, economists, etc. clearly show that London's behavior was consistent with traditional interest rate theory. The relevance and the usefulness of the framework presented here may not be fully known for some considerable time into the future. At the very least, however, it is hoped that this framework will stimulate worthwhile arguments, debates, and discussions.

NOTES

1. Howard Curtis Reed, *The Preeminence of International Financial Centers*, (New York: Praeger Publishers, 1981), pp. 60-61.

2. This evaluation is reflected immediately in the foreign exchange (spot and forward) market value of currencies, and later on, in the nation's collective cost of capital.

3. The sixteen-variable measures are (asterisk indicates variables used in the 1981 study):

   * Capital/Deposit ratio of the large internationally active banks headquartered in the center.

   * Capital/Asset ratio of the large internationally active banks headquartered in the center.

   * Pre-tax Earnings/Capital ratio of the large internationally active banks headquartered in the center.

   * Pre-tax Earnings/Assets ratio of the large internationally active banks headquartered in the center.

   * Revenue/Asset ratio of the large internationally active banks headquartered in the center.

   * Total international currency clearings (daily average) of the center.

   * Size (liabilities) of the center's Eurocurrency market.

   * Total amount of international bonds issued in the center during the year.

   * Foreign financial assets held in the center.

   * Foreign financial liabilities residing in the center.

   * The daily average of the center's stock exchange activity (sales value).

* The number of large internationally active commercial banks headquartered in the center.

* The number of large internationally active foreign banks with offices (agencies, branches, or subsidiaries) in the center.

* The number of foreign financial centers with direct links to the local center and the links are provided by the foreign internationally active banks.

* The center's airline passenger traffic (yearly total).

* The center's airmail/airfreight volume (yearly total).

4. An excellent overview of interest rate theory and structure is given in James C. Van Horne, *Functions and analysis of capital market rates*, (Englewood Cliffs, New Jersey: Prentice-Hall, 1970), Chapter III, IV, and V.

5. An argument could be made that the supplies of capital, supplied after the maximal capital/deposit ratio is exceeded (Point A), would get the additional risk premium. It is highly unlikely that the suppliers of capital recognized this situation. And there is no evidence to support such an argument.

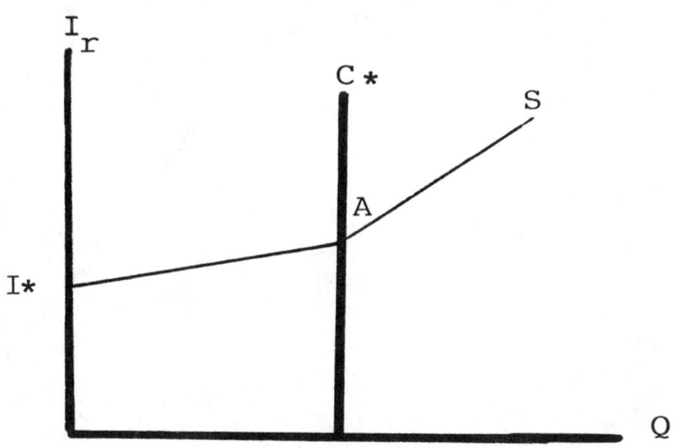

Figure 1

INTERNATIONAL FINANCIAL CENTERS
(Organization and Structures)

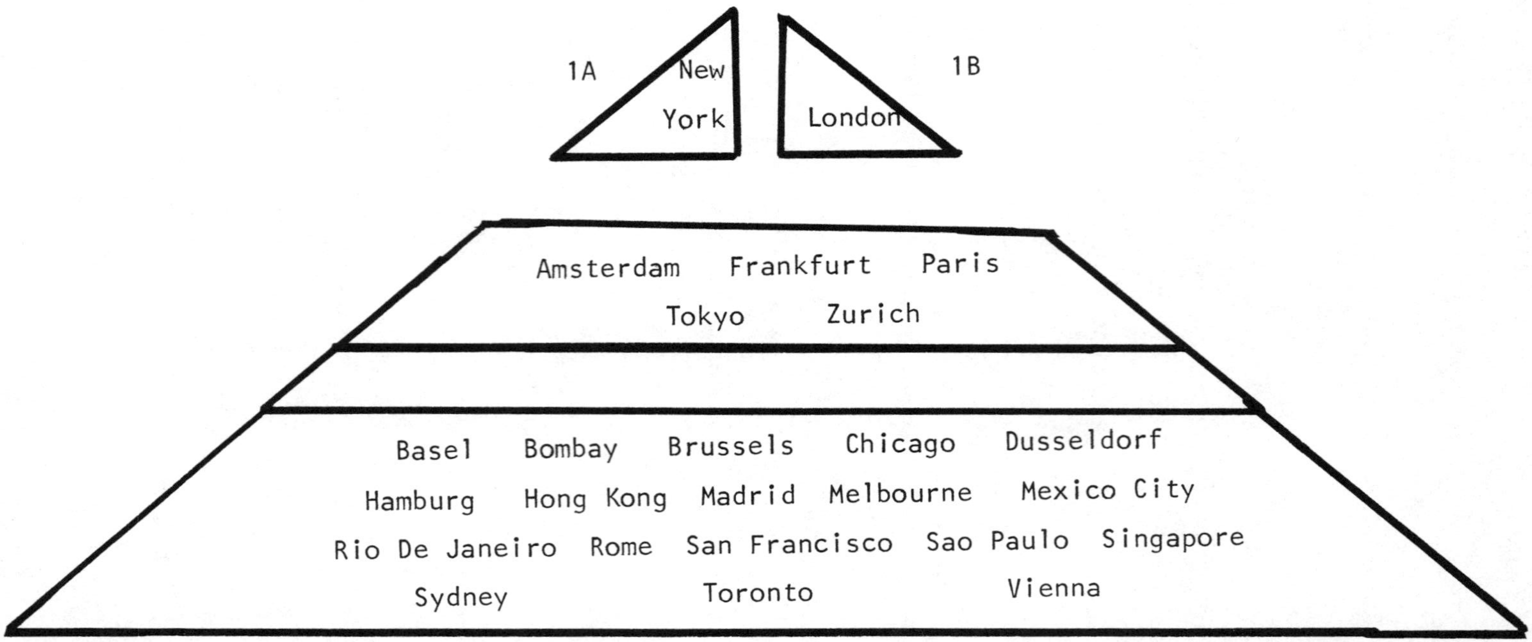

Figure 2

SUPRANATIONAL FINANCIAL
CENTERS

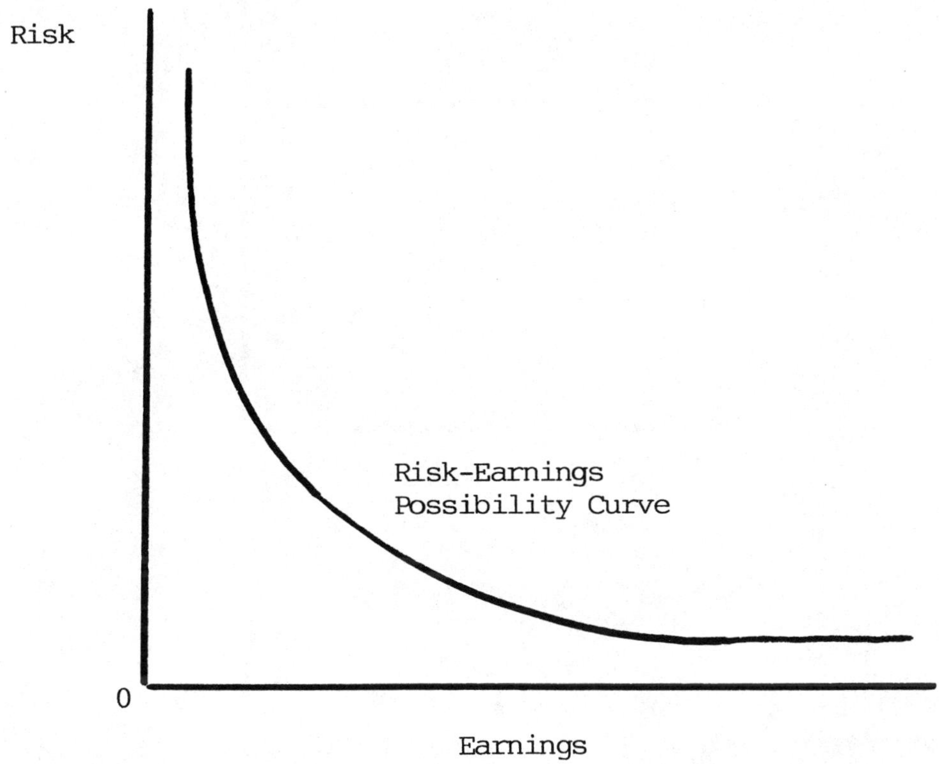

Large Internationally
Active Banks

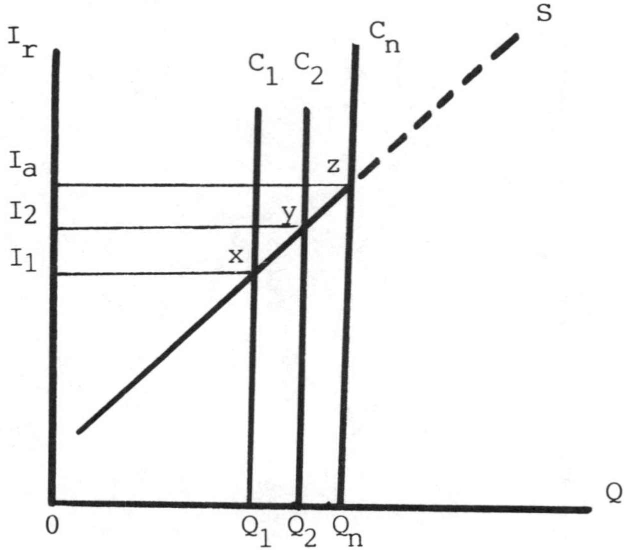

3a

Supranational Financial
Center

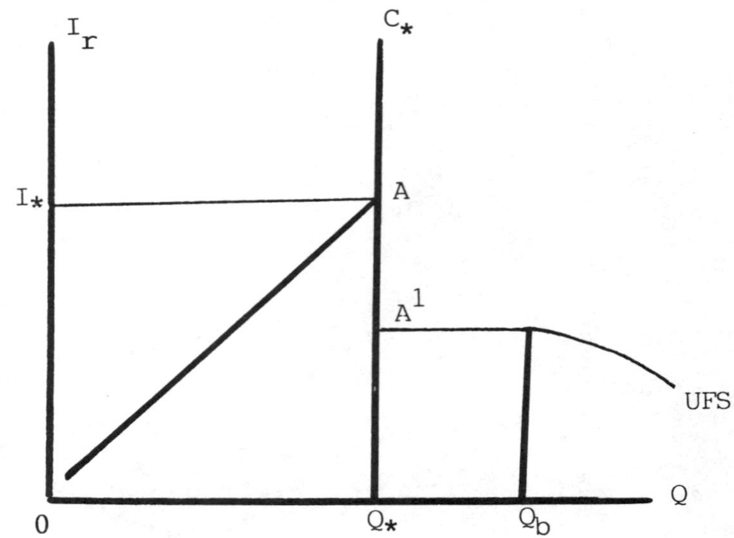

3b

Figure 4

Supranational Financial Center Supply Curves

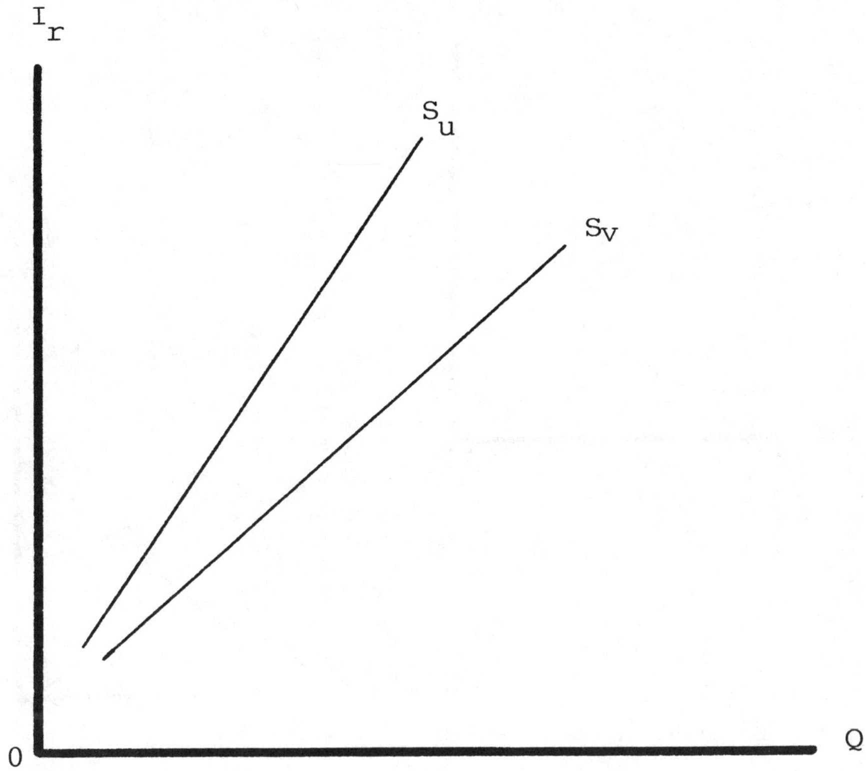

Figure 5
London Supply Curves: 1973/74 and 1979/80

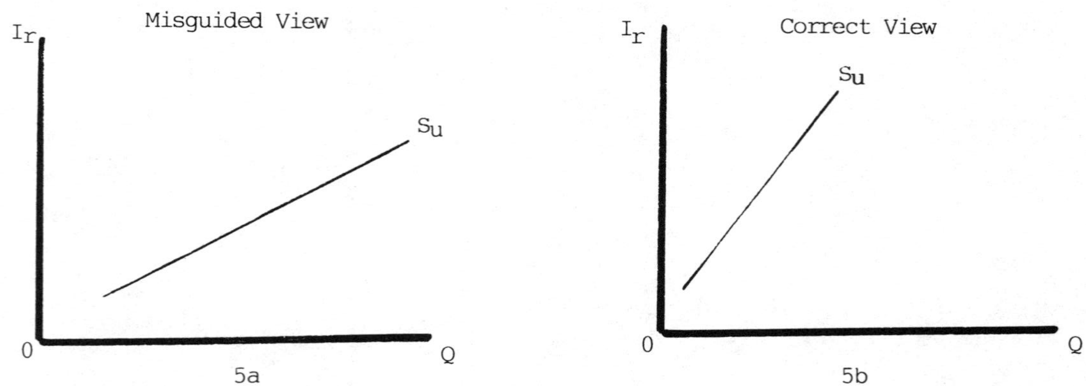

Figure 6
Londond Demand Curve: 1973/74 and 1979/80

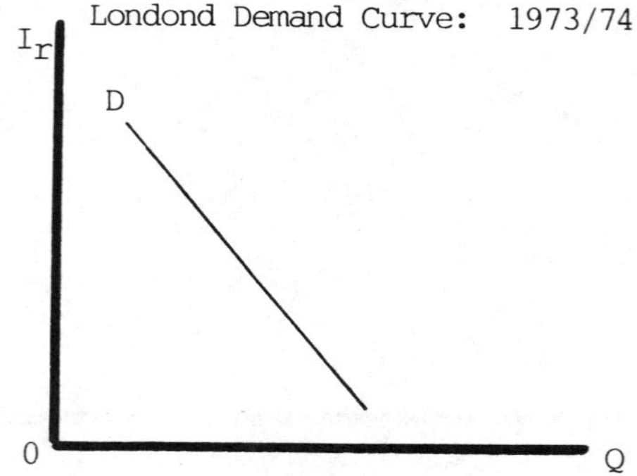

INDEX